Limestone County

Indian Farms
To
Limestone County Plantations

Alabama Plantation Series

Rickey Butch Walker

Copyright 2021 © Bluewater Publications

First Edition

All rights reserved under International and Pan-American Copyright Convention. No part of this publication may be reproduced or transmitted in any form or by any means, electronic or mechanical, including photocopying, recording, or by any information storage and retrieval system, without prior written permission from the publisher.

Bluewater Publications
BWPublications.com

Published in the United States by Bluewater Publications.
Printed in the United States of America.

This work is based on the authors' personal interpretation of research.

Bluewater Publications
books by
Rickey Butch Walker

Cotton Was King, Volume I, Lauderdale County, AL,
ISBN 978-1-934610-99-2, $19.95

Cotton Was King, Volume II, Franklin/Colbert County, AL
ISBN 978-949711-08-8, $19.95

Cotton Was King, Volume III, Lawrence/Colbert County, AL
ISBN 978-1-949711-14-1, $24.95

Appalachian Indians of the Warrior Mountains: History and Culture,
ISBN 978-1-934610-99-2, $19.95

Appalachian Indian Trails of the Chickamauga: Lower Cherokee Settlements,
ISBN 978-1-934610-91-6, $19.95

Celtic Indian Boy of Appalachia: A Scots Irish Cherokee Childhood,
ISBN 978-1-934610-75-6, $19.95

Chickasaw Chief George Colbert: His Family and His County,
ISBN 978-1-934610-71-8, $19.95

Doublehead: Last Chickamauga Cherokee Chief,
ISBN 978-1-934610-97-1, $19.95

Hiking Sipsey: A Family's Fight for Eastern Wilderness,
ISBN 978-1-934610-93-0, $19.95

Soldier's Wife: Cotton Fields to Berlin and Tripoli,
ISBN 978-1-934610-12-1, $19.95

Warrior Mountains Folklore: American Indian and Celtic and History in the Southeast, ISBN 978-1-934610-65-7, $24.95

Warrior Mountains Indian Heritage-Teacher's Edition
ISBN 978-1-934610-27-5, $39.95

Warrior Mountains Indian Heritage-Student Edition,
ISBN 978-1-934610-66-4, $24.95

Limestone County

Acknowledgements

Yolanda Morgan Smith, a local historian, was very helpful in the completion of this book. She provided family information on many of the cotton planters of Limestone County, Alabama. I greatly appreciate her valuable assistance in census and agricultural information used in this book. Without her help, the quality of this book would have been greatly diminished.

I also wish to thank David Curott, Ph.D. and former professor at the University of North Alabama in Florence, Alabama, for editing the manuscript of Cotton Was King, Volume IV, Limestone County. His review and assistance in editing this book was greatly appreciated.

Thanks for my wife, Mary Anne Walker, and my family for allowing me to sacrifice time away from them in completing this book. Their support is very much appreciated.

Contents

Introduction 11

Sims Settlement-1806 24

Fort Hampton 37

Early Limestone County Roads 50

Limestone County, Alabama 62

Planters and Slaves 68

Anderson, Charles D. - Poplar Grove 91

Beaty, Robert 93

Bibb, Thomas - Belle Mina 96

Blackwell, William Henry 106

Bond, Nicholas Pirtle 109

Bradley, Joseph H. 113

Brown, William 116

Cain, Allison Chappell 118

Carroll/Carrell, Grief 121

Cheatham, Christopher - Alba Wood 125

Clark, William Robert 130

Coe, Jesse 135

Coleman, Daniel - Coleman Hill 142

Collier, James - Myrtle Grove 145

Critz, George F. 150

Davis, Captain Nicholas - Walnut Grove 151

Davis, Tinsley 158

Dickerson (Dickinson), Bejamin 161

Dillard, George H. - Oak Mount 163

Donnell, Robert - Pleasant Hill 164

Fisher, Jacob	171
Fletcher Family	174
Gamble, James Hurt - Oak Mount	185
Garrett, Jesse	191
Garrett, Edmond	191
Harris, Captain John Henry - Flower Hill	196
Hine, Silas Jr.	202
Horton, Rodah	207
Houston, George Smith	210
Jackson, James	214
Jones, John Nelson S. - Druid's Grove	218
Jordan, Samuel - Oakland	225
Lane, James M.	227
Maclin, Captain Thomas - Slopeside	229
Malone, George - Cambridge	235
Malone, Thomas	240
Marshall, George, W.	244
Mason, Captain John Richardson	245
Matthews, Luke Sr.	248
McDonald, Captain Jonathan R.	257
Moore, John and Rebecca Fletcher	260
Peebles/Peoples, Sterling	265
Peebles, Henry Jr.	267
Pickett, Sarah Orrick - Myrtle Grove	271
Pryor, Luke Sr. - Sugar Creek	276
Ragland, Samuel Major - Triana	281
Rowe, William	284

Tate, Waddy 285
Trice, William 290
Vest, Samuel M. 291
Ward, William 293
Washington, Starke 293
White, Samuel D. 294
References 296
Index 299

Limestone County

Introduction

The present-day Limestone County, Alabama, was Indian lands for some 14,000 years before the early 1800's when white settlers and cotton land barons with their black slaves arrived in the area. In the aboriginal scene of the Limestone area, paleo hunters were the first humans to enter and live along the Elk River and Tennessee River thousands of years ago. Along the with the paleo nomads, prehistoric cultures of archaic, woodland, and Mississippian people dominated, lived, and thrived along Elk River Shoals 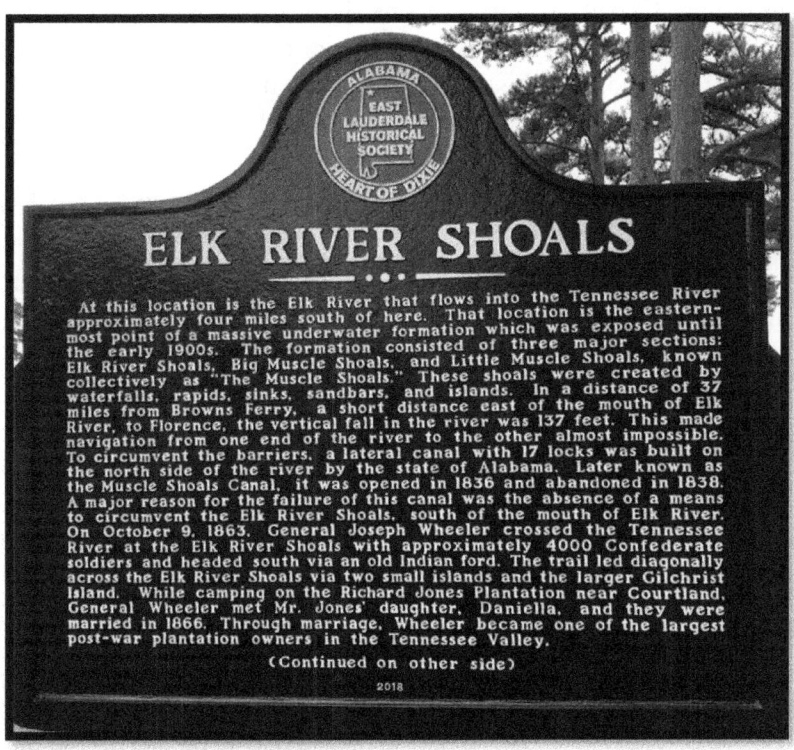 of the Tennessee River including creeks, streams, and springs across the entire Limestone County area. The woodland Copena people and the Mississippians left their mark on the lands of North Alabama by building earthen mounds for burial and ceremonial purposes.

During prehistoric times, large populations of Native American Indian people lived along the Muscle Shoals (Chake Thlocko, Christnnwalee, or Chaka-tsh-locke) of the Tennessee River (Hogoheegee or River of the Cherokees) in North Alabama. For thousands of years, the Muscle Shoals provided prehistoric Southeastern American Indians a staple diet of freshwater mussels of some 80 species and an abundance of wildlife.

Along the Muscle Shoals of the Tennessee River, evidence of sizeable Indian populations still exists in the huge shell middens left by these aboriginal people. Some of the ancient shell mounds over 300 feet long, 100 feet wide, and more than 20 feet high were formed during thousands of years of discarding the shells of mollusks after the meat was cooked and eaten. Artifacts in the areas near some of these old prehistoric shell middens date back to the Paleo Indians who were earliest human inhabitants of the Tennessee Valley.

Prehistoric Indians of Limestone County

The Paleo people lived along the Elk River and Muscle Shoals area of Limestone County from 12,000 BC to 8,000 BC. The Paleo inhabitants were basically nomadic hunters who used spears tipped with beautiful, fluted chert (flint) projectile points. These paleo points have names which include Beaver Lake, Clovis, Cumberland, Folsom, Greenbrier, Quad, Redstone, and others.

The Archaic people lived along the Muscle Shoals from about 8,000 BC to 1,000 BC. These Archaic folks were hunters and gatherers who hunted with atlatl spears tipped with notched projectile points such as the Adena, Big Sandy, Decatur, Dovetail, Hardin, Kirk, Pickwick, Pine Tree, Lost Lake, and others.

The period of Woodland people lasted from about 1,000 BC to AD 1,000. These people were hunters, gatherers, and farmers who practiced ritual burial. They established long term villages with agricultural crops. The Woodland people built huge earthen mounds such as those at Oakville Indian Mounds and Florence. In addition to spears, the Woodland people used bow and arrows to hunt game. Woodland projectile points were basically stemmed and included Bakers Creek, Beacon Island, Flint Creek, Jacks Reef, Limestone, Swan Lake, Wade, and others.

The Mississippian people lived at the Muscle Shoals from AD 1,000 to AD 1540 when Desoto's chroniclers recorded his historic journey through North Alabama. The Mississippians primarily used a bow and arrow for hunting and warfare. Mississippian projectiles were usually small points attached to an arrow and shot with a bow. These points included the Hamilton, Keota, Levanna, Lozenge, Madison, Nova, Nodena, Sand Mountain, and others.

Historic Indian Tribes of Limestone County

During historic times five Indian tribes lived and occupied the area of Elk River and the Muscle Shoals of the Tennessee River in the area that would become Limestone County. These tribes had different languages and cultures and at times they would go to war against each other for control of the valuable river bottom lands of North Alabama.

Yuchi

The historic period of Limestone County began after Desoto traveled through North Alabama in 1540 when the first known written history was recorded. In the earliest historical records, the Yuchi (Euchee) were living along the Elk River in Limestone County at the time of Desoto's expedition. The Yuchi considered themselves the First People of North Alabama and are some of the most pure traditionalists among the various Indian tribes. The Yuchi were known as the "Children of the Sun."

According to the Journal of Muscle Shoals History, "...the Cherokees were not the first Indians to live at the Muscle Shoals on the Tennessee River. This honor belongs to the mound builders, who were followed by the Euchees (Yuchi), a tribe having a unique language and no migration legend. They may have lived at the Shoals in pre-historic times. The Euchee were probably living at the Shoals when Desoto (1540) came through Alabama and were definitely there in 1700 when discovered by some traveling Canadians...the Euchees departed from the Shoals and moved to the mountainous regions of what is now East Tennessee" (Watts, 1973).

Another contingent of the Yuchi migrated south along Black Warriors' Path and settled near the mouth of Euchee Creek and the Chattahoochee River in present-day Russell County, Alabama, near the area where Fort Mitchell would be established. Eventually, a post route from Fort Mitchell and Fort Hampton in Limestone County would be established and known as Mitchell Trace (originally Black Warriors' Path).

John R. Swanton in his book, <u>The Indians of the Southeastern United States</u> (1987), shows the Yuchi (Euchees) living along Elk River in Limestone County and the Tennessee River at the mussel shoals in the early 1700's. However, a few Yuchi remained in the Tennessee Valley maintaining friendly relations with Doublehead and the Chickamauga faction of Lower Cherokee. Some of the Yuchi intermarried with the Cherokee and assisted Doublehead in establishing his domain and Indian alliance along the Muscle Shoals of the Tennessee River.

Cherokee

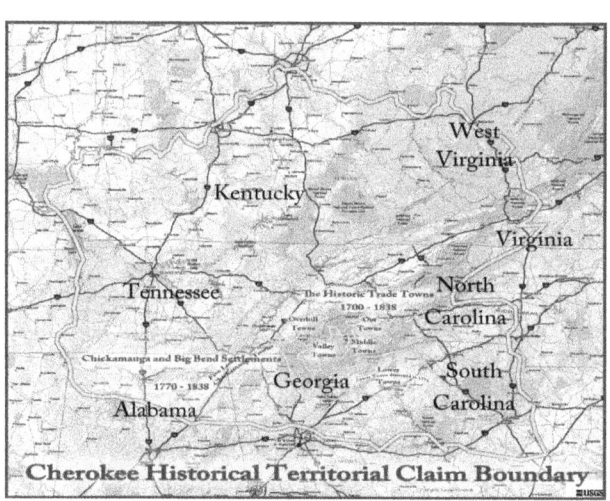

Professor Henry Sale Halbert (January 14, 1837-May 8, 1916) stated, "After moving southward, the maximum boundaries of the Cherokees once included southwest Virginia, the western part of North and South Carolina, north Georgia, east Tennessee, and the Tennessee Valley of North Alabama. Tradition and archaeology agree the Cherokee were occupants of the Tennessee Valley in North Alabama in prehistoric times. How long they have lived in this area is not known, but some time before 1650, they abandoned this region, and retired beyond the Cumberland and Sand Mountain, but reserving their abandoned country as a hunting ground." Limestone County was among the areas of North Alabama that was a part of the Cherokee ancestral hunting grounds.

Shawnee

A few years after the Yuchi and Cherokee moved from the Limestone County area of the Muscle Shoals on the Tennessee River, bands of Shawnee migrated south from the Ohio and Cumberland River Valleys. The Shawnee took possession of the country which the Cherokee and Chickasaw claimed as their primary hunting grounds. The Cherokee became very angry and declared war against the Shawnee. After years of warfare, the Cherokee formed an alliance with the Chickasaw. The two tribes drove the Shawnee from the Tennessee and Cumberland Valleys and forced them back to the Ohio River Valley.

Shortly after Doublehead established his stronghold along the Muscle Shoals, he and other Cherokee leaders allied themselves with the Shawnee. Tecumseh, the great Shawnee leader, actually got his early experience fighting white intruders with the Chickamauga Confederacy.

Chickasaw

After the conflict with the Shawnees ended, the Chickasaws moved east to the Chickasaw Old Fields on Chickasaw Island in the Tennessee River south of present-day Huntsville, Alabama. According to Professor Henry Sale Halbert, "…around the mid 1700's, the Chickasaw's formed the settlement in the Chickasaw Old Fields, which angered the Cherokees very much against their former allies. A great battle was fought in the Chickasaw village in 1769, in which the Chickasaw were victors, but their victory was gained at such a great loss that they retreated from the country, but the Chickasaws continued their claims to lands on both sides of the Tennessee River."

Shortly after the fight with the Cherokee in 1769, the Chickasaws moved west from the Chickasaw Old Fields beyond Caney Creek in the western portion of present-day Colbert County, Alabama. As the Chickasaws moved down the Tennessee River toward Mississippi, Doublehead and his followers moved into and occupied the Muscle Shoals. The Chickamauga faction of Lower Cherokee began reclaiming their ancestral hunting grounds along the Great Bend of the Tennessee River. By 1770 under Doublehead's leadership, they established Cherokee villages on both sides of the Tennessee River along the Muscle Shoals.

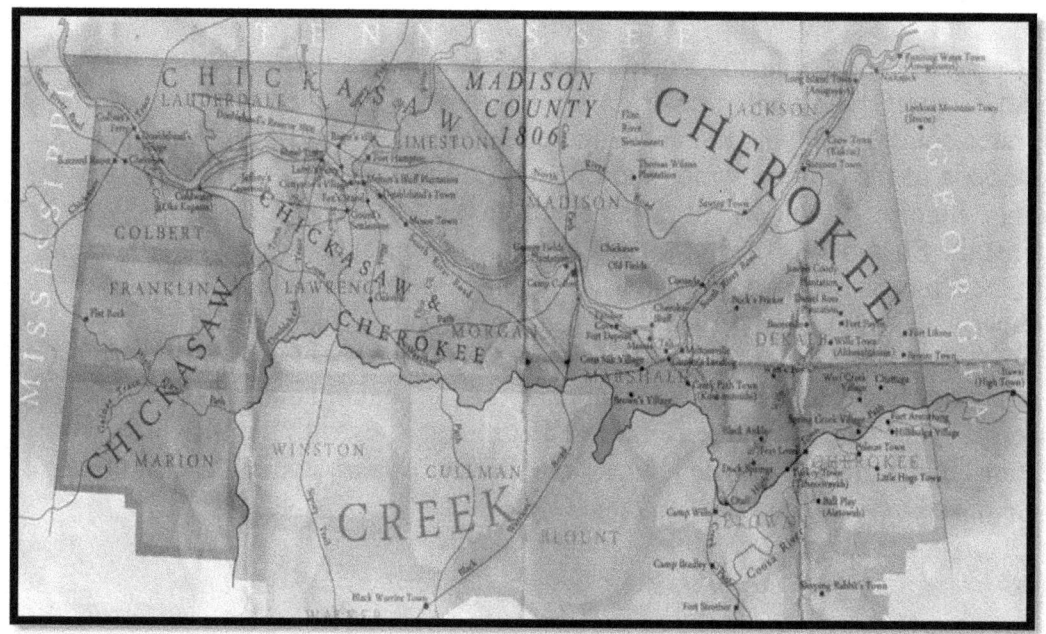

Creek

The Creek Indians claimed their territory extended to the south banks of the Tennessee River including the Muscle Shoals of North Alabama. The boundary line between the Creeks and Cherokees remained in question for many years with the Creeks denying that a boundary existed in the Muscle Shoals area of the Tennessee River; however, as reported by Phil Hawkins, Jr., "In the year 1793, the Cherokees had a settlement at the Muscle Shoals (Shoal Town on Big Muscle Shoals), Doublehead and Katagiskee were the chiefs, and the Creeks had a small settlement…The Cherokee settlement extended southwardly from the shoal probably a mile and a half" (Powell, 1887).

The Upper Creeks befriended Chief Doublehead and became one of his strongest allies. As they had wanted for many years, the Creeks united in a confederacy with Doublehead to carry their war to the white settlers who were invading their frontiers, killing their people, and taking their lands. The Creeks assisted Doublehead in establishing villages along the Muscle Shoals of the Tennessee River and followed him as their leader on many raiding parties into the

Cumberland settlements. At times, as many as 700 Creek warriors would follow Doublehead on the warpath.

Doublehead's Creek alliance began to weaken in the Tennessee Valley after Doublehead agreed to peaceful relations with United States President George Washington on June 26, 1794, meeting in Philadelphia. The break in friendly relations with the Creeks was due in part to the response Doublehead received from Governor William Blount telling him to control the Creeks living in his territory if he wanted to maintain peace. The issue with the Creeks played a major role in Doublehead's acceptance by the government officials; at the time, Doublehead was a lesser of two evils. The bribes offered to Doublehead by the government were of assistance in maintaining peace, controlling the Creeks, and encouraging him to give up Cherokee lands.

French and British Claims of Limestone County

Nina Leftwich states in Two Hundred Years at the Shoals (1935): "Both the French and the English contended for the Indian trade along the western waters; the French planted a post at Muscle Shoals before 1715. Because of the increasing importance of trade with the whites, the Cherokees planted villages near the Muscle Shoals area in the last quarter of the eighteenth century."

According to historical records, the French established a fort about 1715 on the Muscle Shoals of the Tennessee River. By 1763, the English would drive out the French Indian traders and lay claim to the Tennessee Valley. British agents developed an alliance with the Cherokee tribe that lived along Muscle Shoals the Tennessee River. The English goods were much better than those of the French and were usually at a greatly reduced price; therefore, the English effectively undermined French influence in the North Alabama area.

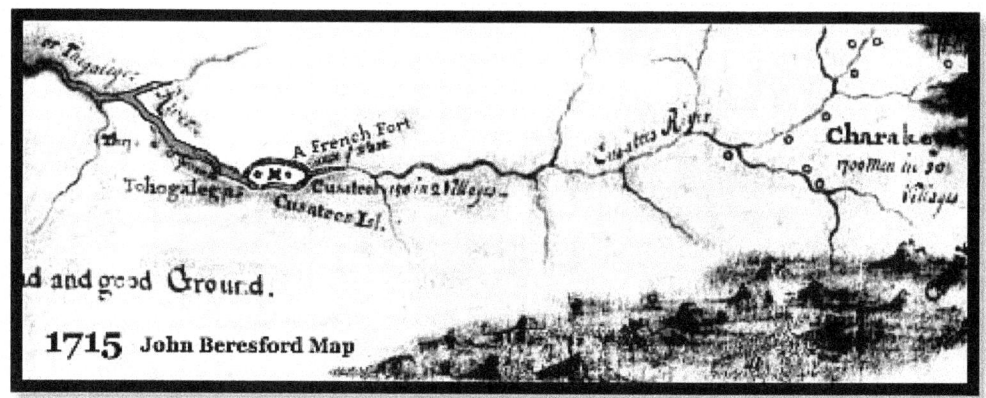

1715 John Beresford Map

Both the Cherokees at the Muscle Shoals and the Chickasaws to the west benefitted from English trade from the British warehouses at Olde Charles Town by way of the Tennessee River Road. In <u>The Dividing Paths</u> (1995), Tom Hatley discusses early trade with the Cherokees along the Tennessee River Road, "This river road was scarcely traveled in the years before 1715...there is no doubt that joint Cherokee and Carolina trade expanded greatly, along with the burgeoning commerce of Charlestown, right up to the 1750's...deerskin loadings remained high at the Charlestown docks, and a significant percentage of these were of Cherokee origin...On the other hand a Charlestown alliance with the tribe would finally give Carolinians access to the long-sought Tennessee River road to the Mississippi."

Standing Turkey, Pigeon, and Ostenaco signed the Royal Proclamation of 1763 in England.

In 1762, three Cherokee leaders, Standing Turkey (the brother of Doublehead), Ostenaco, and the Pigeon, went to England with Lieutenant Henry Timberlake. In 1763, they signed the Royal Proclamation with the King of England which supposed to prohibit British/English subjects from moving west of the Appalachian Mountains and recognize the area as Indian reserve lands. Within some 53 years after the signing of the Royal Proclamation, all Indian land claims would be extinguished in Limestone County, Alabama, and in 75 years, all Indian lands in North Alabama were ceded.

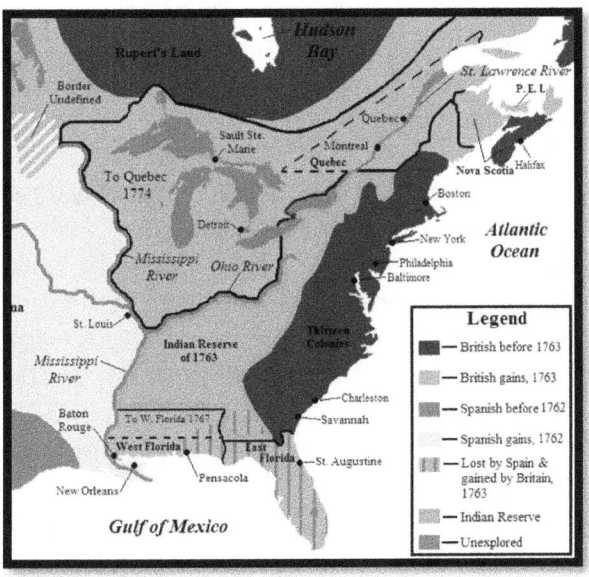

After taking the area from the French, the English merchants from the 13 colonies began establishing alliances with the tribes occupying the entire Tennessee Valley. They built a trading outpost on Chickamauga Creek some 15 miles south of the Tennessee River near present-day Rossville, Georgia, under the control of John McDonald who worked for John Stuart, the British Superintendent of Southwestern Indian Affairs, at Old Charles Town. John McDonald married Anne Shorey, the half-blood Cherokee daughter of the Englishman William Shorey and a full blood Cherokee woman.

From the Chickamauga warehouses and trading post of the British, John McDonald would established trading relations with the Cherokee, Chickasaw, Creek, Shawnee, and other tribes living across the southeastern United States. Cherokee people living in Limestone County and other areas across North Alabama along the Tennessee River would greatly benefit from the English trade.

In the late 1700s, although the French had lost their claim to the Muscle Shoals area to the British, they established a trading post at the Cherokee Town of

Coldwater. The town was located near the mouth of Spring Creek at Tuscumbia Landing on the Tennessee River. Reportedly, Coldwater had 54 people which consisted of 35 Lower Cherokees, 10 Upper Creeks, nine Frenchmen, and some women and children.

On June 13, 1787, Coldwater was destroyed by General James Robertson and his 130 men from Fort Nashboro (Nashville) on the Cumberland River. General Robertson forces killed some 14 Lower Cherokees and six Creeks along with some French traders who were instigating raids on the Cumberland River Settlements. General Robertson's forces burned the Coldwater town and returned to Fort Nashboro, Tennessee; however, Robertson's campaign failed to diminish Chickamauga raids in the area of Nashville, Tennessee. Chickamauga warriors under Doublehead's command would continue their war against the Cumberland settlements into 1795.

Doublehead

In 1770 after the Chickasaw migrated west toward the present-day State of Mississippi, the Chickamauga Cherokee under the leadership of Doublehead established settlements along the Muscle Shoals of North Alabama. From the 1770-1807, Doublehead lived and controlled the area of Limestone County along the Great Bend of the Tennessee River. The Lower Cherokees under Doublehead's leadership established Gunter's at present-day Guntersville, Mouse Town at the crossing at the mouth of Fox's Creek to Cow Ford Landing in Limestone County, Doublehead's Town at the Browns Ferry Road crossing at head of Elk River Shoals, Melton's Bluff on the south bank of the Tennessee River in the middle of Elk River Shoals, Melton's farm in Limestone County, Roger's Ville in Lauderdale County west of Elk River, Gourd's Settlement at present-day Courtland, Shoal Town on the Big Muscle Shoals (area of Big Nance's Creek, Town Creek, and Bluewater Creek), Cold Water at Tuscumbia Landing, Doublehead's Village east of Colbert's Ferry, and other Indian villages along the Tennessee River.

About 1770 prior to the Chickamauga War, Doublehead's Town at the head of Elk River Shoals became the stronghold of Doublehead, his Lower Cherokee family/followers, and their Chickamauga allies of various tribes. Even though there were previous conflicts among the Indian tribes that occupied the area of the Muscle Shoals, Doublehead worked with the tribes of Chickasaw, Creek, and Shawnee to form alliances in order to organize the strongest historic Indian confederacy to ever occupy the Tennessee Valley's Great Bend. Doublehead would rule the Muscle Shoals with an iron fist; under his leadership, the confederacy would protect the Muscle Shoals from white encroachment.

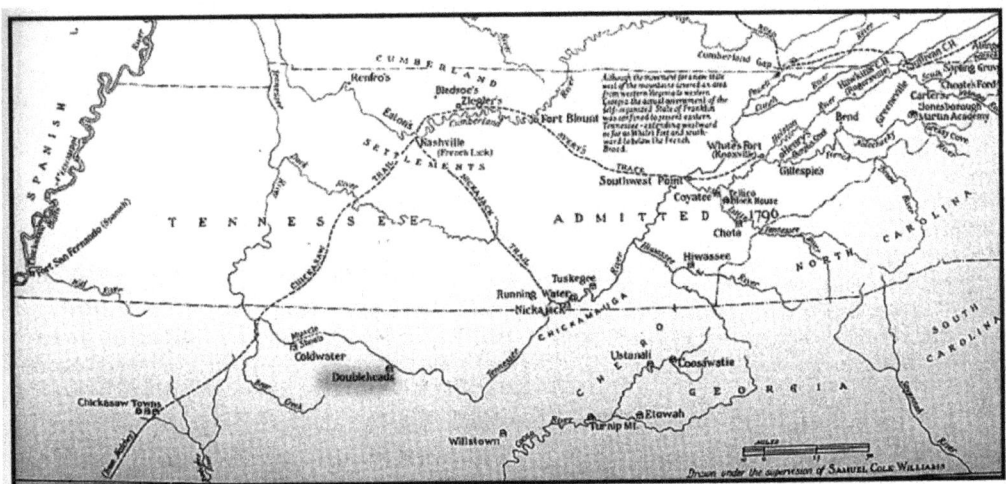

Map from <u>Atlas of American History</u> by James Truslow Adams, showing home site of Doublehead (c. 1770-1802) on south bank of Tennessee River at Brown's Ferry, Lawrence County, Alabama.

The Muscle Shoals towns of Doublehead were used by Chickamauga Confederacy to keep out white land speculators and to fight the Cumberland settlers for the buffalo hunting grounds in middle Tennessee. Two factors were primarily responsible for the start of the Chickamauga War. First, in 1775, the signing of the Treaty of Sycamore Shoals by the old leaders of the Cherokee gives up ancestral lands in Kentucky and middle Tennessee. The treaty infuriated the young Cherokee warriors with Dragging Canoe being most outspoken. Secondly, in the spring of 1776, the colonial armies General Griffin Rutherford and Andrew Williamson invaded the eastern Cherokee territory destroying the Valley, Middle, and Lower Towns in the eastern portion of the Cherokee Nation. Later that year, William Christian's colonial army invaded the Overhill Towns on the Little Tennessee River and forced the old Cherokee leaders to sign the Cherokee Treaty of 1776.

In order to combat the attacks from the colonies, the Indian tribes trading with the British on Chickamauga Creek south of present-day Chattanooga formed the Chickamauga Confederacy. The confederacy included warriors from the tribes of Lower Cherokee, Chickasaw, Upper Creek, and Shawnee. At various times, members of all these tribes were occupying the Muscle Shoals of the Tennessee River. The Chickamauga Confederacy controlled North Alabama, a portion of Tennessee around Chattanooga, and northwest Georgia.

Doublehead-Chickamauga Warrior

Dragging Canoe was the first Chickamauga Cherokee war chief who led and strengthened the southeastern Indian alliance until his death on March 1, 1792. After the death of Dragging Canoe, half-blood John Watts Jr. (the nephew of Doublehead) took over as chief of the Chickamauga Cherokee; however, Watts only controlled the Lower Cherokee villages along Wills Creek and the Coosa River. He did not enjoy the complete loyalty of the federation that had been established by Dragging Canoe. Doublehead filled the role as the supreme authority of the Chickamauga and ruled without submitting to the orders of other leaders in the confederacy. His great strength was the respect, and he had the complete loyalty of the Lower Cherokee along the Muscle Shoals and the Upper Creek faction of the Chickamauga.

As a Chickamauga leader, Doublehead was not only feared by white settlers and politicians, but also by each tribal faction of the Indian alliance. He backed up his stature by vicious blood thirsty attacks on his enemies encroaching on his aboriginal hunting grounds and homelands. Besides the Lower Cherokee, the Creeks were the largest force among the Chickamauga Confederacy and were extremely loyal to Doublehead. The Creeks helped him establish himself as supreme ruler of the Muscle Shoals and Tennessee River Valley. For some 20 years, Doublehead fought white encroachment during the Chickamauga War from 1775 through 1795. The war was a last-ditch attempt to prevent ancestral Indian lands of the Cherokee to be taken over by white folks.

It would be the last twelve years of his life that Doublehead would seek peace with the white settlers. Prior to his death, Doublehead became a very wealthy businessman. According to historic records, it appears that Doublehead owned some 40 black slaves and his brother-in-law John Melton owned some 60 black slaves prior to 1807.

Doublehead's Reserve was given to him by the Cotton Gin Treaty of January 7, 1806. The treaty also secured a cotton gin or a cotton cleaning machine to be placed at Melton's Bluff in Lawrence County, Alabama. Doublehead's Reserve included all the lands ten miles north of the Tennessee River between the Cheewalee (Elk River) and Teekeetanoah (Cypress Creek). A portion of the reserve was in the western middle part of present-day Limestone County along the west side of Range 6 West from near the mouth of Anderson Creek to the mouth of Sugar Creek west of Elk River. Starting in 1806, Doublehead begin leasing lands in his reserve to many white settlers who formed communities in Limestone County such as the Sims Settlement.

Doublehead made shady deals with government officials to his own personal benefit and members of his family. These deals were disliked by many of the Upper Cherokees and used as an excuse for his assassination. After his secret dealing with the government was exposed, Doublehead would realize a widespread decline in his respect. The loss of his feared Chickamauga warrior status would embolden some of his own Cherokee people to murder Doublehead on August 9, 1807.

Doublehead and his Chickamauga alliance would be the last Indian people to occupy and control the valuable piece of real estate along the Muscle Shoals on the Tennessee River known as Chake Thlocko, the Big Ford or Great Crossing Place. The Chickamauga faction of Lower Cherokee lived along the Muscle Shoals until the Turkey Town Treaty of 1816 when they were removed east into their remaining nation or west of the Mississippi River.

During Indian removal, remnants of the great Cherokee Nation passed by Limestone County on their way to lands west of the Mississippi River. Some of the removal contingents went overland through Limestone County and some went by water down the Tennessee River to Waterloo in Lauderdale County where they were placed on steamers and taken west of the Mississippi River. Even though a concerted effort was made to remove all Indian people from the Southeastern United States, many Indian mixed bloods denied their Indian heritage to remain in their ancestral lands of Limestone County and North Alabama.

Sims Settlement-1806

The northeast half of Madison County, including a portion of present-day Limestone County, became the first county in North Alabama. The northeast portion of Limestone County was included in the July 23, 1805, treaty with the Chickasaws and the January 7, 1806, Cotton Gin Treaty with the Cherokees. After Doublehead and his followers signed the treaty, the Chickamauga faction of Lower Cherokees gave up their claims to the land north of the Tennessee River except Doublehead's Reserve to the west. This led to formation of the original Madison County on December 13, 1808.

Many white settlers falsely assumed that the area along Elk River north of the reserve was open to settlement; however, on July 23, 1805, the Chickasaws had only given up the northeast half of present-day Madison County and a small portion of present-day Limestone County. The Chickasaw boundary ran about 45 degrees to the northwest across Tennessee from the mouth of Flint River near Chickasaw Island; however, by treaty, the Chickasaws still owned the land west of that line around the Sims Settlements and Elk River even though the government asked the Chickasaws to voluntarily move their boundary to Caney Creek. Since they did not honor the requested boundary, the Chickasaw lands overlapped Doublehead's Reserve in Limestone and Lauderdale Counties.

Hopewell Treaty

Before the area that became Limestone County was opened to white settlers, it was recognized as Chickasaw land by the United States government in the Hopewell Treaty of January 10, 1786. The treaty with the Chickasaws at Hopewell had an adverse impact on the first white settlers who leased land from Doublehead, or who were squatters in the Sims Settlement area of Elk River of Limestone County.

At the time of the treaty, the United States government was buying an alliance with the Chickasaws even though the Chickamauga faction of Lower Cherokee were living and controlling the area. In 1786, when the Hopewell Treaty was signed, the Chickamauga faction of Lower Cherokee was fighting the Chickamauga War against the United States and the white intruders invading their territory.

The United States government plan was to create conflict between the Chickasaws and Cherokees by recognizing the area as Chickasaw lands. The Chickasaws had suffered great loss at the hands of the Cherokees at Chickasaw Island in 1769. They were smart enough not to pursue war with the Cherokees for the North Alabama lands that included Limestone County; thus, the government plan backfired.

The Cherokees occupied the area of Limestone County from 1770 to the land cessions as part of the Turkey Town Treaty of 1816. The Chickamauga faction of Lower Cherokees lived and controlled the Muscle Shoals, and they had several Cherokee villages along the Tennessee River. During the same time period, historic records do not indicate any Chickasaw settlements along the Muscle Shoals east of George Colbert's Ferry at the Natchez Trace. At the time of the Hopewell Treaty, the Chickasaw had abandoned the Muscle Shoals after their fight with the Cherokee in 1769 at Chickasaw Island (Hobbs Island south of Huntsville).

After Doublehead's death on August 9, 1807, the Chickasaws sought to remove white lease holders of Doublehead's Reserve and white squatters from the area on Elk River that is now present-day Limestone County. Article IV of the 1786 Hopewell Treaty stated, "If an citizen of the United States, or person not being an Indian, shall attempt to settle on any of the lands hereby allotted to the Chickasaws to live and hunt on, such a person shall forfeit the protection of the United States of America, and the Chickasaws may punish him or not as they please." However, the Chickasaws knew better than trying to punish the Cherokees living in the area as long as Doublehead was alive.

With the exception of Madison County and a portion of northeast Limestone County, much of North Alabama continued as the ancestral and historical territory of the Cherokee Nation. Not only was the northeast corner of Limestone County open for settlement but a sizeable area in the midwestern portion of the county was leased to settlers by Doublehead starting in the spring of 1806. These factors led to much confusion for the white settlers leasing and squatting on the lands; however, during the Turkey Town Treaty of September 16-18, 1816, both the Cherokees and Chickasaws gave up their land claims in Limestone County and northwestern portion of North Alabama. When the Indian lands at the Muscle Shoals were ceded to the United States in 1816, John Melton's mixed-blood Cherokee family was living in Limestone County.

Cotton Gin Treaty

Another reason that the area may have been settled by white squatters can be attributed to Doublehead and his white partner/legal advisor Captain John D. Chisholm. They leased Indian lands in Doublehead's Reserve which extended from Elk River to Cypress Creek and some 10 miles north of the Tennessee River. As part of the Cotton Gin Treaty of January 7, 1806, Doublehead was given the reserve for 99 years renewable for 900 years to him and his heirs. The northeast corner of Doublehead's Reserve was a portion of land near the mid-western part of present-day Limestone County west of Elk River and part of the "Over Elk" region of the county.

According to the Cotton Gin Treaty of January 7, 1806, Article 1 states: "The undersigned chiefs and head men of the Cherokee Nation of Indians...relinquish to the United States...all that tract of country which lies to the northward of the river Tennessee and westward of a line to be run from the upper part of the Chickasaw Old Fields...excepting...one tract bounded southerly on the said Tennessee River, at a place called the Muscle Shoals, westerly by a creek called Te Kee, ta, no-eh or Cyprus Creek, and easterly by Chu, wa, lee, or Elk River or creek, and northerly by a line to be drawn from a point on said Elk River ten miles on a direct line from its mouth or Junction with Tennessee River, to a point on the said Cyprus Creek, ten miles on a direct line from its junction with the Tennessee River..." The area of present-day Limestone County which was in Doublehead's Reserve included the land east of the line separating Ranges 6 and 7 West. The Limestone County portion lay in the northeastern corner of Doublehead's Reserve from just northeast of the mouth of Anderson Creek on Elk River to the mouth of Sugar Creek on Elk River and to the west edge of Range 6 West.

Article 2 of the treaty states that "...the Cherokees shall be furnished with a machine for cleaning cotton..." The cotton gin was placed at Melton's Bluff on the Tennessee River in present-day Lawrence County, Alabama. Melton's Bluff was on the south side of the river across from Lucy's Branch.

Article 3 stated: "...the United States...to prevail on the Chickasaw Nation of Indians to agree to the following boundary between that nation and the

Cherokees to the southward of the Tennessee River, viz. beginning at the mouth of Caney Creek near the lower part of the Muscle Shoals, and to run up said creek to its head, and in a direct line from thence to the Flat Stone or Rock, the old corner boundary….the United States…only to endeavor to prevail on the Chickasaw Nation to consent to such a line as the boundary between the two nations."

In the Cotton Gin Treaty of 1806, the United States government agreed to ask the Chickasaws to move their eastern boundary to Caney Creek in present-day Colbert County, but the boundary was not moved until the Turkey Town Treaty of 1816. The government did not compel the Chickasaws to accept Caney Creek as their eastern boundary in 1806 but did so in the Turkey Town Treaty of 1816. Therefore, the 1806 treaty created more confusion by asking the Chickasaws for a voluntary land cession that included all of Limestone County.

Settlement Dispute

The area set aside for Doublehead by the treaty of January 7, 1806, was known as Doublehead's Reserve; the treaty also released the remaining Cherokee land claims of present-day Limestone County to the government. In the fall of 1806, after Doublehead had given up Cherokee land claims north of the Tennessee River except for his reserve, a group of white settlers from east Tennessee led by William and James Sims settled along the Elk River near Buck Island.

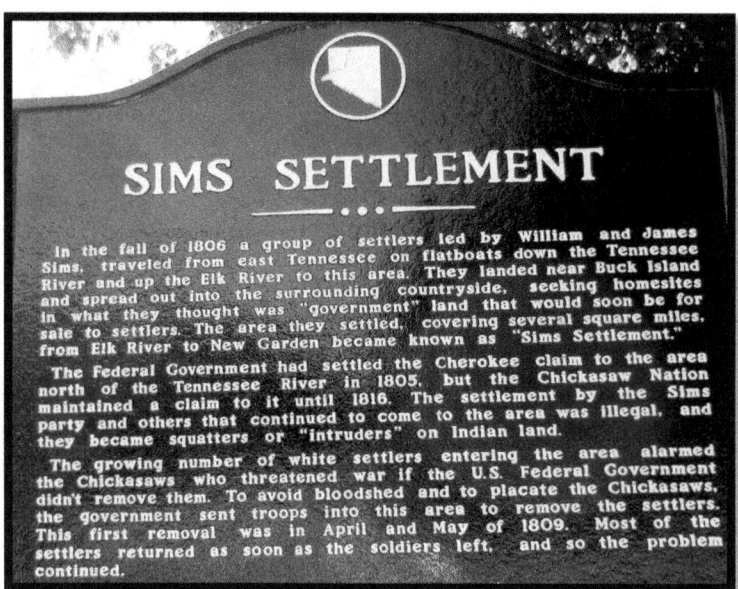

During this same period, Doublehead was leasing lands in his reserve to white settlers.

The Sims settlers came by flatboats by way of the Tennessee River and up Elk River to settle the area that they thought was government lands or Doublehead's Reserve; however, in the 1806 treaty, the Chickasaws did not agree to give up their claims to the land. As long as Doublehead was alive and controlled the area, the white folks in the Sims Settlements had no problems with the Indians, and Doublehead continued to lease lands in his reserve to many white settlers. After the death of Doublehead in 1807, the Chickasaws begin demanding that white settlers be removed from their land claims in present-day Limestone County which eventually resulted in the building of Fort Hampton.

On May 6, 1809, General James Robertson's letter from Nashville, Tennessee, states: "The Chickasaws have been meeting in council. I am now assured that if the white people are not removed off of Doublehead's Reserve by government that the Chickasaw will take measures to do it" (Microcopy 208, roll 4, and number 2303).

According to the Territorial Papers of the United States by Clarence Carter (1934), the Chickasaws pushed for removal of the intruders and the United States recognized Chickasaw claims. The Chickasaws succeeded in having the intruders removed from their lands and inadvertently caused the building of Fort Hampton in Limestone County, Alabama, for that purpose. The following is from the territorial papers:

"In the meantime, the Chickasaws, having learned that the United States had purchased of the Cherokees their supposed claim to the territory as far west as the Tennessee River, including a large region of country to the westward of the limits of the cession of 1805 by the former, construed that fact as a recognition of the sole and absolute title of the Cherokees thereto, and be in consequence very much excited and angered. They were only pacified by an official letter of assurance from the Secretary of War, addressed to Maj. George Colbert, their principal chief, wherein he stated that in purchasing the Cherokee right to the tract in question the United States did not intend to destroy or impair the right of the Chickasaw Nation to the same; but that, being persuaded no actual boundary had ever been agreed on between the Chickasaws and Cherokees and that the

Cherokees had some claim to a portion of the lands, it was thought advisable to purchase that claim, so that whenever the Chickasaws should be disposed to convey their title there should be no dispute with the Cherokees about it."

On September 5, 1810, the intruders on Chickasaw lands petitioned the President and Congress to allow them to stay in present-day Limestone County which at the time was Mississippi Territory. According to the <u>Territorial Papers of the United States</u> concerning the Sims' Settlement on Elk River, the petition of the settlers on the area is as follows:

"To his Excellency James Madison, President of the United States of America, and the honorable Congress assembled: We your petitioners humbly sheweth that a great many of your fellow citizens have unfortunately settled on what is now called Chickasaw land-which has led us into difficultys that tongue cannot express if the orders from the ware department are executed in removeing us off of said land. However in a government like ours founded on the will of the people, we have reason to hope and expect that we shall be treated with as much lennity as the duty you owe to Justice will permit. We therefore wish, Without the shade or colour of falshood, to leve to your consideration the main object of our setling of this country. In the first Place, we understood that all the land on the north side of Tennessee River was purchased of the Indians which was certainly the Case, and further we understood that this was congress land as we call it and by paying of two Dollars per acre we should obtain An undoubted title to our lands and avoide the endless law suits that arise in our neighboring states in the landed property under these and many other impressions of minde that appeared inviteing to us to setle here a great many of us solde our possessions and Came and settled here in the winter and spring of 1807 without any knoledg or intention of violating the laws of government or Infringing on the right of another nation and we remained in this peacefull situation untill the fall of 1807 when General Robertson Came on runing the chickasaw boundary line and he informed us that, though the cherokees had sold this land, yet the chickasaws held a clame to it as their right. And now as booth nations had set up a clame to this land and Government haveing extingushed the cherokee clame; and we who are well acquainted with the boundarys of this country do think in Justice that the cherokees had undoubtedly the best right to this land we could state our reasons for thinking so, in many cases, but we shall only refurr you to one particular, that is when Zacheriah Cocks made a purchase of parte of this country and came in order to settle it he landed on an island in the Mussell Shoals, and was making preparations to in garrison himself but when the Cherokees Understood his intentions they got themselves together and sent in messingers to him telling him if he did not desist and remove his men out of their country they would certainly imbody themselves and cut him off. And Cocks took the alarme And left the Island in the night. And if the Cherokees had not defended this country at that time it may be persumed that it would have been taken from the Chickasaws without asking of them anything about their right to it. For the Cherokees do say that they have held an antiant clame to it which they never lost by sword or treaty untill extinguished by government. And should this be the camse and appeare to your satisfaction that the Cherokees had at least as good a right as the Chickasaw and you haveing that right invested in you-and you are allso willing to pay the Chickasaw for their clame and they refuse to sell it where then can there remain a single doubt In the publick Minde of doing the Chickasaws any kind of unjuistice in making use of the Cherokee clame and saying: if they will not take a reasonable price for their clame we will not remove our fellow citizens off which will bring many women and children to a state of starvation mearly to gratify a heathan nation Who have no better right to this land than we have ourselves And they have by estemation nearly 100,000 acres of land to each man Of their nation and of no more use to government or society than to saunter about upon like so many wolves or bares whilst they who would be a supporte to government and Improve the country must be forsed even to rent poore stony ridges to make a support to rase their famelies on whist there is fine fertile countrys lying uncultivated and we must be debared even from inJoying a small Corner of this land but we believe it Compleatley within your power Whilst you are administering Justice between us and the Chickasaws to say with the greatest propriety that we have once purchased this land and we will not remove our fellow citizens off but let them remain as tennants at will untill the Chickasaws may feell a disposition to sell us their clame therefore we your humble petitioners wish you to take our standing duely into consideration and not say they are a set of dishoneste people who have fled from the lawes of their country and it is no matter what is done With them.for we can support our carractors to be other ways and it is our wish and desire to protect and supporte our own native Government we must informe you that in the settling of this country men was obliged to expose themselves very much and the Climate not helthy a number of respectable men have deceased and left their widows with families Of alphan [orphan] children to rase in the best way they can And you might allmost as well send the sword amongst us as the fammin the time being short that our orders permits us to stay on we wish you to send us an answer to our petition as soon as posable and, for heavens Sake Pause to think what is to become of these poore alphan families who have more need of the help of some friendly parish than to have the strictest orders executed on them who has not a friend in this unfeeling world that is able to asist them Either in geting off of said land or supporting when they are off we are certain in our own minds that if you could have A true representation of our carractor the industry we have made. and the purity of our intentions in settling here together with the justice of our cause you would say in the name of God let them stay on and eat their well earned bread. Perhaps our number may be fare more than you are apprised of from the best calculation that we can make there is Exclusive of Doubleheads Reserve, 2250 souls on what is called Chickasaw land and all of us could live tollerabie comfortable if we Could remain on our improvements but the distance is so great if we are removed off that we cannot take our produce with Us and a great many not in a circumstance to purchase more will in consequence of this be brought to a deplorable situation We shall therefore conclude in hopes that on a due consideration we shall find favour in the sight of your most honourable Body which will in duty binde your petitioners to ever Pray &c."

At least 86 of the signers of the petition are found in the <u>Old Land Records of Limestone County, Alabama</u> (Cowart, 1984), and they are noted by an asterisk; those families returned to the area after Limestone County was created. The white settlers of Doublehead's Reserve and the Sims Settlement on Elk River who signed the 1810 petition are listed below as follows

Jonathan Adams*,
Thomas Adams*,
William Adams Jr.,
William Adams Sr.*,
John Allen*,
John Allman,
David Allred,
Harda Allred,
James Anderson*,
George Arbuthnot,
Clemen Arman(?),

M. Armstrong,
Andrew Arnett,
James Ball,
George Bankhead,
John Bankhead,
John Bartell,
Christopher Baylor,
Jessey Beavers,
John Bell*,
James Bevers,
John Bidell,

John Billinsly,
Francis Bird,
Joan Black*,
John Black Jr.,
John Black Sr.,
Levi Black,
William Black*,
Jonathan Blair*,
Andrew Blithe,
Jacob Blithe,
Abner Borden,

James Borden,
Nicholess Borden,
Damarias Bowling,
William Bowling Jr,
William Bowling Sr,
Joseph Bradley*,
Samuel Bradley*,
James Braden,
Hugh Brandon,
Jaret Brandon,
Mathew Brewer,
Thomas Brighton,
Abraham Brown*,
George Brown*,
Isham Brown,
James Brown,
Joseph Brunson,
Joshua Brunson,
Mathew Brunston,
Josha Bruntson,
James Burleson,
John Burleson,
Jonathan Burleson,
Joseph Burleson,
Adam Burney*,
James Burney,
James Caldwell,
Joseph Calvert,
John Calwell,
Abner Camnon*,
David Capshaw*,
Wm. W. Capshaw,
Joseph Carnes,
William Carnes,
John Carnham,
Benjmin Carrel,
Patsey Carter,

John Chambers*,
William Chambers,
Moses Chot,
William Cochran,
Jonathan Cochron,
Lovill Coffman*,
Betsey Cooper,
George Cooper,
Jessy Cooper,
John Cooper,
John Cooper Jr.,
John Cooper Sr.,
Leire Cooper,
Levi Cooper Jr.,
Levi Cooper Sr.,
William Cooper Jr.,
William Cooper Sr.,
William Conway,
Allen Cotton,
John Cotton,
John Coward,
Fuller Cox,
Samuel Cox*,
William Cox*,
John Crage*,
James Craig*,
William Cramer,
Robert Cravens,
Redden Crisp,
Moses Crosen,
Henry Croslin,
John Croslin,
Benjamin Cross*,
Henry Cross*,
Shaderick Cross,
Gilly Crowson,
Isaac Crowson,

Levi Cummins*,
Francis Daugherty,
John Daugherty,
Edward Davis,
Henry Davis,
Henson Day,
Bernard Devan*,
Chale Dever,
Jessy Dillion,
Thomas Dodd,
Rawleigh Dodson,
David Dudden,
James Dunahoo,
Alexander Dunham,
James Dunham,
Alexander Dutton,
Charles Easely,
Samuel Easely,
William Ellis*,
Joseph England,
John Eppler,
Jonathan Eppler,
Henry Evans,
Joseph Evans*,
Edmond Fears,
George Fergel,
William Ferrell,
James Ford,
Joseph Foster,
Robert Foury,
Simon Foy,
Issac Fraey,
Bridges Freeman,
Amos French*,
Benjamin French*,
Edward Frost,
James Garner,

Elisha Garritt,
Cornelius Gatliff,
John Gebbens,
Robert Gebbins,
James Gibbons,
Joseph Gibbons,
Saml Gibbons,
Aaron Gibson*,
Isaac Gibson,
James Green,
Philmer Green Sr.,
Jonathan Greenhaw*
William Greenhaw*,
Clouds Greenhow,
GreenberyGreenhow
Robert Gresham*,
Ann Grin(?),
John Hamlin,
John Hakins,
Nathanniel Hannet,
James Harbin,
Jessee Harbin,
Nathaniel Harbin,
Thomas Hardy,
Amerida Hatton,
John Hatton,
Robert Hatton,
George Hauge,
Thomas Henderson*
H. T. Hendry,
Joseph L. Hendry,
James William Hill*,
James Hodge*,
John Hodge,
William Hodge,
John Hodges,

Robert Hodges Jr.,
Milly Hogwood,
George Honbre,
James Hood,
William Hood Jr.,
William Hood Sr.,
William Hooker,
Harmon Horn,
Elye Hornback,
Charles Hulsey,
Hardin Hulsey,
James Humphrs*,
William Humphrs,
James Isaac,
Benjamin Ishmal,
Anderson Jackson,
Joel James,
Ann Johnstons,
Joseph Jones*,
Joseph L. Jones,
Caleb Juett,
Joseph Keen,
James Kellett,
Joseph Kellett,
William Kellett,
Prier Kile,
Thomas Kile,
William Kile *,
John Kim,
Daniel Kinny,
John Kirkendall,
Abraham Kirkelot,
Benjamin Land,
Isaac Lane*,
Caty Lawrence,
James Leath,

William Lilly,
Richard Linville*,
George Loften,
Lennard Lofton,
James Long,
Joseph Looker,
Aaron Luisley,
Beverly Luster,
David Luster,
James Luster,
Jesop Luster,
John Luster,
John Lynn,
Henry Lysby,
Asa Magge,
William Magers(?),
Elijah Major,
James Major,
Obediah Martin,
William Martin*,
Alexander Masky,
Reel Matcok,
Berry Matlock,
William Mayer,
Duncan McAntire,
James McConnell,
Jas. M. McConnell,
Sami McConnell,
George McCown,
David McCutcheon,
John McCutcheon,
Robert McGowen,
William McGowen,
Henry McGuin,
Daniel McIntyre,
Jeremiah McKellins,
James McKenny*,

John McKenny*,
Ruben McKenny*,
Roland McKenny,
Robert McKenny*,
Wm. McKenny*,
James McMahan,
Christiana McRavey,
Drankey Medders,
Abraham Miller,
Alex Miller,
David Miller,
Henry Miller,
James Miller*,
John Miller*,
George Mitchell*,
John Mitchell Sr.*,
John Mitchell Jr.,
Mark Mitchell,
Alexander Moor,
Amos Moor,
Robert Moor,
Shadrach Morres,
James Mossy,
John Mowery*,
James Mullens,
Thomas Mullin,
William Mullins*,
Benjamin Murrell*,
Isaac Murrell,
Richard Murrell*,
William Murrell,
John Myers,
James Neill,
John Nelson,
Samuel Nelson,
William Nelson*,
James Norman,
Michael Odaniell,
Hirram O'Neel,
Mitchell O'Neel,
Tiery O'Neel,
John Paine,
Jesse Panton,
John Panton,
David Parker*,
John Parmerly,
William Payne,
Joshua Perkins,
Isaac Perrett,
Beverly Philips,
Joel Philips,
Andrew Pickens,
James Pickins,
Thomas Pool*,
James Preed,
Samuel Preed Jr.,
Samuel Preed Sr.,
Elijah Price,
Thomas Price*,
Polly Prigman,
Jacob Pyeatt,
James Pyeatt,
George Ogel,
Benjamin Osbourn,
Elisha Rainbolt,
John Ray*,
John Read,
Thomas Read*,
James Redey,
Thomas Redus*,
John Reed*,
Malachi Reeves,
James Renn,
James Reynolds,
Jessey Richardson*,
William Riggs,
Ely Robertson*,
Mahaley Robertson,
Michel Robertson,
Richard Robertson*,
Samuel Robertson *,
John Rogers,
John Rosson,
Simon Rosson,
Jeremiah Rowlen,
John Runnels,
John Sanders*,
Reuben Sanders,
John Sauls,
John Scaggs,
Jacob Scallern,
John Scallern,
John Sessoms,
Fredrich Shaly,
George Shaly,
Michael Shaly,
Owen Shannon,
Owin Shannon Sr.,
Isack Shipman,
Edward Shoat,
Valentine Shoat,
Aaron Shote,
John Shote,
David Simon,
Abraham Sims,
Elizebeth Sims,
Grizell Sims,
James Sims*,
Charles Skaggs Jr.,
Charles Skaggs Sr.,

Thomas Skagg*,
James Slaughter*,
William Slaughter*,
Alexander Smith*,
Andrew Smith,
Bryan Smith,
Charles Smith,
Ezekiel Smith,
Felps Smith,
James Smith*,
John Smith Jr.,
John Smith Sr.*,
Matt Smith,
Reuben Smith,
Samuel Smith*,
William Smith,
William Smith,
William Smith Jr.,
William Smith Sr.*,
Robert Stenson*,
William Stephens,
James Steward,
William Stinson,
Marckel Stockdon,
Lewis Tacket,
Any Taylor,
Ellken Taylor,
Gabriel Taylor,
George Taylor,
Hanum Taylor,
John Taylor,
John Taylor Jr.,
John Taylor Sr.*,
Robert Taylor*,
William Taylor*,
Elkin Tayler,
John Tayler*,
John Thomas*,
David Thompson,
Robert Thresher,
Eli Tidwell Jr.,
Eli Tidwell Sr.,
Millenton Tidwell,
Millin Tidwell,
John Toliver,
Archable Tremble,
Walter Tremble,
John Trimble,
Micheal Trimble,
Cabot Turner,
Benjamin Tutt,
John Umphres,
John Vans,
William Voss,
John Wager,
John Wainwright,
Robert Wallis,
David Water,
John Webb*,
Larkin Webb,
John Welch,
William Welch Sr.,
Susan Wigges,
Betsey Williams,
Charles Williams*,
Sally Williams,
George S. Wilson*,
Calvin Wittey,
Robert Wood,
James Wooley,
John Wynn*."

On October 1, 1810, the petition was received by the United States government and was addressed to James Madison, President of United States. As noted in the petition, there were 2,250 people living on Doublehead's Reserve and the Sims Settlement; however, a fraction of those signed the petition. Probably, a lot of women and children were not included as signers of the petition. The petition was signed by 450 white settlers who had homes and farms on Doublehead's Reserve and Sims Settlement of present-day Limestone County. They were referred to as intruders because the Chickasaw still claimed the territory.

Fort Hampton

After the August 9, 1807, assassination of Doublehead, his reserve leases were voided by the United States government. The white settlers were told that their land claims were invalid and belonged to the Chickasaw Nation. The government tried to force the people who had leased lands in Doublehead's Reserve and settled lands in the Sims Settlement to give up their claims and leave.

After the white settlers refused to leave, the Chickasaws demanded that the illegal squatters be removed from their lands by the government. At the time, some of those lands along the river were still occupied by Chickamauga Cherokees. In order to appease the Chickasaws, the United States government built Fort Hampton to remove these white squatters from the lands west of Madison County that still belonged to the Chickasaws by the Hopewell Treaty of January 10, 1786.

Starting on August 4, 1810, Fort Hampton was built on a hill east of Elk River and north of the Tennessee River near the old North River Road in Mississippi Territory. The fort became the home to the soldiers who were required by duty to remove the intruders from land claims of the Chickasaw Indians. Even though the Chickasaws had not lived on those lands around Elk River or the Muscle Shoals after 1770, the United States still recognized their claims.

Fort Hampton became a United States Army garrison that was erected to remove white settlers from Doublehead's Reserve, the Sims Settlement, and to keep additional white squatters off Chickasaw land claims. "Lt. Colonel Robert Purdy of the 7th U.S. Infantry located Fort Hampton on a hill east of the (Elk) river on August 4, 1810" (Dunnavant, 1993). The fort was built a few miles east of Elk River in present-day Limestone County near the North River Road or present-day Highway 72. It was one of the only forts built to protect Indian lands from white encroachment.

After the 1816 treaty, the Chickasaws lands were recognized as being west of Caney Creek in present-day Colbert County. Finally on March 26, 1818, the United States Congress approved legislation that allowed the Sims settlers to acquire the land that they had struggled to keep since moving into the area in 1806.

John Melton

At the time Fort Hampton was built to remove white settlers, some members of the Chickamauga faction of Lower Cherokees were occupying the area of the Muscle Shoals. The John and Ocuma Melton family lived in the area of present-day Limestone County between Fort Hampton and the Tennessee River prior to the Turkey Town Treaty of 1816. Irishman John Melton was the white brother-in-law of Doublehead; Ocuma, the youngest sister of Doublehead, was the Cherokee wife of John.

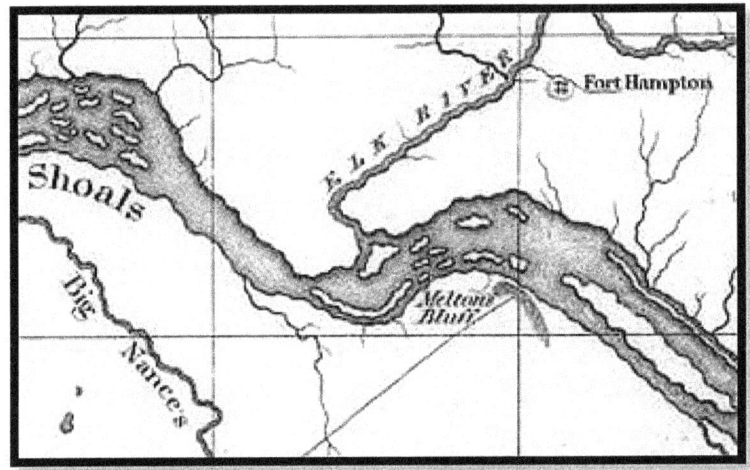

Melton's Bluff-1817 peel and Sannoner map

After the June 26, 1794, Treaty of Philadelphia, Doublehead became a business man and cotton planter with the assistance of his brother-in-law John Melton. Doublehead and Melton owned some 100 black slaves, and with their slave labor, they became very successful farmers of cotton, corn, and livestock including beef cattle that Doublehead sold to the United States military.

Originally, John and Ocuma Melton lived near the middle of Elk River Shoals on the south bank of the Tennessee River at the Cherokee village known as Melton's Bluff. Ocuma, the Cherokee wife of Irishman John Melton, was born about 1750. She was the daughter of Great Eagle (Willenawah) and the sister of Red Bird, Wurteh, Old Tassel, Standing Turkey, Big Nance (Nancy), Doublehead, Pumpkin Boy, Sequechee, WahHatchie, and UlauHatchy.

By 1780, John and Ocuma had followed Doublehead to the Muscle Shoals. They settled near Doublehead, the brother of Ocuma, on the Elk River Shoals area of the Tennessee River in North Alabama. Doublehead lived at Doublehead's Town at the head of the Elk River Shoals near Browns Ferry while his sister Ocuma settled at Melton's Buff some eight miles downstream from her brother.

Melton's Bluff was a Chickamauga Cherokee Indian town that was located in present-day Lawrence, County, Alabama, between Mallard Creek and Spring Creek. For many years, the high flat land above the river bluff was the home of Ocuma and John Melton, and they had several children including Charles, David, Lewis, Elick, Thomas, James, Merida, and Rhea's wife. Rhea was the son-in-law of John Melton, but the name of his wife was unknown.

According to Anne Newport Royall in Letters from Alabama 1817-1822, John and Ocuma owned large farms on both sides of the river and a great number of slaves. They farmed cotton which was a very important Cherokee product with the use of black slaves. Their farming operations were primarily the flat fertile lands along the two upstream shoals which included Elk River Shoals and Big Muscle Shoals of the Tennessee River.

In 1813 during the Creek Indian War and some two years prior to the death of her husband, Ocuma and John moved to the north side of the river in present-day Limestone County, Alabama. They moved from Melton's Bluff on the south side of the Tennessee River for fear of attacks by the Creeks and to be near Fort Hampton for protection. John and Ocuma Melton had a home and farm in present-day Limestone County south of Fort Hampton and north of the Tennessee River.

According to Anne Royall in Letters from Alabama 1817-1822, "John Melton lived in a fine house on the north side of the river and died rich in a good old age." According to local folklore, John Melton was buried in the McNutt Cemetery in Limestone County; there is no known record of Ocuma's burial site.

On June 7, 1815, John Melton died while living in present-day Limestone County on the north side of the river; his Cherokee wife Ocuma probably lived there until the 1816 treaty took the Indian lands. Shortly after his death, John Melton's wife wrote a letter to Cherokee Indian agent Colonel Return J. Meigs; she was voicing her concerns about her husband's brother on the Duck River getting all the property they had accumulated. The letter written by Ocuma was dated June 30, 1815 (Microcopy 208, roll 7, and number 3229).

Mrs. Ocuma Melton's letter to Colonel Meigs is as follows: "My husband John Melton died at his residence below Ft. Hampton 7 instant. He became a resident of Cherokee Nation 35 years ago and married me not long afterward according to established custom of my nation. He died of considerable property which I am told me and my children will be deprived of by his brother, a citizen of the United States who resides on Duck River in Tennessee. Please advise me what to do."

Family of John and Ocuma Melton

In the Lawrence County cotton book, a mistake was made in the children of John and Ocuma Melton. It was stated that Merida Melton, probably one of John Melton's daughters or granddaughters which is not correct. Below is the correction for Merida Melton, who was supposedly the half Irish-half Cherokee son of John and Ocuma Melton.

Merida (Merrida) Melton

Merida Melton was listed in the 1820 census of Lawrence County, Alabama, as a white male over 21 years of age. The census reported a total of eight individuals in the household of Merida Melton as follows: White males over 21, 2; White males under 21, 2; White females over 21, 1; White females under 21, 3. The census indicates that Merida Melton was born before 1799; he could very well be the son of John Melton who died on June 7, 1815.

On September 18, 1818, Merida Melton of Lawrence County, Alabama, entered 80.13 acres of land in the South ½ of the Southeast ¼ of Section 15 in Township 7 South and Range 9 West (Cowart, 1991). The land he entered was on the northwest edge of present-day William B. Bankhead National Forest south of Mt. Hope, Alabama. Merida Melton forfeited his claim to the land in 1829 and left Lawrence County, Alabama.

According to the descendants of Merida Melton, he moved west and married a woman by the name of Mary Edington. One of their daughters, Leah Ann Melton who married William Reynolds, died on October 20, 1906, at Marion in Linn County, Iowa. Another daughter Elizabeth Melton moved to Tennessee with her husband and his family. It is believed that other children migrated to Texas.

Thomas Melton

Thomas Melton was found in the 1820 United States Census of Lawrence County, Alabama. The census reported a total of five individuals in the household of Thomas Melton as follows: White males over 21, 1; White males under 21, 2; White females over 21, 1; White females under 21, 1. The census indicates that Thomas Melton was born before 1799; he could very well be the son of John Melton who died on June 7, 1815. He was also mentioned as a son of John Melton in William Lindsey McDonald's, Lore of the River (2007).

Charles Melton

After his father and mother, John and Ocuma, moved to the north side of the Tennessee River in Limestone County, Alabama, their son Charles lived and traded from the Melton's Bluff home. During the Indian boundary surveys in April 1816, General John Coffee would stop at Melton's Bluff and trade with Charles Melton. After the Turkey Town Treaty of September 1816, Charles Melton moved eastward along the Tennessee River to about three miles above Guntersville, Alabama. About 1817, Charles established an Indian town known as Melton's Village or Meltonsville at the mouth of Watts Town Creek or later Town Creek in Marshall County, Alabama.

Oliver D. Street in Indians of Marshall County refers to Charles Melton as an Indian from Melton's Bluff who settled Meltonsville in Marshall County, Alabama. This village was named for Charles Melton, who was born at Melton's Bluff; Charles Melton was the half-blood Cherokee son of Irishman John Melton and his Cherokee wife Ocuma.

David Melton

On November 22, 1816, half blood Cherokee David Melton, son of John and Ocuma Melton, sold his family's land and black slaves to General Andrew Jackson; therefore, when Andrew Jackson purchased Melton's Bluff, he also purchased Melton's slaves. David Melton signed the deed on November 22, 1816, that gave General Andrew Jackson all the Cherokee land at Melton's Bluff. The lands claimed by David Melton's family were given to Jackson in the first legal deed to white people in present-day Lawrence County, Alabama; Jackson kept the land until 1827.

In 1816 after the sale of Melton's Bluff to Andrew Jackson, David Melton moved west to be with his Old Settlers people many of whom were his relatives. The Old Settlers left the Muscle Shoals area in 1810; the passports were issued in January and February 1810.

After moving west, David Melton, formerly of Melton's Bluff, signed the 1834 treaty between the Cherokees West, Comanche, Wichita, Osage, and other tribes (the Kiowa did not attend). Also, both David Melton and Lewis Melton, sons of John and Ocuma Melton, signed the Cherokee Articles of Union on behalf of the Old Settlers; the articles unified the Old Settlers and the Cherokees who arrived in the west in March 1839 with Trail of Tears.

Elick Melton

While living at Melton's Bluff in Lawrence County, Alabama, Elick Melton signed a letter with The Gourd asking for Negro Fox to be returned to the Cherokees after members of the Burleson family attacked and killed three of their Cherokee people. These Cherokee men were killed at Mouse Town which was located on the border of present-day Lawrence County and Morgan County, Alabama, at the mouth of Fox's Creek and the Tennessee River.

James Melton

James Melton made quite a reputation for himself as a boat pilot or guide. This involved meeting the boats at the upper end of the Muscle Shoals and piloting them through the dangerous and often deadly passage over that part of the river. There were a number of these pilots who operated from Melton's Bluff. They would meet the boats at the upper end of the Elk River Shoals and guide them through the treacherous shoals of the river. These men would disembark below the Shoals at Colbert's Ferry at the Natchez Trace crossing and walk back to Melton's Bluff.

John Melton's son James was mentioned by General John Coffee. James had a reputation as an excellent pilot or guide. James became identified with the bluff that was named for his father. A number of early historians refer to James Melton as the half-blood Cherokee Indian from Melton's Bluff who guided keelboats through the Muscle Shoals.

James Melton worked mainly as a pilot for Malcolm Gilchrist who settled near Melton's Bluff before Alabama became a state. Gilchrist, whose ancestors came from Scotland, became the "Commodore Vanderbilt" of the lower Tennessee River. Malcolm, a land speculator, owned a fleet of flatboats that navigated the river from Muscle Shoals to New Orleans and made for him quite a fortune.

Lewis Melton

Lewis Melton lived at Melton's Bluff when the Lower Cherokees relinquished their claims to most of their lands north of the Tennessee River in Lauderdale and Limestone Counties except Doublehead's Reserve. The treaty was signed at Washington, D.C., on January 7, 1806. After the 1806 treaty, Lewis' son Moses Melton, the grandson of John Melton, was made a beneficiary of one of the tracts of land reserved by the provisions of the Cotton Gin Treaty. The land Moses received was just west of Melton's Bluff near Spring Creek. He was given the reserve as follows: "…and the other reserved tract, of said Moses Melton and of Charles Hicks in equal shares."

After the Turkey Town Treaty of 1816, Lewis Melton moved west with the Old Settlers along with his brother David Melton. After the Trail of Tears Cherokees arrived west in 1839, Lewis signed for the reunification of the Cherokee Nation with his brother David.

(Rhea's Wife) Melton

Rhea's wife was the daughter of John and Ocuma Melton. Rhea was a white man and river boat pilot who guided boats through the Muscle Shoals. He was the guide to Anne Royall when she visited the Muscle Shoals, "I learned he was from Rockbridge County, Virginia; had piloted boats through the Muscle Shoals, fifteen years; sometimes four at a time, at ten dollars each. He sails down one day, and walks back the next. He never met, in all that time, with an accident! There are several of these pilots" (Royall, 1969).

Rhea's wife was not named, but on January 12, 1818, Anne N. Royall's <u>Letters from Alabama 1817-1822</u> talks about John Melton's son-in-law Rhea. Rhea had guided boats through the Shoals for some 15 years. On January 14, 1818, Royall also tells about John Melton's half-blood daughter (Rhea's Wife) leaving Melton's Bluff for lands in the west. Royall says that Rhea's wife left Melton's Bluff last fall for Indian Territory in Arkansas which would have been the Fall of 1817.

Lucy's Branch

In 1832, Finch "Lucy" was born to a black female slave and Cherokee father on the former farmland of John Melton. It is thought by some historians that the black female was a slave of the Cherokee Indian family of John Melton. Lucy was born into slavery as a mixed blood Cherokee and black daughter of an unknown black female and Cherokee Indian male. Lucy was thought to be the half-blood daughter of one of John and Ocuma Melton's half-blood Cherokee-Irish sons.

It is historically recorded that some of the Cherokee half-blood children of John and Ocuma Melton remained in the Muscle Shoals area of North Alabama after 1816. James Melton worked as a keel boat guide for Malcolm Gilchrist, who entered a lot of land in Limestone County. Two other children of John and Ocuma Melton, Thomas and Merida, are recorded in the 1820 census of Lawrence County, Alabama. Charles Melton stayed in North Alabama, and he established the Cherokee village of Meltonsville at the mouth of Town Creek northeast of Guntersville.

Eventually, Lucy married a slave known as Meredith Bedingfield who probably got his last name from his master or white owner. In <u>Old Land Records of Limestone County, Alabama</u> (Cowart, 1984), Charles Bedingfield was the only white landowner in Limestone County listed with that last name. The Bedingfield black family name probably came from a white slave owner with that last name.

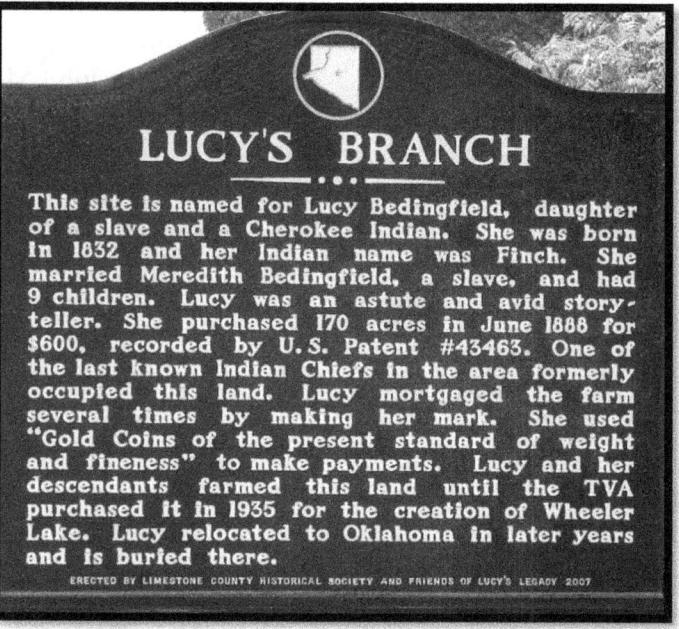

On March 17, 1818, Charles Bedingfield entered 91 acres not far northwest of Lucy's Branch near Elk River in the west ½ of the southeast ¼ of Section 30 of Township 2 South and Range 6 West in Limestone County (Cowart, 1984). On May 23, 1828, Charles also entered 78.81 acres on the west side of Elk River in Section 12 of Township 3 South and Range 7 West in Lauderdale County (Cowart, 1996). According to the 1860 Lauderdale County, Alabama, Slave Schedules, Charles Bedingfield owned 29 black slaves; he was the only slave owner in the area with the last name Bedingfield. Therefore, Meredith Bedingfield, the husband of Lucy, was more than likely a slave of Charles Bedingfield; the land of Charles on Elk River was not far west from Lucy's Branch.

The slaves that General Andrew Jackson purchased from David Melton on November 22, 1816, were still farming cotton in the vicinity of Lucy's Branch. At his death on June 7, 1815, John Melton was living in Limestone County near Lucy's Branch. Since the 1818 land entered by Charles Bedingfield was near the old John Melton farm, it is highly probable that the Bedingfield slaves and the former black slaves Jackson obtained from the Cherokee family of John Melton's half-blood Cherokee-Irish sons were the ancestors of the mixed blood black and Indian lady known as Lucy Bedingfield.

Lucy's Branch on the Tennessee River in Limestone County is named after this famous mixed blood black and Cherokee Indian lady. Lucy once owned, lived, and farmed the old John Melton place in the southwest corner of Limestone County; John Melton was last known to live on that site prior to his death. In the later years of her life, Lucy moved to Oklahoma where some of the Cherokee Melton family had moved in 1816. Lucy died and was buried in Oklahoma.

Cuttyatoy

Cuttyatoy was a fierce and aggressive Lower Cherokee warrior who fought with Dragging Canoe and Doublehead during the Chickamauga War. He was fighting the encroachment of whites to prevent settlement of the Big Bend of the Tennessee River and to protect Cherokee lands. In 1788, Cuttyatoy led an attack on a keelboat belonging to the Brown Family near the Lower Towns of Dragging Canoe. During the raid led by Cuttyatoy, the Brown Family father was killed along with two of his boys. Cuttyatoy took several of the black slaves of the Brown family.

The Creeks and Lower Cherokees took Jane Brown, two daughters and two sons captive. One of the captive white boys was Joseph Brown, who was fifteen years old at that time. Later, Cuttyatoy tried to kill Joseph Brown, but he was protected by his Indian owner. After the raid on the Brown Family, Cuttyatoy moved west along the Tennessee River and lived near the lower end of the Elk River Shoals of the Tennessee River. His village was thought to be on Gilchrist Island across the river from the mouth of Elk River near the south bank of the Tennessee River at the mouth of Spring Creek.

In time, Joseph Brown escaped and joined the army commanded by General Andrew Jackson, and Joseph became a colonel during the Creek Indian War. During the Battle of Talladega on November 9, 1813, Colonel Joseph Brown learned from mixed blood Charles Butler where his father's slaves were being held by Cuttyatoy.

According to the American Whig Review, Volume 15, Issue 87, March 1852, page 247: "Colonel (Joseph) Brown...a participant in the battle of Talledega (November 9, 1813)...met Charles Butler... and learned from him that...Chief Cuttyatoy, was still alive...he was then living on an island in the Tennessee River, near the mouth of Elle (Elk) River, and that he had with him several Negroes... taken by him at Nickajack on the 9th of May, 1788... with ten picked men, Brown proceeded to the island, went to the head man's (Cuttyatoy) lodge and exhibited to him General (Andrew) Jackson's order, and demanded that Cuttyatoy's Negroes be immediately sent over to Fort Hampton...In crossing the river, Colonel Brown and his men took up the Negroes, and Cuttyatoy's wife behind them, to carry them over the water while the Indian men crossed on a raft (Browns Ferry) higher up (stream)." Colonel Joseph Brown and his men reached Fort Hampton that morning while Cuttyatoy and his men arrived in the afternoon.

By the time Cuttyatoy reached Fort Hampton, the slaves had already been sent to Huntsville. Colonel Joseph Brown, who was also a preacher, spared the life of old Cuttyatoy, and said, "I will let God take care of him."

Joseph Brown became a landowner just three miles west of Pulaski, Tennessee, in the community known as Bodenham; he moved there from Columbia, Tennessee. When he was 95 years old, Joseph Brown was leaning the back of his chair to the fireplace on a cold January day. His chair tipped over, and he fell into the fire. Joseph Brown was severely burned, and he died two weeks later.

Reverend Joseph Brown was buried in the Mt. Moriah Cemetery some two miles west of Pulaski, Tennessee. His tombstone indicates that his date of birth was August 2, 1772, and his date of death was February 4, 1868.

David Crockett

On August 30, 1813, the red stick Creeks went to war with the United States by attacking Fort Mims known as "Fort Mims Massacre." In November 1813, the Army of Tennessee Volunteers under the command of General John Coffee marched south out of Tennessee, and his army crossed the Tennessee River from Limestone County to Melton's Bluff in Lawrence County, Alabama. David Crockett, a soldier in Coffee's command, had volunteered for 90 days of military service on September 20, 1813, and he was a scout for Francis Jones Company of the second regiment of volunteer Mounted Riflemen.

According to David Crockett, "After we passed Huntsville, we struck on the river at the Muscle Shoals, and at a place on them called Melton's Bluff. This river is here about two miles wide, and a rough bottom; so much so, indeed, in many places, as to be dangerous; and in fording it this time, we left several of the horses belonging to our men, with their feet fast in the crevices of the rocks" (Crockett, 1987). His military unit crossed the Tennessee River from present-day Limestone County to Melton's Bluff in present-day Lawrence County. However, Crockett was not with Jackson's army on March 27, 1814, when the Creeks were defeated at the Battle of Horseshoe Bend.

In August 1814, General Andrew Jackson sought support from the Tennessee militia to remove the British forces from New Orleans. On September 28, 1814, David Crockett re-enlisted for a six-month tour of military duty as a third sergeant in Captain John Cowan's company. In October 1814, David Crockett was a member of the military unit of the Tennessee Mounted Gunman that crossed the Tennessee River from Limestone County to Melton's Bluff.

In David Crockett's words, "I determined to go again with them, for I wanted a small taste of British fighting…I fixed up and joined old Major Russell again; but we couldn't start with the main army, but followed on, in a little time, after them. In a day or two, we had a hundred and thirty men in our company; and we went over and crossed at the Muscle Shoals at the same place where I had crossed when first out, and where we burned Black Warriors' Town" (Crockett, 1987). The unit saw little action since they were several days behind the rest of the troops.

It appears that David Crockett (8/17/1786-3/6/1836) had family members living near the Sims Settlement in Limestone County. In 1818, Robert Crockett, who is thought to be an uncle of David, is listed as a trustee for the Town of Bridgewater near Sims Landing. Bridgewater is located at a horseshoe bend of Elk River about ten miles north of Fort Hampton and about 15 miles south of Elkton, Tennessee. John Crockett, the father of the David Crockett, had a brother named Robert Crockett (1755-2/26/1836). David Crockett had a son he named Robert Patton Crockett, who was born in 1816 (Find A Grave).

Early Limestone County Roads

The very first trails and roads across Limestone County were Indian routes which utilized shallow areas or fords to cross the Tennessee River, Elk River, and the numerous streams across the area. At water crossing of these trails and roads, Indian people, and later settlers utilized shoals, dugouts/boats, rafts, or ferries to ford the numerous streams in Limestone County.

According to <u>Letters from Alabama, 1817-1822</u>, when the area first opened to white settlers in January 1818, Anne Newport Royall came from Huntsville, crossed Limestone County, to Florence on the north side of the Tennessee River. Royall traveled portions of old Indian trails that probably included Browns Ferry Road, Snake Road, or the North River Road that crossed Elk River near the mouth of Anderson Creek. She crossed the Tennessee River at Florence and traveled east on the south side of the Tennessee River to Melton's Bluff along the South River Road. During her trip, she crossed major streams with the aid of a boat or ferry, and sometimes, horses would swim the stream if it was too deep to ford.

On April 24, 1818, Doctor Calvin Jones started a journal of his trip from Raleigh, North Carolina, to North Alabama; Dr. Jones was accompanied by Billy who was his black servant. He was another early traveler to the Muscle Shoals of the Limestone County area who documented his travels in a personal journal. Jones traveled along Peter Avery's Trace from White's Fort (Knoxville) to Fort Nashborough (Nashville, Tennessee). From Nashville, he traveled south toward Columbia along the Great South Trail or Old Huntsville Road where he probably forked off to Elkton, Tennessee. After 39 days of travel, Dr. Jones passed through Limestone County near Fort Hampton and crossed the Tennessee River from the Lucy's Branch area to Melton's Bluff in Lawrence County, Alabama.

During the spring and summer of 1818, Dr. Calvin Jones traveled through the area of Limestone County and North Alabama which was taken by the Turkey Town Treaty of September 1816. He was looking for an investment in cotton grounds of the former Chickasaw and Cherokee lands that were being sold at the

Huntsville Land Office. Jones was more interested in the cotton lands that lay to the south of the Tennessee River between Melton's Bluff and Tuscumbia.

Dr. Jones and Billy left Melton's Bluff on a large flatboat loaded with 100 bales of cotton and two hogshead of tobacco and made their way through the Muscle Shoals towards Tuscumbia. He noted that the water near the mouth of Elk River was from two to three feet deep, and that he counted 180 islands between Melton's Bluff and Tuscumbia. He stated that the Big Spring at Tuscumbia was certainly fine, after which he traveled farther southwest to visit with Pitman Colbert on the Natchez Trace.

Browns Ferry Road

As early as 1790, maps of the State of Franklin show Browns Ferry as the home site of Doublehead. Also, Albert James Pickett's <u>Alabama History</u>, written in 1851, states: "In December 1801, settlers came down the river and stopped at the home of Doublehead at the head of the Shoals. They then traveled over land to the BigBee (Tombigbee River) Settlements." Doublehead was noted as living at Browns Ferry in present-day Lawrence County until 1802 when he moved to Bluewater Creek in Lauderdale County.

The Browns Ferry Road was an Indian route that crossed the Tennessee River at the Doublehead's Town near the head of Elk River Shoals between Limestone County on the north side and Lawrence County on the south side of the river. Browns Ferry Road ran from Hunt's Spring in present-day Huntsville to Tanner in Limestone County where it crossed the Old Jasper Road and continued to the Browns Ferry crossing of the Tennessee River.

After crossing the river, the road passed through Doublehead's Town and Fox's Stand to the southwest and continued to Gourd's Settlement (Courtland) where it joined the Gaines Trace leading to Cotton Gin Port, Mississippi. Gaines Trace was laid out by Captain Edmund Pendelton Gaines starting on December 26, 1807, at Melton's Bluff, to Courtland, and then to Cotton Gin Port on the Tombigbee River.

After the Turkey Town Treaty of 1816, which took the Indian land claims to the area, Browns Ferry continued to operate as a river crossing of the Browns

Ferry Road. By 1818, settlers and wealthy cotton planters with their black slaves begin to pour into the great Tennessee Valley of Limestone County by way of the Browns Ferry Road from Huntsville and points east and north of the Tennessee River. Fine cotton plantations were established along the old Indian trail in Limestone County. Many early cotton planters crossed the river from Limestone County at Browns Ferry to claim lands and develop their plantations around the Courtland area of Lawrence County.

One of the last crossings documented at Brown's Ferry was by the army of Confederate General Nathan Bedford Forrest on April 23, 1863. He moved his cavalry along the Browns Ferry Road to protect Courtland from Union General Grenville M. Dodge's eight thousand troops. After Dodge retreated to Corinth, Mississippi, Forrest chased Colonel Streight across North Alabama and made the famous capture of some fifteen hundred Union soldiers with his five hundred cavalry men.

General Wade Hampton's forces, for whom Fort Hampton was named, established other early roads along the north bank of the Tennessee River running in and out of Fort Hampton which provided better access to Melton's Bluff and Browns Ferry. The troops of General Hampton widened a nearby Indian trail to a wagon road starting about three miles from Huntsville which connected Hayes Point to Browns Ferry. According to <u>The Old Southwest 1795-1830</u> (1989) by Thomas Clark and John Guice, "The Secretary of War had ordered General Wade Hampton to open a wagon road from Muscle Shoals to Fort Stoddert along another route surveyed by Edmund P. Gaines."

Browns Ferry

Probably, the most famous Indian ferry of these early Tennessee River crossings in Limestone County was Browns Ferry. The Browns Ferry Road from Hunt's Spring (Huntsville) to Gourd's Settlement (Courtland) crossed the Tennessee River at Browns Ferry from Limestone County into Lawrence County.

Browns Ferry was named in honor of a half blood Cherokee known as Captain John Brown. The Brown Indian family operated ferries from Chattanooga to the Browns Ferry site at the eastern end of Elk River Shoals. In the late 1770's, the Brown Indian family migrated westward with Doublehead and the Chickamauga Cherokees; they brought with them their family business of operating river ferries.

In November 1813, Cuttyatoy and his men crossed the Tennessee River on a large raft at Browns Ferry on their way to Fort Hampton. After the Turkey Town Treaty of 1816, Captain John Brown moved east into the Cherokee Nation and established the Town of Otali, which means end of mountain. The Cherokee town became present-day Attala, Alabama, at the south end of Lookout Mountain on the Coosa River.

Cherokee Captain John Brown's stepdaughter by his second marriage was named Betsy. It is thought that Betsy married Joshua Cox who was assigned the area as of February 14, 1818; Cox owned an additional 153.3 acres in Section 13 of Township 4 South and Range 6 West in Limestone County (Cowart, 1984). While Betsy helped with the operation of the ferry with her husband, it was known for a brief time as Cox's Ferry.

Later, the Browns Ferry area was purchased by a man by the name of Brice M. Garner of Fayetteville, Tennessee. Brice M. Garner also owned an island near the northeast side of the ferry which he acquired in Limestone County. On July 19, 1821, Garner entered 71.67 acres of an island near the north side of Browns Ferry in Section 13 of Township 4 South and Range 6 West in Limestone County (Cowart, 1984). After Garner purchased the property, the Tennessee River crossing became known for a short time as Garner's Ferry which is mentioned in records in the Lawrence County Archives.

On September 7, 1818, Joshua Cox was assigned 3.4 acres on the south bank of the Tennessee River at Browns Ferry in Section 13 of Township 4 South and Range 6 West in Lawrence County; he also owned an adjacent 80 acres. The same 3.4 acres of Cox was purchased by Brice M. Garner on July 19, 1821 (Cowart, 1991). Eventually both names of the ferry when owned by Joshua Cox and Brice M. Garner reverted back to its original name; today, the river crossing is still known as Browns Ferry. Today, the north side of the Tennessee River at Browns Ferry is the site of the Browns Ferry Nuclear Plant in Limestone County, Alabama.

Black Warriors' Path or Mitchell Trace

Black Warriors' Path crossed the middle of Elk River Shoals at Melton's Bluff and passed by Fort Hampton. This is the route that was crossed by military units which David Crockett wrote about in his book, "A Narrative of the Life of David Crockett." The Indian trail ran from St. Augustine, Florida, to Nashville, Tennessee, and was later called Mitchell Trace after a post route was established from Fort Mitchell in Russell County, Alabama, to Fort Hampton in Limestone County, Alabama. The route continued to Elkton, Tennessee, and then north to French Lick or Big Lick (Nashville, Tennessee).

Mitchell's Trace, earlier known as the Black Warriors' Path, was a post route from Fort Hampton to Fort Mitchell on the Chattahoochee River. Fort Mitchell was named for David Brady Mitchell, a Scotsman listed in the territorial papers as Governor, General, and Indian Agent. Mitchell Trace crossed the Mulberry Fork of the Warrior River at Baltimore Ford, a few miles northeast of its junction with the Sipsey Fork. The Black Warriors' Path was widened to a wagon road from Fort Hampton to Elkton, Tennessee.

Many early travelers from the north followed Black Warriors' Path from Nashville, to Columbia, to Elkton, and then to Melton's Bluff in Lawrence County, Alabama. According to the book Historic Limestone County, "Early in 1818 there was an attempt to sell plots in a community to be called "Bridgewater" near Sims Landing, just upstream from Buck Island (on Elk River)...Bridgewater was located 15 miles below Elkton, 10 miles above Fort Hampton, and opposite the great bend in the Elk that almost circled round bottom near Sims settlements...The prospectus predicted that the nearest road from Melton's Bluff in Lawrence County to Nashville would touch Bridgewater" (Dunnavant, 1993). The Black Warriors' Path ran north to slightly northeast from Melton's Bluff toward Nashville.

The Gaines Trace joined Mitchell Trace at Melton's Bluff and was also a trade route from the Muscle Shoals to the French Landing at Cotton Gin Port on the Tombigbee River which led downstream to Mobile. The Gaines Trace route was laid out through Cherokee and Chickasaw territory by Captain Edmund Pendleton Gaines in December 1807, just four months after the death of

Doublehead on August 9, 1807. Captain Gaines was married to Barbara Blount, the daughter of Governor William Blount of the Southwest Territory.

North River Road

One of the early primitive trails or roads used by the Indians and early settlers to bypass the Muscle Shoals on the north side of the Tennessee River included the North River Road. This was another major Indian trail that passed through Limestone County by present-day Athens and Fort Hampton and connected Indian villages along the north bank of the Tennessee River.

The road ran through Cherokee territory from Crow Town near Stephenson, to Sawtee Town west of Scottsboro, to the Flint River villages east of Huntsville. From Huntsville west, a portion of the route was known as Snake Road which continued through Doublehead's Reserve to Roger's Ville west of Elk River, to Shoal Town where Doublehead's final home was located west of Elgin. From Fort Hampton to the west, the road passed through the Cherokee town of Roger's Ville that was listed in the Cherokee census of 1809 by Indian agent Return Jonathan Meigs. According to the 1809 census, Rogers' Ville had 20 Cherokee males, ten Cherokee females, and six white folks.

The North River Road was originally an Indian trail that was widened to a wagon road from Huntsville in Madison County, to Athens in Limestone County, to Fort Hampton, and then to Florence in Lauderdale County. In early January of 1818, Anne Newport Royall was one of the first documented writers of North Alabama to travel along the road from Huntsville to Florence. In January and February of 1818, many of the first cotton planters from Huntsville traveled west to claim the former Indian lands opened by the Turkey Town Treaty of 1816. Many of the wealthy cotton planters followed this early road into Limestone County to begin their cotton plantations. In 1823, the Indian path became a post route between Athens in Limestone County to Florence in Lauderdale County. In 1836, Addison Binford was given permission to operate a ferry on the post route from Athens to Florence during high water periods that prevented fording Elk River. In 1837, Terry Bradley began operating a ferry crossing of Elk River near the mouth of Anderson Creek.

The North River Road continued west where it eventually connected to Memphis, Tennessee, at the mouth of the Wolf River with its junction to the Mississippi River in Shelby County, Tennessee. In the early years of Limestone County, wagons and stagecoaches operated along the old Indian trail of the North River Road. In 1849, the Patrick Stagecoach Line started operation between Huntsville, Alabama, and Memphis, Tennessee. Around the 1850s, several cotton planters with their black slaves left Limestone County, Alabama, and moved west to settle in Shelby County, Tennessee, near Memphis.

Old Jasper Road

The Old Jasper Road was originally an Indian trail that ran north from Tuscaloosa to Jasper and eventually connected to Nashville, Tennessee. The route was part of the Nashville to Mobile Traces. After crossing the Sipsey Fork, the Jasper Road followed the old Indian trail along the dividing ridge between Rock Creek and Brushy Creek for nearly twenty-five miles without crossing a creek or stream creating a route across present-day Winston County that was passable year-round. The route crossed the West Fork of Flint Creek a few miles north of present-day Neel and continued to the Decatur crossing of the Tennessee River at Rhodes Ferry. Dr. Henry Rhodes of Decatur, Alabama, was an early landowner and established the ferry crossing around 1818.

At Rhodes Ferry, the route north crossed into Limestone County and continued to Athens and on to Nashville, Tennessee. Just north of the Tennessee River in Limestone County, the route passed through the Slopeside Plantation of Thomas Maclin, Flower Hill Plantation of John Henry Harris, Tanner, then to Athens and points north. The railroad corridor from Decatur to Athens to Nashville paralleled the Old Jasper Road.

In the 1830s, Rhodes Ferry became the eastern end of the Decatur-Tuscumbia Railroad that was used to transport cotton and other products around the treacherous Muscle Shoals which included Elk River Shoals, Big Muscle Shoals, and Little Muscle Shoals. Prior to the rail line through Athens, cotton produced in Limestone County could be transported south along the Old Jasper Road then ferried across the Tennessee River to the railroad where it could be carried around the shoals and eventually to New Orleans. In the late 1830s, the early rail line was used during Indian removal to transport Cherokee and Creek

Indians around the Muscle Shoals to Tuscumbia Landing and then to points west of the Mississippi River.

Burleson Trace

On September 5, 1810, James Burleson, John Burleson, Jonathan Burleson, and Joseph Burleson signed the petition to stay on Chickasaw land in the Limestone County portion of Mississippi Territory. James, John, and Joseph were brothers that migrated into the area of the Tennessee River and Elk River prior to Indian removal; Jonathan Burleson was the son of John. From 1807, members of the Burleson family lived in Limestone, Madison, Morgan, and Lawrence Counties of North Alabama.

Prior to the land being taken from the Chickasaw and Cherokee in September 1816, members of the Burleson family were leasing and farming lands of the Cherokee, but they were most often associated with a Cherokee village of Mouse Town near the mouth of Fox's Creek. For a short time, they supposedly operated a ferry from the east mouth of Fox's Creek at Mouse Town to Cow Ford Landing in present-day Limestone County; the road led north from Cow Ford Landing to Athens.

Burleson Indian Fight

The Cherokee village of Mouse Town was also called Moneetown by James Edmonds Saunders in his book <u>Early Settlers of Alabama</u> (1899). The Cherokee village was located a few miles upstream of Browns Ferry on the east side of the mouth of Fox's Creek in present-day Morgan County. Saunders (1899) states, "Joseph Burleson and his brother James came into this county some time before the Indians were removed….James Burleson settled with his family on the north side of the mountain, on Fox's Creek. Here, near an Indian village called Moneetown (Mouse Town), the family became involved in a feud in consequence of the imprudence of a son-in-law named Martin, and the consequence was that James Burleson and his son, Edward, killed three Cherokees and fled to Missouri."

On August 12, 1816, four members of the Burleson Family along with four other white settlers were accused of murdering two Cherokees at Mouse

Town at the mouth of Fox's Creek. In a letter of August 15, 1816, the Indians give an account of two of their fellow Cherokee Indians killed at Mouse Town east of Elk River Shoals. "James Burleson and seven other white men killed two Cherokees. Hope you will cause whites to give up Negro Fox as he is considered one of our people and we wish to try him by our law." Signed by Gourd (X), Charles Melton (X), William Rains, Isaac Wade, Breton Wider, Joseph Slaughter, John Lambe, Nelson Bonds, Walter Evans, Elick Melton, and William Phillips (Microcopy 208, roll 7, and number 3533).

Other white settlers living and farming in the area identify the people who killed the two Cherokees as follows: "The Indians were killed by Edward Burleson, James Burleson, John Burleson, Joseph Burleson, Robert Thrasher, Martin Tailer (Taylor), Charles Tailer (Taylor), and John Bird. They have left and gone to Madison County." Signed: Thomas Lovell, David Danault, William Fears, Don White, Lemuel Lovell, William Cosby, Rudolph McDaniel, George Cosby, Sam Cosby, Robert W. Woods, Sam B. McClure (Microcopy 208, roll 7, and number 3534).

On August 12, 1816, white settlers sent the following letter from Mississippi Territory to the chiefs of the Cherokees in order for the innocent to avoid retaliation and punishment, "To any of the Chiefs or hed men of the Chirokee Nation. Wee feel it our Duty to let you know who commited that offence against your subjects so that the inesant may not suffer. The offence was committed on the twelveth Inst by these under named: James Burleston, John Burleson, Robt. Thrasher, Martin Tailer, Charle Tailer, John Bird, Edward Burleson, and Joseph Burleson. These are all wee have any knowledg of they have left the settlement and gone in to Madison County where they will be delt with acording to law as soon as it can be put in force against them and as for old fox he has went of with those men that committed this offene therfore wee subscribe our names on the other side."

On August 25, 1816, additional information is given in a letter from Mississippi Territory to Colonel Louis Winston (1784-1824), native of Virginia, who was appointed the district attorney general for Madison County in 1809. The letter is as follows: "Requesting him (Winston) to have apprehended certain men who murdered two Cherokees. Two Indians were killed August 12, a few miles above Melton's at head of Shoals by white men having with them Negro Black

Fox who belonged to Cherokee Nation...signed by: Thomas Lovell, David Davolt, William Fears, David White, Lemuel Lovell, William Cosby, Rudolph McDaniel, George Cosby, Sam Cosby, Robert W. Woods, Sam B. McClure informing Winston that James Burleson, John Burleson, Robert Thrasher, Martin Taylor, Charles Taylor, John Bird, Edward Burleson, and Joseph Burleson were of the number who committed the deed and there were others in party whose names we do not know. All have gone to Madison County" (Microcopy 208, roll 7, and number 3544).

On September 5, 1816, The National Intelligenser in Washington D.C. gives editorially a letter dated August 13, 1816, from James Burleson to Colonel Louis Winston. Burleson tries to explain the fight between his family and the Cherokees on Fox's Creek. James Burleson states: "That he, Burleson, and others who had settled near Meltons Bluff (Mouse Town), on the south side of the Tennessee River to the number of eight men were attacked by a party of Cherokees armed with guns and war clubs, the number not known, on the night of the 11th inst. The whites resisted and three Indians were killed and one wounded. The fear of the Indians caused consternation among the settlers, and many moved away leaving promising crops."

On September 10, 1816, The National Intelligenser adds details concerning the disturbance from information at Huntsville dated August 17, 1816. "It seems that a Mr. (Martin) Taylor had rented a field from some Cherokees. In his absence they offered some insult to Mrs. Taylor, who escaped to the home of her father, James Burleson. Burleson, Taylor and others went to the Indian settlement, where they found a number collected. They demanded an explanation. The Indians raised a yell and said fight. An attempt was made by the whites to cut them off from their arms. This produced a conflict."

According to a letter from Waco, Texas, May 9, 1882, and printed in The Moulton Advertiser on May 25, 1882, page 2, column 4: "Gen. Ed Burleson of Texas Revolutionary fame…was engaged in the killing of some Indians at Mouse Town on Foxe's Creek, east of Courtland in 1817, for which he fled the country, went to Missouri, thence to Texas."

Joseph Burleson

Even though Joseph Burleson was one of the men accused of killing the two or three Cherokees at Mouse Town, he moved to Moulton, and by 1818, became a trustee for the town. On September 11, 1818, Joseph Burleson entered 82.54 acres in the southwest corner of Moulton in Section 32 of Township 6 South and Range 7 West; his son Aaron entered some 514 acres near Moulton in 1818 (Cowart 1991). "When Moulton was established Joseph (Burleson) kept the best public house in it....Aaron (son of Joseph), had considerable reputation as an Indian fighter" (Saunders, 1899). Joseph served as a trustee of Moulton from 1818 through 1827.

On December 26, 1822, the Alabama legislature authorized Joseph Burleson and associates to build the Burleson Trace from Moulton to Pikeville, Alabama, where he also owned land at the forks of the Buttahatchee. The Alabama act completed the Burleson Trace from Mouse Town, where a ferry crossed the Tennessee River from Cow Ford Landing in Limestone County, to Pikeville in Marion County, Alabama.

Prior to the railroad from Decatur to Tuscumbia which circumvented the Muscle Shoals, cotton and farm products could be offloaded at Mouse Town. Goods from Limestone County could be transported to Cow Ford Landing, ferried to the south side of the Tennessee River, and sent south toward the Gulf of Mexico via Burleson Trace which connected to both the Byler Road and Jackson's Military Road.

On the south side of the Tennessee River, the Burleson Trace passed south through the Boxwood Plantation of Samuel Elliott near the Lawrence and Morgan County lines. In September 1818, Samuel Elliott Sr. came to the Tennessee Valley area of Fox's Creek from Wilson County, Tennessee, and entered land in the drainage of Fox's Creek in Lawrence County, Alabama.

After the Burlesons moved from the area of Fox's Creek, George Peck operated a landing on the south side of the Tennessee River in Morgan County near Mouse Town. On July 11, 1818, George entered 80.24 acres in the East ½ of the Northwest ¼ of Section 29 in Township 5 South and Range 4 West in Morgan County, Alabama; he was listed as an assignee of J. Burleson (Cowart, 1981). George Peck, who owned Peck's Landing, was married to Celia Fennel, the daughter of Wylie Fennel; George died in 1826. He was a brother-in-law to James Fennel of the Walnut Grove Plantation; James was one of the founders of Decatur. The Burleson Trace passed south through the plantations of the Elliotts and Fennels; then it basically followed the present-day route of the Old Moulton Road to Moulton.

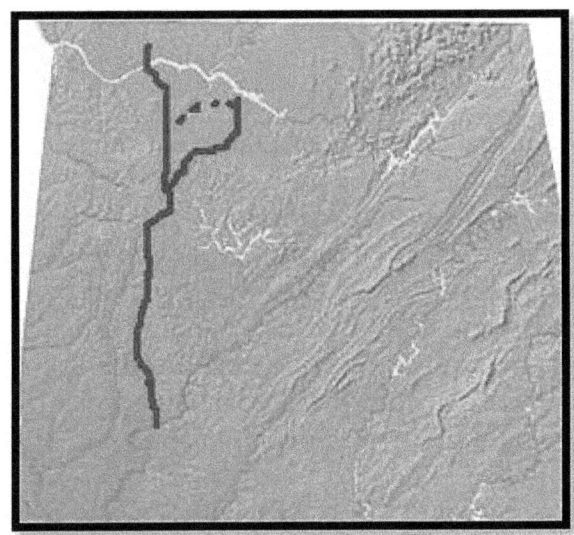

Byler Road-Shoals Creek to Tuscaloosa
Burleson Trace-Mouse Town to Moulton

Burleson Trace intersected the Byler Road which led to the falls of the Black Warrior River at present-day Northport; the trace also intersected Jackson's Military Road at Pikeville. From Northport, goods could be transported to Mobile, and from Pikeville, the products could be transported to New Orleans via Jackson's Military Road. The Burleson Trace route avoided the very dangerous and hazardous Elk River Shoals, Big Muscle Shoals and Little Muscle Shoals of the Tennessee River.

By state law where the Burleson Trace ran concurrent with the Byler Road portion starting at Ebenezer Martin Gap to Haleyville, Joseph was not allowed to collect a toll. The road was originally authorized as Burleson Trace, but later the portion from Moulton to the Byler Road became known as the Byler Road Fork: today in Moulton, the route is called the Byler Road. About 1833, Joseph Burleson left Alabama and moved to Texas where his family became famous in the fight against Mexico and founding of the State of Texas.

Limestone County, Alabama

In the late 1770s, the first white folks arrived in the Limestone County area as intermarried families of the Chickamauga faction of Lower Cherokees. In his 1809 census of the Cherokee Indians, Indian agent Return J. Meigs enumerated many whites living in Cherokees villages along the Big Bend of the Tennessee River. According to the census, nearly all the Cherokee towns and communities in North Alabama contained white folks; Gunter's Landing had 554 inhabitants with 45 being whites. Some the original Cherokees that lived in the Limestone County were not removed until 1816. Today, descendants of those mixed blood remnants of Cherokees still call Limestone County home.

On July 23, 1805, the northeastern corner of Limestone County that was in the original Madison County was ceded by a treaty with the Chickasaws. In the treaty, the Madison County boundaries were to run from the mouth of Flint River with the western boundary going northwest approximately 45 degrees into the State of Tennessee. The eastern boundary of Madison County followed a somewhat a jagged or wavy line north from the mouth and along Flint River into Tennessee. However, the area of Madison which included the northeastern corner of present-day Limestone County was not ceded by the Chickamauga faction of Lower Cherokee until the Cotton Gin Treaty of January 7, 1806, which was negotiated by Doublehead.

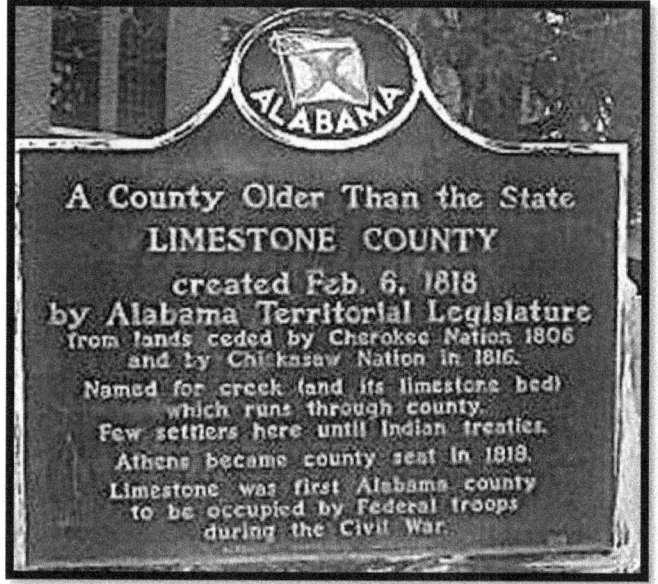

In 1806 after signing the Cotton Gin Treaty, Doublehead leased lands in his reserve to many white settlers along Elk River in present-day Limestone County. After Doublehead's death in 1807, many Cherokees in the area sought passports to move west of the Mississippi River; these passports to lands west of the Mississippi River were approved in January and February 1810. The death of Doublehead and the Cherokee "Old Settlers" moving from the Muscle Shoals prompted the Chickasaws to insist on the government to remove white settlers. Starting about 1810, early white settlers by and large were removed from Chickasaw land by military forces stationed at Fort Hampton.

On December 13, 1808, Mississippi Territory Governor Robert Holmes signed a proclamation creating Madison County, named in honor of President James Madison. Madison formally became the first county in North Alabama created from the Mississippi Territory which included the northeastern corner of present-day Limestone County; Mississippi Territory was designated on April 17, 1798.

The portion of Limestone County that was originally included in Madison County was located in Township 1 South and Range 3 West, Township 2 South and Range 3 West, and Township 1 South and Range 4 West. This northeast corner of present-day Limestone County was secured by treaties with the Chickasaws and the Chickamauga faction of Lower Cherokees under Doublehead's leadership.

In September 1816, the remaining Indian land claims to north and east of the Tennessee River in the area of Madison County and northeastern Limestone County were ceded by both the Cherokee and Chickasaw tribes. "On March 1, 1817, Congress carved the Alabama Territory out of the existing Mississippi Territory, which had included land in what is now both states. On May 8, 1817, possibly uninformed about action in Washington, Mississippi Territory Governor David Holmes announced creation of Elk County on lands that would become Limestone County. Elk County was bounded on the west and south by the Tennessee River and on the east by Madison County" (Dunnavant, 1993).

In September 1817, William Wyatt Bibb of Georgia was appointed the first governor of the newly created Alabama Territory by United States President

James Monroe. William was elected governor of the State of Alabama two years later, and he died not long after taking office when he was thrown from his horse. His brother, Thomas Bibb, succeeded him as governor.

After Indian removal from the area, Limestone County was created by an act of the Alabama Territorial Legislature on February 6, 1818, from lands comprising Elk County of previously Mississippi Territory. The legislature established Limestone County as its eastern boundary along the longitude line separating Range 2 West and Range 3 West; therefore, the northwestern corner of the original Madison County became part of the newly created Limestone County. The western boundary of Limestone County became the longitude line separating Range 6 West and Range 7 West except the point that the range line to the south intersects Elk River, then the boundary followed Elk River to the Tennessee River; therefore, the extreme southwestern corner of Limestone County lying east of Elk River and north of the Tennessee River is in Range 7 West of present-day Limestone County. The northern border was the Tennessee state line with the southern border the Tennessee River. On December 14, 1819, Limestone County officially became a part of the State of Alabama when the territory was admitted into the union as a state.

Malcolm Gilchrist

The Turkey Town Treaty of September 1816 opened the area to legal white settlement and attracted interest from land speculators. Malcolm Gilchrist Jr. was an early land speculator of Muscle Shoals area, and he became one of the largest landowners in Limestone County. When the Indian lands in North Alabama were sold at public auction in 1818, Malcolm Gilchrist Jr. bought large tracts of land as investments, and then he resold these lands to cotton planters reaping large profits. Gilchrist personally surveyed every parcel of land before he purchased it; therefore, valley planters knew that they were getting good cotton lands when Gilchrist offered it to them.

Between February 10, 1818, and September 26, 1837, Malcolm Gilchrist entered some 5,775 acres of land in Limestone County, Alabama, most of which was purchased in 1818 along the Tennessee River. On April 10, 1838, Malcolm's brother Daniel entered approximately 877 acres in Limestone County (Cowart,

1984). Malcolm Jr. and Daniel Gilchrist were the sons of Malcolm Sr. who was born in Cantire, Scotland, and first came to North Carolina where he married Catherine Buie; the Gilchrists moved to Maury County, Tennessee, in 1809 (Saunders, 1899). The Gilchrist boys made their home in Lawrence County, Alabama, near Melton's Bluff. Malcolm Jr. was born in 1786, and Daniel was born on December 22, 1788. According to the 1850 Lawrence County, Alabama, Slave Schedule, Daniel Gilchrist owned 87 black slaves, and Malcolm Jr. owned 10 slaves.

In addition to buying and selling cotton land, Malcolm Gilchrist Jr. was a cotton freighter. The planters who lived east of the Muscle Shoals were at a disadvantage in transporting their cotton to the markets. Malcolm came to the rescue of planters along and east of the Muscle Shoals by building large fleets of flatboats. Gilchrist had the confidence of the cotton planters and enough capital to purchase a large number of boats. He would employ a steersman for each boat and four more to work the oars. His cotton boats successfully challenged the almost impassable barriers in the Tennessee River at the Muscle Shoals. Malcolm Gilchrist Jr. had a Midas Touch; by shipping cotton and land speculation, Malcolm amassed a great fortune when "Cotton Was King."

Over Elk Region

The whole northwestern corner of Limestone County was isolated from the rest of the county by Elk River which was difficult to cross during high water. This area of land in Limestone County to the north and west of Elk River became known as the "Over Elk" region, a portion of which was in Doublehead's Reserve. Because of high water during flooding periods, the "Over Elk" area was not readily accessible to the county seat of government in Athens, Alabama. For many years, the first settlers of Limestone County in the "Over Elk" region had to depend on shallow fords, boats, rafts, and private ferries to cross Elk River in order to access the county seat.

In 1819, the Limestone County Commissioners established "fees for crossing over ferries on the Elk and Tennessee Rivers. The commissioners set the rate for crossing a man and horse at Browns Ferry at 25 cents: $1.25 for every loaded wagon and team" (Dunnavant, 1993).

A ferry at Elk River Mills was authorized and operated by two members of the Vaughn family-Isham and William B. On November 27, 1812, Manoah and William Vaughn entered 160.3 acres of land in Section 21 of Township 3 South and Range 2 East in Madison County (Cowart, 1979).

In the 1850 Limestone County, Alabama, Slave Schedules, James Vaughn owned 14 black slaves, and William P. Vaughn owned 11 black slaves in 1860. Both James and William Vaughn entered 158.84 acres in Section 14 of Township 3 South and Range 3 West in Limestone County. James Vaughn entered the land on June 21, 1831, and William entered his on October 21, 1854. On March 18, 1892, Andrew J. Vaughn entered 40 acres on Elk River in Section 26 of Township 2 South and Range 6 West (Cowart, 1979 and 1984).

On July 12, 1876, the first permanent bridge was built across Elk River. Some 3,000 people attended a huge celebration of the bridge which was held at the plantation of James E. Horton, Sr. In the 1860 Limestone County, Alabama, Slave Schedules, James and R. C. Horton owned 39 and 47 slaves, respectfully.

Athens

By 1803, the Big Spring site that became the Town of Athens was attracting the attention of white settlers. According to Dunnavant (1993), "Jim Craig and his family are reported to have come to the Big Spring that was to become the site of Athens in 1803. They encamped just north of the spring, but the Chickasaws apparently made them less than welcome and they left. Samuel Robertson and his family came to the spring in 1808 and established a trading post at what would become the southeastern corner of the courthouse square. Soldiers from Fort Hampton later forced him to give up the post to William Wilder, an event that led to an eventual fight and Wilder's death when Robertson returned to reclaim his land."

Two of the principal founding fathers of Athens were Robert W. Beaty and John D. Carroll; they were cotton planters and owners of black slaves. On February 9, 1818, Robert W. Beaty and John D. Carroll purchased 159.9 acres in the northeast ¼ of Section 8 of Township 3 South and Range 4 West in Limestone County, Alabama (Cowart, 1984). They bought the present-day Athens area at a government land auction in Huntsville, Alabama. Their land was surveyed by

Ernest Hine, who laid out the square plan of typical southern towns of the time period. The Town of Athens began development on land that Beaty and Carroll jointly owned and sold as lots.

On November 19, 1818, Athens, first called Athenson, became one of the oldest incorporated towns in North Alabama. The town is in Limestone County of north central Alabama some 15 miles south of the border of the State of Tennessee. Athens, named after Athens, Greece, became a very prosperous agricultural center of wealthy cotton planters and slave owners who settled in Limestone County.

On December 3, 1819, Athens became the county seat of Limestone County before Alabama was admitted into the Union on December 14, 1819. Samuel Tanner, the namesake of the Community of Tanner, was the first mayor of Athens. In 1822, "The Athenian" was established as Athens first newspaper. In 1822, a charter for the Athens Female Academy was granted by the state. The school eventually became Athens State University, the longest operating and oldest institution of higher education in Alabama.

Athens was the home to three Alabama governors as follows:
1. Thomas Bibb was a cotton planter and owner of 257 black slaves. He was resident of Athens, and he became Alabama's second governor. Thomas was chosen to serve after his brother and first Governor of Alabama, William Wyatt Bibb died after falling from a horse. The Thomas Bibb home still stands in the City of Athens.
2. Joshua Lanier Martin (December 5, 1799-November 2, 1856) was a resident of Athens; he became the 12th Governor of Alabama. He was a member of the Democratic Party and served as governor from 1845 to 1847. Joshua Martin's wife was Sarah Ann Mason; she was the sister to Captain John Richardson Mason who married Glorvinia Beaty, daughter of Robert Beaty.
3. George Smith Houston was a cotton planter and owner of 78 black slaves. In 1831, he first married Mary Jackson Beaty, Robert Beaty's daughter, and they lived in Athens. He became the 24th Governor of Alabama in 1874, some nine years after the end of the Civil War. He was the first post Reconstruction Democratic governor and served until 1878. George S. Houston's home still stands in the City of Athens.

By 1859, the Tennessee and Alabama Railroad was completed, and Athens was a stop on the rail line from Decatur in Morgan County, Alabama, to Nashville, Tennessee. Cotton and the railroad provided for economic development and growth of Athens. But, within a few years, the Civil War would wreak havoc for Athens.

In April 1862, Union forces occupied the City of Athens. On May 1, 1862, the Confederate cavalry forced Union troops to retreat to Huntsville; however, Union forces under the command of Colonel John Basil Turchin retook Athens the next day. Union soldiers looted and terrorized the town in what became widely known as the "Sack of Athens." After the Civil War, the economy of Athens boomed again. Again, Athens became an important cotton and rail location of North Alabama.

Planters and Slaves

For several years after Indian removal, a mass influx of wealthy white cotton planters with their black slaves arrived in Limestone County, Alabama, of the Tennessee Valley; this mass migration was known as Alabama Fever. The vast majority of the planters originated in Virginia, and they were seeking better land to grow their cotton. The 1816 Indian land cessions by the Chickasaws and Cherokees open vast tracts of land in northwest Alabama, and many of the Virginia cotton planters sought the rich farmlands along the Tennessee and Elk Rivers of Limestone County.

The 1820, 1830, 1840, 1850, and 1860 censuses included many individual slave owners and black slaves that lived in Limestone County, Alabama, that are not included in this book; only those with 10 or more slaves are listed. According to 1860 Limestone County, Alabama, United States Census, the population included 8,085 black slaves that were held by 661 slave owners.

After 1860, the Civil War ended the ownership of slaves, and many of the Limestone cotton planters lost everything. However, some planter families managed to hold on to vast tracts of land in the Tennessee River Valley. Today, those prior slave owning families that hold hundreds of acres of land still benefit economically from the land by renting to farmers or by farming the land themselves.

The following tables list the slave owners in alphabetical order by last name and cover the 1820 through 1860 census records for Limestone County, Alabama. Some years of slave ownership, numbers of slaves were missing or not recorded, and very few planters owned slaves over the span of 40 years of reporting.

Limestone County Slave Owners	1820	1830	1840	1850	1860
A---ant, James		19			
Adams, Thomas	10				
Adkinson, James		20			
Airs, Samuel				23	
Akin, William				12	
Allen, Asa F.		33	32	23	36
Allen, Benjamin	12				
Allen, James W.				27	
Allen, Mary			18	17	
Allen, Robert B.					20
Allen, William T.				7	12
Allison, James			16		
Allison, John Sr.			13	10	
Anderson, Charles D.				44	63
Anderson, George R.				8	
Andrews, Eliza A.			27		
Andrews, Richard			10		
Arledge, James Cyrus	0	15	16		
Arnett, James	10				
Ashford, Thomas Harrison Jr.					32
Askew, Abner Eli	6	15			
Aslego, Isaac					14
Athens, Alabama					29
Atkinson, Jesse			14		22
Bailey, David			12		
Banks, Equilla				13	
Bap, Thomas				18	
Barker, George R.				40	
Barley, Elizabeth					10
Barnes, A. T.			11		

Limestone County Slave Owners	1820	1830	1840	1850	1860
Bass, Thomas			15	6	12
Bates, Fleming	18	25			
Batts, Frederick			10		
Baugh, William A.					20
Beaty (Beatty), Robert	4	19			
Beckham, Abner			10		
Beckham, John			8		
Bennett, Benjamin L.			50	4	
Bennett, James			33		
Bennett, John		16			
Benson, Martin	13	14			
Benson, Nathaniel W.			12	19	
Benson, William			13		
Bibb, Joseph W?		25			
Bibb, Robert T.				69	40
Bibb, Thomas Sr.	110	257			
Bibb, Thomas Jr.			61	59	57
Bibb, William			48		
Bill, Sarah R.				11	
Binford, Abner H.				25	41
Binford, Addison D.		36	62		
Binford, E. M.					22
Binford, H. A.					41
Binford, John J.				15	16
Binford, John M.-deceased			15		
Bird, Edmund E.				24	
Bird, Pleasant			19		
Bird, William	10				
Black, John			19		
Black, William		6	8		

Limestone County Slave Owners	1820	1830	1840	1850	1860
Blackburn, Francis				34	31
Blackwell, Bouldin C.				24	
Blackwell, Eliza W.				43	
Blackwell, Samuel			36	42	14
Blackwell, William H. Sr. & Jr.			39	60	21
Blackwood, James	9				
Blackwood, John				7	
Blair, John S.				25	
Blair, Jonathan	23				
Blas__igh, John L.					59
Blessing, Phil				13	
Bond, Nicholas P.	45	20			
Bonner, Willis				22	
Booth, George				8	
Bradley, Archelaus M.			16		
Bradley, Joseph H.				115	
Bradley, Palmyra					33
Bramett, James				39	
Bridgeforth, James W.					39
Bridgeforth, Robert L.				17	17
Bridges, Tenen B.				47	
Brister, Nancy				12	
Brown, William					147
Bullard, William W.				64	
Bumpass, J. A.				24	
Burkes, John P.				10	
Burns, William	10	17			
Burt, John M.				26	
Cain, Allison Chapppell				31	51
Cain, James H.					53

Limestone County Slave Owners	1820	1830	1840	1850	1860
Cain, Thomas. J.					13
Canice?, Grief		14			
Cannon, Daniel A.					16
Cannon, David	8				
Carrell, Grief	16				
Carrell (Carriel), John D.	12				
Cartwright, Hezikiah B.			11	15	44
Cheatham, Christopher	28				
Clarke, Robert				15	
Clarke, William	35	23	11	10	
Clay, A. J.					16
Clay, Sam			17		
Clement, Edmond	11				
Coe, Jesse	40	114			
Coffman, James D.					27
Coffman, Mark M.			14		
Coleman, Daniel-estate					140
Coleman, David				13	
Coleman, E. F.					14
Coleman, Ruffin		20			
Collier, Joseph		18			
Collier, Joshua				13	
Collier, Thomas B.			30	81	49
Collins, Alfred			16	7	
Coman, A. P.					16
Common, J. W.			23		
Copeland, Nathan W.					23
Copeland, William			18		
Copeland, Rickets	12				
Cordle, Charles W.				24	

Limestone County Slave Owners	1820	1830	1840	1850	1860
Cotton, Thomas		56			
Cox, Bradley (Bartley)		28	12	14	
Cox, James			12		
Craig, David H.	2	10	18		
Craig, Elenor				15	
Craig, James	0	35	8		
Crenshaw, Freeman	10	14	18		
Crenshaw, James W.				12	
Crenshaw, Samuel				16	
Crenshaw, Truman		15			
Crenshaw, William M.					19
Cright, John			20		
Critz, George F.					13
Crutcher, Reuben			21	21	20
Dabney, R. C.					24
Dancey, David		35			
David, Robert C.			9	9	10
Davis, Benjamin	10				
Davis, John	9	16	10	11	12
Davis, Nathaniel	0	3	7	4	
Davis, Nicholas	21	55	81	114	
Davis, Tinsley	32				
Davis				6	
Dawson, T. B.			18		
Dement, Josiah B.					11
Denny, A.					12
Denny, Willis			8		
Devan, Bernard (Barney)	25				
Dickerson, Benjamin	150	39			
Dillard, George	30	22			

Limestone County Slave Owners	1820	1830	1840	1850	1860
Donaldson, Nancy				10	
Donnell, James W. S.	12	12	13		
Donnell, Robert	11	26	34	10	
Donoho, John	11				
Dorch, Robert		33			
Dunkin, Benjamin		16			
Duncan, James M.			8		
Dunn, Gray			8		
Dunn, Willis				14	
Dupuy, James W.	10				
Easter, Champion (Champ)		27	41		
Easter, Milton T.					14
Easter, Samuel W.					35
Eddins, Joel	12				
Edmund, William				13	
Edmundson, Amos? J.		17			
Edmundson, William	14				
Ellison, John	9				
Ellison, Thomas	0	19			
English, James	14	15			
English, Nancy			18		
English, Partick	12				
Farmer, Tandy R.			8		30
Favour, John			9		
Featherstone, Howell C.	1	8	16	23	17
Fielding, William				8	
Finn, Edward			13		
Fisher, Jacob	26	31	37	20	
Fisher, William (Will)		13	14		
Flannagan, Sam			12		

Limestone County Slave Owners	1820	1830	1840	1850	1860
Fletcher, Edward A.			18	41	61
Fletcher, James N.			30	78	103
Fletcher, John James			20	39	27
Fletcher, Richard M.					14
Flian?, W. H.					21
Floyd, N.					24
Ford, Richard			21		
Forte (Foote), Garvin P.				20	26
Fox, Benjamin	24				
Fox, John		42			
Frazier (Frazer), John				15	13
Fritz, John F.			39		
Gamble, James Hurt			37	50	93
Gamble, John Hicks					54
Gamble, Ruffin Coleman				20	50
Garner, Brice M.	15				
Garrett, Edmond		22	27	41	
Garrett, Jesse				90	
Garrett, Peter				19	34
Garrett, William H.				21	
Garrison, R.			19		
Gilbert, David			35		43
Gilbert, David C.					10
Gilbert, Thomas	25				15
Gilbert, Thomas H.					27
Gill, Gardner			10		
Glago, Ruben				8	
Glaize, B.					10
Golightly, James	8		14		
Golightly, Mary	9				

Limestone County Slave Owners	1820	1830	1840	1850	1860
Gordon, David M.					15
Gordon, James	6				
Gravitt, Jesse			75		
Gray, James	10				
Gray, Matthew		15			
Gray, Nancy			11		
Gray, Thomas	2		14		
Gray, Walter	16	37			
Green, Balaam		30			
Green, Robert			15		
Griffin, Thomas R.					28
Grigsby, Edward W.			50	59	68
Grigsby, James			24		
Grigsby, John		24	30	49	68
Grigsby, John P.					28
Halbert, John			9		
Hall, H. Y.			17		
Hall, William	8	9	11		
Hancock, Clem			10		
Hancock, Nath.			27		
Hanson, William R.					25
Hardin, John	7	13	17	17	
Hardin, L. T.			8		
Hardy, John S.					15
Hargrove, James	10	15		17	
Harris, A. S.				12	
Harris, John Hunter	26	47	66	82	83
Harris, John R.			25	24	23
Harris, Mary	22				
Harris, Schuyler				30	40

Limestone County Slave Owners	1820	1830	1840	1850	1860
Harris, Thomas	9				
Harris, William W.		37	33	30	24
Harrison, Benjamin			22		
Harrison, John P.			22		
Harrison, Joseph	10				
Harrison, William H.			10	10	
Harrison, William L.				19	
Hartwell, J. W.					11
Harvey, George H.					14
Harwell, William M.					18
Hatchett, C. A.					11
Hatchett, Edward			13	25	20
Henderson, Bennett E.	20				
Henderson, Isaac			8		
Henderson, Margaret					19
Henderson, Thomas			9		
Higgs, James		15			
Hill, Joel	20				
Hine, Calvin	12				
Hine (Hind), Edward				23	27
Hine, Silas	50	42	34		
Hine, James Harrison				33	47
Hine, William A.				11	
Hine (s), Charlotte				17	25
Hines, Richard G.			16		
Hinnel?, Will (William)		26			
Hobbs, David		51			
Hobbs, Ira E.		54	32	10	
Hobbs, John E.			14		
Hobbs, Thomas Hubbard					83

Limestone County Slave Owners	1820	1830	1840	1850	1860
Hold, William					19
Holt, Henry			6	21	41
Holt, John D.			0	11	17
Hooks, Garie (Gorrie)	10				
Horton, James E.					39
Horton, Rodah V.					47
Houston, George S.			21	49	78
Howell, Jourden	10				
Hubbard, Benjamin	8				
Hudson, Charles O.					16
Hughes, Beverly	12				
Hughey, Robert H.					11
Humphrey, B. P.					31
Hundley, John H.			19	47	41
Hunt (Hurt), James H.			8	22	35
Hussey, E. M.					36
Hutchins, Christopher	7				
Hyde, Isaac			10		
Hyde, Jemima					12
Irwin, John P.			19		
Jackson, James-Forks of Cypress	100				
Johnson, Anderson	45				
Johnston, James F.				8	
Johnston (Johnson), Joseph	5	25			
Johnston, Nancy			10		
Johnston, William			26		
Jones, Alexander P.				36	65
Jones, Alfred			8		
Jones, Benjamin B.	14				
Jones, Charles H.					11

Limestone County Slave Owners	1820	1830	1840	1850	1860
Jones, Clinton			24		
Jones, Hamilton			30		
Jones, Hardy		18	22		
Jones, J. H. W.					14
Jones, John H.	17			53	170
Jones, John J.	3	13	21	28	
Jones, John N. S.		73	73	115	
Jones, Llewallen	50				
Jones, Obadiah	16				
Jones, Sam P.			9		74
Jones, Susanna		23			
Jones, Thomas E.	16				
Jordan, Elizabeth		24		88	
Jordan (Jourdan), Samuel	40	77	84		
Kemp,			25		
Kendall, Moses	12				
Kerby, William M.		57			
Key, Samuel D.		17			
Keyes, G. & N.		37			
Keys, Ruth				26	
King, Elizabeth		22			
Kimbell (Campbell), Henry W.				28	38
Land, Charles	20				
Lane, George W.			44		
Lane, James M.			37	61	74
Lane, John		24			
Lane, Sampson	9				
Lane, Thompson		34			
Lanier, Thomas		12			
Legg, Andrew C.					43

Limestone County Slave Owners	1820	1830	1840	1850	1860
Lemaster, James L.		18			
Lemmond, William (Will)		50			
Leonard, John			15		
Leonard, Thomas	2	14			
Leslie, James				17	43
Little, George W.	12				
Lockhart, H. B.					44
Lockhart, James B. (P.)	9			40	49
Lookingbell, Christian	15				
Love, Elizabeth			14	12	
Love, Thomas				11	
Love, William	9	18			
Lowell, James F.				23	
Lucas, Edwin N.				26	21
Lucas, John H.		23			
Lucas, John R.		29			
Lucker, Hartwell		17			
Lynch, N.					12
Lynch, Thomas				9	
Lynch, William N.				17	
Maclin, Benjamin W.			41	59	77
Maclin, (Mackin, Maclien) Thomas		88	76		
Malone, Booth		48			
Malone, Franklin		23	16	8	
Malone, George		28	42		
Malone, James C.			39	30	18
Malone, James H.				48	89
Malone, James M.				27	32
Malone, John D.			26	13	14
Malone, John N.				7	45

Limestone County Slave Owners	1820	1830	1840	1850	1860
Malone, John P.		22			
Malone, R. D.			17	27	
Malone, Stith				13	
Malone, Thomas H.	50	35	30		
Malone, Thomas C.		27	21		
Malone, William E.	20		44		
Maples, A. K.			19		
Maples, Holloway	12				
Maples, John	14	34	91		
Maples, Malcolm G.					76
Marge (Maxye), Robert V.	70				
Marshall, George				50	
Marshall, Josiah W.		13			
Marshall, Thomas			31		
Martin, Frances C.					21
Martin, William	12				
Martindale, Elizabeth					40
Mason, Elizabeth	13				
Mason, John R.			54	111	134
Mason, William					61
Massey (Mapey), Edward	7	15			
Massey, John	10				
Massey (Maper), Judith		14	12		
Matthews, Judith			19	21	
Matthews, Kitty			90		
Matthews, Luke		41	112	57	203
Matthews, Robert		14			
Matthews, Samuel			44	67	
Matthews, Thomas	30	69			
Matthews, William Washington			22	30	

Limestone County Slave Owners	1820	1830	1840	1850	1860
May, Joseph E.		25			
McClay?, S.?					13
McCargo, Robert F.			26	37	
McClellan, T. J.				11	18
McClure, William W.				94	
McCrary, Benjamin P.				34	
McDonald, Jonathan				69	103
McGaughey, David				7	
McGaughey, S.					12
McGee, Abraham	8				
McJohn, Nancy		25			
McKinney, Alex			14		
McKinney, James			9	28	30
McKinney, John	0		8		
McKinney, Mex L.					11
McKinney, Sarah			11		
McKinsey, Daniel	9				
McWilliams, Andrew	0	5	10	15	15
McWilliams, A. R.					14
McWilliams, John	1	5	9		
Mechin, B. W.					76
Meal(s), James A.					15
Memphis-Charleston RR					37
Miller, William			12		
Millhouse, Anna				10	
Millhouse, C. A.					26
Millhouse, John E.			14	27	8
Minor, One					25
Mitchell, Cullin			32		
Mitchell, James			8	17	

Limestone County Slave Owners	1820	1830	1840	1850	1860
Mitchell, Samuel F.				27	16
Mitchell, Thomas B.		22			
Montgomery, James			9		
Moore, Alfred				61	
Moore, John H.	17	23	29	23	
Moore, John L.			25		
Moore, John M.					16
Moore, Joseph A.					12
Moore, Samuel B.					112
Moore, William H.				18	
Moran, William		42			
Morton, Quinn	12				
Murry, Amos			18		
Neal, Sylvanus			8		
Nelson, Frederick (Fred) B.	0	4	8		
Nelson, Lewis A.				12	24
Nelson, Stephen G.			10	15	14
Nelson, William	10				
Newby, Matthew				14	
O'Banum			17		
Odum, Charles		20			
Odum, William			26		
Parham, John B.				7	
Parham, Nicholas			9		
Parham, Nicholas C.			21		
Parham, William			13	20	24
Parker, Charlotte		14			
Parker, Thomas	15				
Parker, William C.			45		
Pate				30	

Limestone County Slave Owners	1820	1830	1840	1850	1860
Peebles (Peoples), Henry	30	21	32		
Peebles, John T.				9	
Peebles, Robert B.				22	80
Peebles, Washington				11	37
Peete, Benjamin B.		68	23		28
Peete, Richard			34		
Peete, Samuel					45
Peoples (Peebles), Joseph D.	32	67			
Perkins, C?. S.					27
Perkins, N.		14			
Pettus, Alice T.		29			
Petty, Abner T.			8		
Petty (Pettey), Gaden		15			
Petty, George			34		
Petty, George J.			21		
Petty (Pettey), Joseph M.					18
Phillips, Anthony	12	15			
Phillips, George			8		
Phillips, Thomas				21	
Phillips, William W.			26		14
Philpot, F.					17
Pickett, J.					16
Pickett, Sarah O.				61	69
Pickett, Steptoe, Sr and Jr.		30	46	57Jr	16Jr
Pitts, John	14				
Pope, Leroy	59				
Posey, Jesse H.	13				
Poston, Zephaneah	35				
Pruiet, Jesse H.			24		
Pryor, Luke Sr. and Jr.			2	39	76Jr

Limestone County Slave Owners	1820	1830	1840	1850	1860
Ragland, Samuel				54	
Raney (Ramsy?), John		29	18		
Rawlins, Sam W.			9		
Reddus, Alfred H.					15
Reddus, Calvin					29
Reddus, Thomas			11		65
Reddus, William			12	13	14
Reed, Benjamin F.			8		
Rice, Elisha H. (K.)		26			
Rice, John, Mary P. Rice					94
Rice, Tate	27				
Richardson, N. D.					8
Richardson, William			11	15	23
Roberts, Benjamin				7	
Roberts, F.				10	
Roberts, George			10		
Roberts, James	9	10	11		
Roberts, Matthew H.			28	47	47
Robertson, Martha H.				13	
Robertson, Stokes				16	
Robertson, W. H.					20
Robertson, William W.			8		
Robinson, Hardy	8				
Robinson, M. H.					13
Robinson, Stokes			8		
Rodgers, R. M.			12		
Rowe, William		24	44		
Russell, A.					11
Russell, James				14	22
Sanders, Sarah				13	

Limestone County Slave Owners	1820	1830	1840	1850	1860
Sanders, W. L.					12
Sandifer, William (Will)		31	55		
Saunders, William			38		
Scallion, Nancy				11	
Scott, Jane	17				
Scruggs, Edmund P. B. Y.				59	
Shuttleworth, Elijah			16		
Simpson, Ned.				57	
Slap, C. W.					11
Slaughter, J. K.					23
Silvers, John	55				
Simmons, Ann	10				
Sims, Hickman			25		
Smith, Gabriel		35			
Smith, John N.	2		22		
Smith, John W.	15				
Smith, W. B.					16
Solomon, Marshall	18				
Sowell, James F.			20		
Stanback, George			10		
Stanley, James			13		
Stinnett, Abigail			16		
Stinnett, C. Clay					39
Stinnett, William	10				
Sweaney, Arthur M.				11	
Sykes, Benjamin		23			
Tanner, L. S.					15
Tate, Enos	7		32		
Tate, John	16				
Tate, Mrs.					19

Limestone County Slave Owners	1820	1830	1840	1850	1860
Tate, Nancy				41	31
Tate, Waddy	100	80	83	38	
Tate, William (Will) R.		21	23	30	
Teague, Harriet B.			8	6	
Terry, Nathaniel			110	24	
Thatch, Thomas H.		17	40		
Thomas, Charles K.				11	
Thomas, Micajah	13	31	43		
Thomas, Theophilus	20	13			
Thomason, William (Will)		28			
Thompson, Neal			32	22	13
Thompson, S. C.			41		
Tilman, Reuben		15			
Tisdale, Shirley			16	21	37
Titus, James	12				
Townson, Brice M.			22	38	55
Travis, T. G.			61		
Trice, William	35				
Trotter, J. R.			12		
Tucker, Bennett		18	14		
Tucker, H. P.			22		
Tucker, James		22	34	37	51
Turner, William E.				17	
Turnipseed, Andrew	0	23			
Tweedy, Joseph M.		26	17		
Tweedy, T. T.					14
Vasser, E. H.			31		
Vasser, Richard W.				9	98
Vaughan, James			9	14	
Vaughan, William P.					11

Limestone County Slave Owners	1820	1830	1840	1850	1860
Vest, Samuel M.				53	
Waddel, Nancy			10		
Walker, James W.	72	90			
Walker, R. S.			21		
Wall, William	11				
Walton, Edmond		23	38		
Walton, M. A.					75
Ward, William				68	
Warrick, Benjamin			51		
Washington, Thomas T.			15		
Washington, Starke	22	14			
Waters, David M.					15
Watkins, Edmund				20	
Watkins, R. J. (T.)					37
Wear, M. T.					17
Webb, James		23			
Webb, John		22	36		
Webb, Mary S.				40	
Webb, Robinson (Robert)		19	26	32	
Welborn, Chapley R.	13				
White, Effy (Eppy)	5	14			
White, John D.	1	17			
White, M.					92
White, Samuel D.		22	61	118	
Whittaker, William	9				
Wholeapple, Jane			10		
Wiggins, J.? A					19
Wilaes, John		27			
Wilbourne, John K.			19		
Wilkinson, John B.		32			

Limestone County Slave Owners	1820	1830	1840	1850	1860
Wilkinson, John Y.				19	
Wilkinson, Ruben				9	
Wilkerson, George			46		
Wilkerson, James			10		
Williams, Thomas			11		
Williamson, James		17			
Winn, John H. J.			8	10	
Winsett, Elizabeth			18		
Winston, Joel W.	17				
Wofford, Andrew			9		
Wofford, John	5	17			
Wood, Alexander				9	
Wood, Edward (Edmund)	8	20	31		
Wood, Thomas			14		
Woodruff, James W.			12	35	83
Wooley, Jack				18	
Wooley, Joel	4	8	13		26
Word, William			8		
Wright, Claibourne			12		
Wright, Robert C.				7	
Yale, Enos C.		33			
Yarborough, Albert G.					24
Yarborough, Henry	14	17	61		
Yarborough, James					40
Yarborough, John N.					39
Yarborough, William H.					42

Anderson, Charles D. - Poplar Grove

Major Charles Dandridge Anderson was born about 1810 in Bedford County, Virginia. He was the son of Jesse Anderson (Find A Grave Memorial #123651445) and Elizabeth West Jones (Find A Grave Memorial #123651494). Charles Dandridge Anderson was the grandson of John Anderson and double nephew of Llewellyn Jones who were Revolutionary War soldiers.

On June 21, 1791, Elizabeth West Jones (1775-September 1849) married Jesse Anderson (1767-1818). A year later in 1792, Elizabeth's brother Llewellyn Jones married Mary Lighfoot Anderson, who was the sister of her husband, Jesse Anderson. Llewellyn Jones (1760-1/26/1820) owned a lot of land and at least three cotton plantations: Avalon Plantation at present-day University of Alabama at Huntsville (UAH), Druid's Grove Plantation near Greenbrier, and Seclusion Plantation near Town Creek in Lawrence County.

On October 25, 1841, Charles D. Anderson married Mary Anne Harrison in Bedford County, Virginia. She was born on November 15, 1815, in Brunswick County, Virginia. Mary was the daughter of Benjamin Harrison.

Charles D. Anderson and Mary Anne Harrison Anderson had the following children:
1. Elizabeth W. Anderson was born about 1843.
2. Mary A. H. Anderson Harris was born about 1848.
3. Harriet R. Anderson was born about 1853.

The Poplar Grove Plantation of Charles D. Anderson was near Tanner in Limestone County, Alabama. According to the 1850 Limestone County, Alabama, Slave Schedules of District 3, Charles D. Anderson owned 44 black slaves.

On August 26, 1850, Charles Dandridge Anderson and William L. Harrison paid $1.25/acre for 83 acres in the west ½ of the southeast ¼ of Section 31 of Township 3 South and Range 2 West in Madison County, Alabama. On March 21, 1855, Charles D. Anderson paid 12.5 cents/acre for 177.17 acres of land in the northwest ¼ of Section 31 of Township 3 South and Range 2 West in

Madison County, Alabama. The land Charles bought lay just east of the Limestone-Madison County lines.

On January 14, 1853, Mary Anne Harrison Anderson died in Limestone County, Alabama. She was buried in the Anderson Cemetery in Limestone County, Alabama.

In 1860 Limestone County, Alabama, Slave Schedules of District 3, Charles Dandridge Anderson owned 63 black slaves. The 1860 Limestone County, Alabama, United States Census, District One listed the following: Charles D. Anderson, male, 50, white, Virginia; Elizabeth W. Anderson, female, 17 Alabama; Mary A. H. Anderson, female, 12 Alabama; Harriet R. Anderson, female, 7, Alabama; and Robert S. Anderson, male, 44, Virginia.

On May 14, 1873, Major Charles Dandridge Anderson died at his Poplar Grove Plantation in Limestone County, Alabama. Major Anderson was in the 21st Alabama Infantry during the Civil War.

Anderson Cemetery #1 is located on the north side of the Browns Ferry Road in Limestone County, Alabama. The Anderson Cemetery was also presented in the book <u>Limestone County, Alabama Cemeteries</u> (Linda H. Smith, 2/1/1992).

1. Anderson, Mary Ann, wife of Charles D. and daughter of Benjamin Harrison. She died on January 14, 1853 (Find A Grave Memorial# 36041887).
2. Jones, Francis M., wife of Clinton Jones, born Virginia in February 1802, and she died in Alabama on October 12, 1845. She lived a consistent Christian and died the death of the righteous. Clinton C. Jones married Frances Ann Thatch on December 14, 1846. Frances was the daughter of Henry Thatch of Mooresville. After Frances died, Clinton Jones married Sarah Gray in 1847.
3. Roberts, Sarah B., Consort of J. F. Roberts, June 5, 1828-June 18, 1849.
4. Tinnin, Robert, born in Orange City, North Carolina on November 6, 1801, and died on March 31, 1847.

Beaty, Robert

On June 12, 1762, Colonel Robert Beaty was born in British Virgin Islands, and he came to America as a child. Robert grew up in Virginia, and moved to Madison County, Alabama.

On August 9 and 11, 1809, Robert Beaty entered some 480 acres of land in Madison County of Mississippi Territory. On February 17, 1810, he entered an additional 160 acres in Township 4 South and Range 1 West in Madison County of Mississippi Territory (Cowart, 1979).

On September 20, 1809, Robert Beaty married Sarah Parrott in Madison County, Alabama. Robert Beaty and Sarah Parrott Beaty had the following children:

1. Lucretia Beaty was born June 10, 1811, and she died on May 7, 1822, at 10 years, 10 months, 27 days. Lucretia is buried in the Houston Cemetery in Limestone County, Alabama.
2. Narcissa Beaty was born November 22, 1813. She married Major James W. Crenshaw at Athens on Friday, February 18, 1831; James owned 12 black slaves in 1850. Narissa died about 1834 at 21 years, 8 months, 19 days. She is buried in the Houston Cemetery in Limestone County, Alabama. Her son Robert F. Crenshaw is buried in the same grave as his mother; he was only 22 days old.
3. Mary Jackson Beaty was born April 16, 1815, in Alabama, and she died April 20, 1856. Mary was the wife of George Smith Houston who became Governor of Alabama in 1874.
4. Napoleon Beaty was born April 24, 1817, and he died March 29, 1853, in Pettis County, Missouri.
5. Glorvinia Beaty was born September 26, 1818, and she died on June 24, 1894. See more about Glorvinia Beaty under John Richardson Mason.
6. Jerome Beaty was born November 18, 1820, and he died December 27, 1830, at 10 yrs, one month, nine days. Jerome is buried in the Houston Cemetery in Limestone County, Alabama.

By February 1818, Robert Beaty was entering land in Limestone County, Alabama. In February 1818, Robert Beaty entered 1600 acres in Townships 2, 3, 4 South and Ranges 3, 4, 6 West in Limestone County, Alabama. On November 2, 1829, Robert entered an additional 80.6 acres in Section 9 of Township 3 South and Range 4 West in Limestone County, Alabama (Cowart, 1984).

On February 9, 1818, Robert Beaty and John D. Carroll purchased 159.9 acres which became Athens, Alabama. According to Wikipedia: "Robert Beaty was one of the original founders of Athens. An Irish immigrant who settled in Virginia, Beaty and his associates purchased 160 acres around a spring and began subdividing the land for sale in 1818. A small village of log structures had formed by 1826 and began to be replaced by permanent homes over the next decade."

According to the 1820 Limestone County, Alabama Census, the Robert Beaty household had one white male over 21, one white male under 21, two white females over 21, and four white females under 21. The census indicates 11 people of color and four black slaves.

In 1822, Robert Beaty began building his home which still stands in the Robert Beaty Historic District in the City of Athens. The district contains 86 contributing properties representing architectural styles including Federal, Greek Revival, Italianate, Eastlake, Victorian, and Spanish Colonial Revival. The district was listed on the National Register of Historic Places in 1984.

In 1826, Robert Beaty completed his large, magnificent brick house in Federal style. The home was built on South Beaty Street, and he planned to use the house as the family plantation residence.

In the 1830 Limestone County, Alabama Census, the Robert Beaty household had one male 5-10 years, one male 10-15 years, one male 30-40 years, one male 70-80, one female 5-10 years, four females 10-15 years, one female 15-20 years, one female 30-40 years, and one female 40-50 years. In 1830, Robert Beaty owned 19 black slaves.

According to the 1840 Limestone County, Alabama Census, the Sarah Beaty household had one female 50-60 years, one female 20-30 years, one female

5-10 years, one male 15-20 years, and two males 10-15 years. In 1840, no slaves are indicated.

On June 10, 1837, Robert Beaty died in Pettis County, Missouri, while on a business trip. Robert was buried in the Providence Baptist Church Cemetery at Smithton in Pettis County, Missouri.

After 1840, Sarah Parrott Beaty, the wife of Robert Beaty, died in Limestone County, Alabama. Sarah P. Beaty was in the 1840 Limestone County, Alabama census.

The Robert Beaty home was inherited by Edmond Peter Garrett, and he sold the home to Athens State College in 1961. Today, the Beaty house is for sale by Athens State University. The college used the home for the college president, but renovation costs became too high; therefore, the home was put up for sale. The log cabin slave quarters at the back of the Beaty house was restored and served as a guest house. The Robert Beaty house is located at 211 Beaty Street South, Athens, Alabama.

Robert Beaty Home

Bibb, Thomas - Belle Mina

On May 8, 1783, Thomas Bibb was born in Amelia County, Virginia; he was the son of William and Sally Wyatt Bibb. Thomas received his education in Elbert County, Georgia, where he grew to manhood. The siblings of Thomas Bibb were born in Virginia and are as follows:
1. William Wyatt Bibb
2. Reverend Peyton Bibb
3. John Dandridge Bibb
4. Benajah Smith Bibb

In May 1803, according to Find A Grave, Thomas Bibb married Parmelia Thompson (1784-1854) in South Carolina. Some sources say they married in 1805 in Elbert County, Georgia. Parmelia was the daughter of Robert Thompson and Sarah Watkins, natives of Amelia County, Virginia.

By August 9, 1809, based on Old Land Records of Madison County, Alabama, by Margaret Matthews Cowart (1984), Thomas and Parmelia moved to Madison County in the Mississippi Territory where he became a planter and merchant. Between August 9, 1809, and September 28, 1821, Thomas Bibb entered some 4,072 acres in Madison County, Alabama (Cowart, 1984).

Thomas Bibb

Starting in 1809 through November 1818, based on early land records, Thomas Bibb was a land speculator and owned some 22,600 acres of land in the six counties taken from the Cherokee and Chickasaw Indians. The following is the approximate acreage of land in these

North Alabama counties: Madison 4,070 acres, most entered in August 1809; Limestone 2,650 acres, entered in February 1818; Lauderdale, 4,900 acres entered in March 1818; Morgan, 600 acres, most entered in July 1818; Lawrence County, 8,600 acres, entered in September 1818; and Franklin County (Colbert), about 1800 acres, entered in November 1818.

About February 1818, the family moved to Limestone County where Thomas entered additional land. Thomas and Parmelia had the following children:
1. Adeline Bibb (1806-1894) married James Bradley in 1822.
2. Emily Julie Bibb (11/20/1808-9/2/1849) married James Pleasants in1824.
3. Thomas Bibb Jr. (1810-1861) married Anna Corbin Pickett in 1857.
4. William Dandridge "Will" Bibb (1810-1880) married Mary Mitchell in 1840.
5. David Porter Bibb (12/31/1814-7/8/1865) married Mary Chambers Betts in 1835.
6. Elmira Bibb (1816-1887) married Archibald Mills in 1833.
7. Robert Thompson Bibb (1818-1861) married Ann Bradley in 1843.
8. Eliza Parmelia Bibb (1821-1899) married Arthur Moseley Hopkins in 1837.
9. Peyton Dandridge Bibb was born in December 1823, and he died in January 1824. His newspaper obituary stated, "Died in this place Saturday evening last, Peyton Dandridge Bibb, infant son of Thomas Bibb, Esq., aged 4 month, 22 days."
10. Nimrod Bibb (unknown-1868)
11. Benjamin Franklin Bibb (Unknown-1875)
12. Benjamin Franklin Bibb (1829-1920)

On February 6,7,10, 1818, Thomas Bibb Sr. entered about 2,650 acres of land in Limestone County, Alabama. From 1831 through 1841, Thomas Bibb Jr. entered an additional 1,600 acres in the county (Cowart, 1984). All the land the father and son entered was in Townships 4, 5 South and Ranges 3, 4 West. Jointly, Thomas Bibb Sr. and Jr. owned some 4,200 acres of land and were among the largest landowners in Limestone County at the time.

In 1819, Thomas Bibb Sr. served as a Delegate to the Alabama State Constitutional Convention from Limestone County. That same year, he was elected to the senate of Alabama and chosen as senate president. By law, Thomas Bibb took the office of governor upon the death of his brother, Governor William Wyatt Bibb.

In 1820 based on Limestone County, Alabama, Slave Schedules, Thomas Bibb was one of the largest slave holders in Limestone County. In 1820, Thomas Bibb Sr. owned 110 black slaves. He sought out skilled slave labor to make bricks and to harvest timber with crosscut saws for lumber to build his home.

On July 10, 1820, while Thomas was serving as president of the Alabama senate, his brother William was accidentally killed in a fall from his horse. At the time, William Wyatt Bibb was serving as the first Governor of Alabama. Previously, William Wyatt Bibb was a physician, and he entered politics in the early 1800s. William served in the Georgia House and Senate and the United States Congress before he was appointed to be the Governor of Alabama Territory from 1817 through 1819. When Alabama became a state on December 14, 1819, William became the first Governor of the State of Alabama.

From July 1820 to December 1821, Thomas Bibb served as the second governor of Alabama. During his term, the state government was formally moved from Huntsville to Cahaba. He did not run for re-election at the end of his term. He also served as director of the Huntsville branch of the Bank of the State of Alabama. In 1828 and 1829, he was elected a representative to the State legislature.

In 1826, Thomas completed his home at Belle Mina Plantation in Limestone County, Alabama. The plantation was originally called Belle Manor but changed because southern people were mispronouncing the original name. The Town of Belle Mina developed around the huge plantation of Thomas Bibb and the railroad station in the town. The railroad was intended to pass through the nearby Town of Mooresville, but the residents did not want it built too close to their homes and businesses; therefore, it ran through Belle Mina.

Belle Mina

    According to Wikipedia, "Prior to the construction of the main house, Bibb had to have a sawmill and a brick kiln built. As the area was still being converted from a frontier, there was no sawed lumber or ready-made brick available. Bibb obtained skilled slave artisans to produce the construction materials and build the house. It took him several years to find a highly skilled slave mason and an expert carpenter. The house was basically complete by 1826, although work on various buildings of the plantation continued up to 1835."

    On June 17, 1829, Robert Thompson, father-in-law of Thomas Bibb, died at Belle Mina in Limestone County, Alabama. Robert "Old Blue" Thompson was born in 1757 in Amelia, Virginia.

    According to the 1830 Limestone County, Alabama, census records, Thomas Bibb Sr. owned 257 black slaves; he may have had slaves at other plantations. The Limestone County slaves worked his cotton crop, and that year, they produced 164 bales of cotton.

Belle Mina-Rear View
Library of Congress

In 1836, in addition to his country home at Belle Mina, Thomas built a town house for him and his wife on Williams Street in Huntsville, Alabama. Based on land records, Thomas and Parmelia had lived in Madison County as early as August 1809. Thomas also lived in Huntsville in 1820, when the first state capital of Alabama was located there. He served as the second governor of Alabama after the death of his brother. After his term as governor ended, his wife wanted to remain in the town where she enjoyed the social circles. Thomas Bibb had the financial resources to build their grand mansion in Huntsville. Nearby, he also gave a Huntsville home to

Thomas Bibb Home
Huntsville, Alabama

his daughter Adeline Bibb and her husband James Bradley.

Supposedly, Thomas enjoyed living at his home at Belle Mina because of his love for the serenity and quietness of the country life. While living in Huntsville, Thomas made many trips back to the old home place at Belle Mina.

On July 19, 1838, David Porter Bibb, son of Thomas Bibb Sr., moved to Louisiana after his son Porter Bibb was born in Limestone County, Alabama. A few years prior to his death, Thomas Bibb Sr. had moved to Louisiana. Thomas owned property in New Orleans and had cotton and sugar cane plantations nearby. On December 18, 1939, Lockhart Bibb was born in Louisiana; his father David Porter Bibb was probably there when he was born.

On September 20, 1839, Thomas Bibb Sr. died at Mobile in Mobile County, Alabama. He was buried in Maple Hill Cemetery in Block 9, Lot 15, Space 1 at Huntsville in Madison County, Alabama (Find A Grave Memorial# 7418818). According to local folklore, the ghost of Thomas Bibb cannot sleep; on some quiet moonlight nights, the hustle and bustle of the apparition of Governor Thomas Bibb can be seen and heard going back and forth between Maple Hill Cemetery and his Belle Mina Plantation home.

On November 7, 1844, Sarah Watkins Thompson, the mother-in-law of Thomas Bibb, died at Huntsville in Madison County, Alabama. Sarah, the wife of Robert Thompson, was born on June 20, 1760, in Prince Edward, Virginia.

On September 5, 1854, Pamelia Thompson Bibb, wife of Thomas Bibb Sr., died in Huntsville. She was buried in Maple Hill Cemetery at Huntsville in Madison County, Alabama, Plot: Block 5, Row 3 (Find A Grave Memorial# 7418818).

In 1941, the Belle Mina Plantation was purchased by Dr. and Mrs. Berthold Kennedy; they renovated the plantation mansion in the 1940s and again in 1967. They added a kitchen wing and garage including some minor interior modifications to the house.

On October 31, 1972, the Belle Mina Plantation house and surrounding nine acres were added to the National Register of Historic Places. Today, the old Belle Mina plantation home of Thomas Bibb Sr. is used as a private residence.

Thomas Bibb Jr.

Based on land records it would appear that Thomas Bibb Jr. was born in Madison County, Alabama; however, some say that he was born in Elbert County, Georgia. Since Thomas Bibb Sr. was entering tracts of land in Madison County in 1809, he was either purchasing the land in absentia or he was living in the area in order to identify the tracts he was buying. The following is a chronological timeline for Thomas Bibb Jr.:

1. In 1810, Thomas Bibb Jr. was born in Alabama (Mississippi Territory) to Thomas Bibb Sr. (1782-1839) and Pamelia Thompson (1784-1854) of Elbert County, Georgia.
2. From 1831-1841, Thomas Bibb Jr. entered some 1,600 acres in Limestone County, Alabama (Cowart, 1984).
3. In 1840 according to census records, Thomas Bibb Jr. owned 61 black slaves.
4. In 1850 based on the Limestone County, Alabama, Slave Schedules, Thomas Jr. owned 59 black slaves.
5. In 1857, Thomas Bibb Jr. (1810-1861) married Anna Corbin Pickett.
6. The 1860, Limestone County, Alabama, Slave Schedules indicates Thomas owned 57 black slaves.

7. In 1861, Thomas Bibb Jr. died.

Bibb, David Porter - Woodside

On December 31, 1814, David Porter Bibb was born to Thomas Bibb Sr. (1782-1839) and Pamelia Thompson (1784-1854) from Elbert County, Georgia. The father of David Porter Bibb, Thomas Bibb, was entering land in Madison County of Mississippi Territory in 1809.

In 1835, David Porter Bibb married Mary P. Chambers Betts (1814-1898), and they had the following children:
1. Henry Chambers Bibb was born on June 9, 1836, and he died in October 1873. Dr. Henry C. Bibb is buried in Bibb Cemetery at Mooresville in Limestone County, Alabama (Find A Grave Memorial# 68294015).

2. Porter Bibb was born on July 19, 1838, and he died on February 9, 1915, at 76 years old. Captain Porter Bibb is buried in Bibb Cemetery at Mooresville in Limestone County, Alabama (Find A Grave Memorial# 11287514).
3. Lockhart Bibb was born on December 18, 1839, and he died on December 30, 1907, at Paris in Lamar County, Texas. Lockhart is buried in Bibb Cemetery at Mooresville in Limestone County, Alabama. According to the <u>New Decatur Advertiser</u>, January 9, 1908: "Those of us who were living here at about the time the Gordon School was built, will remember Mr. Lockhart Bibb who was principal of that institution. After he left here, he taught in many places finally landing in Paris, Texas, where he died on the 30th of last month. He was interred at Belle Mina in the family burial ground. He leaves a widow and five children" (Find A Grave Memorial# 11287615).
4. Mary Chambers Bibb Eggleston was born on October 23, 1841, and she died on January 12, 1873. Mary is buried in Bibb Cemetery at

Mooresville in Limestone County, Alabama (Find A Grave Memorial# 114407096).

In 1861 just before the Civil War, David Porter Bibb built a grand plantation home known as Woodside. Porter had the home constructed for his daughter Mary Chambers Bibb as a wedding present when she married William Fleming Eggleston (1841-1913).

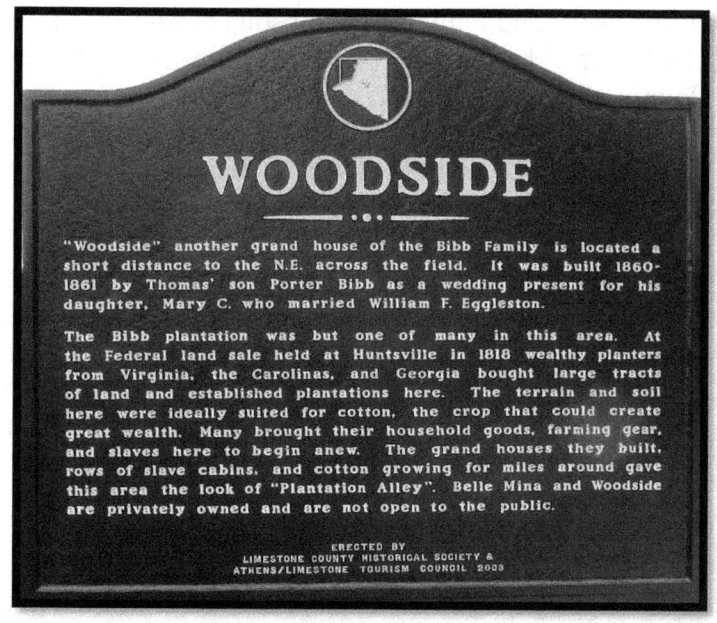

William F. Eggleston was the youngest son of Samuel O. Eggleston, a cotton planter who owned 48 black slaves. The 1850 Lawrence County, Alabama, United States Census, House Number 218 listed the following: Samuel O. Eggleston, male, 53, Virginia; Eliza J. F. Eggleston, female, 49 Virginia; M. O. Eggleston, male, 21, Alabama; M. L. Eggleston, male, 18, Alabama; Caroline V. Eggleston, female, 16, Alabama; Marcellus A. Eggleston, male, 13 Alabama; and, William F. Eggleston, male, 9, Alabama. In the 1860 census, William F. Eggleston was listed as 19 years old, and he still living at the household of his parents at that time.

According to Wikipedia: "Woodside is a historic residence in Belle Mina, Alabama. The land on which the house was built was originally part of Alabama Governor Thomas Bibb's estate, Belle Mina. The two houses stand one-half mile apart. Woodside is a two-story Greek revival house, originally with a central, double-height portico that was extended to the full width of the façade in the early 1900s. The house has a center-hall plan, with two rooms on either side of a hallway on both floors. The rear of the house was originally a pair of one-story wings, but a second story was added in an early 20th-century renovation. Greek

Revival details continue inside the house, such as mantels and architrave-framed panels in the stairwell."

On July 8, 1865, David Porter Bibb died at the age of 50. He is buried in

Woodside

the Bibb Cemetery at Mooresville in Limestone County, Alabama (Find A Grave Memorial# 11287587). On February 18, 1898, Mary P. Chambers Betts Bibb (David's wife) died at the age of 83. She is buried in the Bibb Cemetery Mooresville in Limestone County, Alabama (Find A Grave Memorial# 114402144).

In 1982, the Woodside plantation house was listed on the National Register of Historic Places in 1982. Today, the Woodside home is used as a private residence.

Bibb, Robert Thompson

In 1818, Robert Thompson Bibb was born in Alabama to Thomas Bibb and Parmelia Thompson. The wife of Robert T. Bibb was Ann Bradley, who was born in 1827. According to Early Settlers of Alabama, "Robert T. Bibb (1818-1861) of Nashville, Tennessee, married Ann Bradley in 1843; they had no children" (Saunders, 1899).

According to the 1850 Limestone County, Alabama, United States Census, House Number 389, Robert T. Bibb was a 33-year-old white male born in Alabama. Also listed with Robert was Ann Bibb a 23-year-old female born in Alabama.

In the 1850 Limestone County, Alabama, Slave Schedule, Robert Thompson Bibb owned 69 black slaves. In 1860, Robert T. Bibb owned 40 slaves.

According to the 1850 Limestone County, Alabama, Agricultural Census, Robert T. Bibb owned 1,100 acres of improved land and 1,340 acres of unimproved land worth $44,800. He also had $550 worth of farming equipment and livestock valued at 3,345.

Robert Thompson Bibb is listed in the United States Civil War Confederate Papers of Citizens or Businesses. Robert died in 1861.

Blackwell, William Henry

On November 27, 1792, William Henry Blackwell was born in Fauquier County, Virginia. He was the son of Samuel Blackwell Sr. and Elizabeth Tyler. William also had a brother named Samuel Blackwell Jr. who came to Alabama with William and entered land adjacent to his brother.

On December 14, 1817, William Henry Blackwell married Eliza Wyatt Collier who was born on May 21, 1797. She was the daughter of James Collier and Elizabeth Bouldin of Virginia.

William Henry Blackwell and Eliza Wyatt Collier Blackwell had the following children:
1. Bouldin Collier Blackwell was born on December 16, 1818; he married Mary Collier Slaughter (1823-1883). In the 1850 Limestone County, Alabama Census, Bouldin C. Blackwell owned 24 black slaves. On October 13, 1859, Bouldin died and was buried in the Blackwell-Collier Cemetery in Limestone County, Alabama (Find A Grave Memorial# 70347643).
2. Samuel Blackwell was born about 1824; he married Sarah Virginia Pickett. Sarah was the daughter of Steptoe and Sarah Orrick Chilton Pickett.
3. Wyatt Blackwell was born about 1827; he married Diana Jane Collier. Diana was the daughter of Dr. James Bouldin Collier.
4. Martha "Mattie" Wyatt Blackwell was born on October 20, 1833, in Limestone County; she married John Scott Pickett. On January 24, 1897, Mattie died and was buried in the Karnes City Cemetery in Karnes County, Texas (Find A Grave Memorial# 50983134).
5. William Henry Blackwell Jr. was born about 1835; on December 11, 1877, he married Maud Hunley in Limestone County. In 1899, William died and was buried in the Decatur City Cemetery in Morgan County, Alabama (Find A Grave Memorial# 184346066).
6. Lucy Steptoe Blackwell was born about 1837; she never married.
7. Mary Ann Battle Blackwell was born on January 16, 1838; in 1858, she married Joseph John Wiggs who died in Little Rock, Arkansas. On February 28, 1875, Mary Ann Battle Blackwell Wiggs died and was buried in the Oakland and Fraternal Historic Cemetery Park at Little Rock in Pulaski County, Arkansas (Find A Grave Memorial# 160002219).

On February 4, 1818, William H. Blackwell entered 78.94 acres in Section 19 of Township 5 South and Range 2 West in Madison County, Alabama (Cowart, 1979). On September 15, 1818, William entered 180 acres in Section 24 of Township 5 South and Range 3 West in Limestone County, Alabama (Cowart, 1984). William entered additional acreage, but these two tracts were the earliest entries on record.

According to the 1830 Limestone County, Alabama, United States Census, William H. Blackwell owned 39 black slaves. Also listed near William was Samuel Blackwell who owned 36 slaves in 1830.

In the 1840 Limestone County, Alabama, United States Census, William H. Blackwell owned 60 black slaves. In 1840, Samuel owned 42 slaves in Limestone County.

On November 26, 1846, William Henry Blackwell Sr. died in Limestone County, Alabama. William was buried in the Blackwell-Collier Cemetery in Limestone County, Alabama (Find A Grave Memorial# 70347693).

According to the 1850 Limestone County, Alabama, United States Census, Eliza W. Blackwell was a 32-year-old female born in Virginia. Also living in her household was Lucy Blackwell, Female, 20, Alabama; Martha Blackwell, Female, 17, Alabama; William H. Blackwell, Male, 15, Alabama; and Mary A. Blackwell, Female, 13, Alabama.

In the 1850 Limestone County, Alabama, United States Census, Eliza W. Blackwell, wife of William H. Blackwell, owned 43 black slaves. According to the 1850 Limestone County, Alabama, Agricultural Census, Eliza W. Blackwell owned 440 acres of improved land and 190 acres of unimproved land worth $8,700. She also had $605 worth of farming equipment and livestock valued at $1,550.

In the 1850 Limestone County, Alabama, United States Census, Bouldin C. Blackwell was a 32-year-old male born in South Carolina. Also, living in his household was Mary S. Blackwell, Female, 25, Alabama; Ann S. Blackwell, Female, 2, Alabama; Eliza Blackwell, Female, 11months, Alabama; Samuel Blackwell, Male, 26, Alabama; Wyatt C. Blackwell, Male, 23, Alabama; and Diana J. Blackwell, Female, 19, Alabama.

On July 25, 1856, Eliza Wyatt Collier Blackwell died in Limestone County at age 59. She was buried in the Blackwell-Collier Cemetery in Limestone County, Alabama (Find A Grave Memorial# 70347757).

In the 1860 Limestone County, Alabama, United States Census, William H. Blackwell was a 25-year-old male born in Alabama. Also, living in his household was Lucy Blackwell, Female, 23, Alabama; Martha Blackwell, Female, 21, Alabama; and Samuel Blackwell, Male, 34, Alabama.

In the 1860 Limestone County, Alabama Census, William H. Blackwell Jr. owned 21 black slaves. In 1860, William H. Blackwell had a real estate value of $5,800 and a personal estate value of $19,438. Lucy Blackwell had a real estate value of $5,800 and a personal estate value of $15,839. Mary A. Blackwell had a real estate value of $5,800 and a personal estate value of $16,138. Samuel Blackwell had a personal estate value of $30,500.

Samuel, son of William Henry Blackwell and Eliza Wyatt Collier Blackwell moved to Arkansas before 1870. In the 1870 Batesville, Independence County, Arkansas, United States Census, William H. Pickett was a 44-year-old farmer born in Alabama. Also living in his household was Annie R. Pickett, Female, 39, Alabama; Ida G. Pickett, Female, 15, Alabama; Elizabeth B. Pickett, Female, 13, Alabama; Samuel Blackwell, Male, 48, Alabama; Sarah V. Blackwell, Female, 38, Alabama; and two servants.

Bond, Nicholas Pirtle

On March 5, 1779, Nicholas Pirtle Bond was born at Harpers Ferry in Jefferson County, West Virginia. His parents were William (George) Bond (1719) and Elizabeth Gordon (1723). In 1743, William Bond married Elizabeth Gordon; they had the following children: Stephen, George, Isaac, Sarah, Elizabeth, Nicholas Pirtle Bond, William, and 5 others.

On December 18, 1800, Nicholas Pirtle Bond married Margaret Ann (Peggy) Fryar (1781-1862). Margaret was born in Pennsylvania on April 25, 1781. Nicholas and Margaret Bond migrated to Knoxville, Tennessee, from West Virginia, near Harper s Ferry. By February 7, 1818, they were entering land in Limestone County, Alabama.

Nicholas Pirtle Bond and Margaret Ann (Peggy) Fryar Bond had nine children:
1. William Bond (1801-1816)
2. George Bond (1803-1815)
3. Dr. Samuel Bond (1804-1862)
4. Melinda Bond (1806-1826)
5. John I. Bond (1808-1871)
6. Margaret Ann Bond (1810-1815)
7. Ashincton Bond (1812-1815)
8. Washington Bond (1813-1874)
9. Newton Bond (9/24/1815-1/23/1854)

In early 1800, two brothers of Nicholas P. Bond were entering land in Mississippi Territory in what is now Madison County, Alabama. On October 31, 1812, Stephen Bond entered 160 acres in Section 26 of Township 3 South and Range 1 East in Madison County, Alabama. On July 24, 1813, Isaac Bond entered 160.18 acres of land in Section 9 of Township 2 South and Range 1 East in Madison County, Alabama.

Nicholas P. Bond probably followed his brothers Stephen and Isaac to Madison County in Mississippi Territory. Probably while there in March 1814, Nicholas Pirtle Bond served in the Creek War under General Andrew Jackson at the Battle of Horseshoe Bend.

On February 7, 1818, Nicholas P. Bond entered 160.25 acres in Section 8 of Township 5 South and Range 3 West in Limestone County, Alabama. On the same day, he entered 162.11 acres in Section 9 of Township 5 South and Range 3 West in Limestone County, Alabama (Cowart, 1984).

The 1820 Limestone County, Alabama Census lists the following for Nicholas P. Bond: White Males over 21: 1, White Males under 21: 4, White Females over 21: 1, White Females under 21: 1, Total Whites: 7, Free Persons of Color: 1, Slaves: 45, Number of acres cultivated: 4, Number of either hands or bales: 12, Average Weight per bale: 310 pounds.

The 1830 Limestone County, Alabama, United States Census gives the following for Nicholas P. Bond household: White Males: 15-20 years: 2, 20-30 years: 1, 50-60 years: 1, White Females: 50-60 years: 1, Slaves: 25.

On July 26, 1831, Nicholas passed away in Limestone County, Alabama, at Mooresville in Limestone County, Alabama. After Nicholas Pirtle Bond died, his wife, Margaret Ann Fryar Bond, and children moved to Shelby County, Tennessee. Margaret Ann Fryar Bond died on September 10, 1882. Margaret was buried in the Bartlett-Ellendale Cemetery in Shelby County, Tennessee.

Dr. Samuel Bond

On December 10, 1804, Dr. Samuel Bond was born in Knox County, Tennessee; he was the son of Nicholas Pirtle Bond and Margaret Ann "Peggy" Fryar Bond. When he was 12 years old, Samuel moved with his parents to Limestone County, Alabama. He practiced medicine under Dr. Henry C. Bibb of Mooresville in Limestone County.

Samuel Bond married Alice Mary Tate who was born on May 8, 1811. In 1831, Samuel moved to Shelby County, Tennessee, where he established the Cedar Hall Plantation.

Samuel Bond Home
Cedar Hall

In 1854, Samuel Bond purchased the Longwood Plantation in Carroll Parish, Louisiana. He kept the Louisiana plantation for about seven years.

On May 24, 1855, Alice Mary Tate Bond, the wife of Samuel Bond died. She was buried in the Bartlett-Ellendale Cemetery in Shelby County, Tennessee.

In 1861 after the start of the Civil War, Dr. Samuel Bond sold the Longwood Plantation. The estate consisted of 1,534 acres of land, 107 black slaves, corn fodder, 40 mules, and cattle that were valued at $48,000 to Joseph R. Parks.

On August 8, 1862, Samuel Bond died near Memphis, Tennessee. He was buried in the Bartlett-Ellendale Cemetery in Shelby County, Tennessee.

John Bond

On October 9, 1808, John Bond was born in Knox County, Tennessee. John was the son of Nicholas Pirtle Bond and Margaret Ann (Peggy) Fryar Bond.

On February 16, 1832, John married Susan Elizabeth Massey in Limestone County, Alabama. She was born on February 16, 1816.

The father of Susan Elizabeth Massey was Edward Massey of Spotsylvania County, Virginia. Edward was the son of Reuben Massey, a Revolutionary War Patriot. According to the 1830 Limestone County, Alabama Census, Edward Massey owned 15 black slaves, and he died in Limestone County, Alabama, in 1830.

John Bond and Susan Elizabeth Massey Bond had the following children:
1. Nicholas Pirtle Bond (12/9/1833-12/29/1896) married Ellen Preddy,
2. John Nicholas Bond married Maggie Shipp,
3. Susan Margaret Bond married Charles P. Winkler,
4. William Edward Bond died at age 11,
5. Robert Donnell Bond married Fanny Board,
6. Newton Henry Bond married Mary McCoy,
7. Sarah Anne Bond married ? Graven,
8. Malinda Zula Bond; never married,
9. Fannie Parmelia Bond (1855-1883) married Joe B. Mayo,
10. Elizabeth Love Bond married S.F. McKenry,
11. Mary Lucy Bond.

On December 31, 1865, Susan Elizabeth Massey Bond died in Shelby County, Tennessee. She was buried in the Bartlett-Ellendale Cemetery.

On August 4, 1871, John Bond died, and he was buried in the Bartlett-Ellendale Cemetery in Shelby County, Tennessee.

Bradley, Joseph H.

According to census records, Joseph H. Bradley was born in 1812 in North Carolina. During the census, Susanna Bradley, who was born in 1794, was living in his household. If Susanna Bradley was his mother, she would have been 18 years old when she had Joseph H. Bradley.

On September 5, 1810, Joseph Bradley was one of the original Sims Settlers who signed the petition to President James Madison. Joseph H. Bradley was probably related to the Joseph Bradley who lived in the area from 1806 to 1810.

On July 24, 1812, and October 3, 1812, Joseph Bradley entered two 160.1-acre tracts in Section 2 of Township 1 South and Range 3 West in the northeast corner of old Madison County in Mississippi Territory. The land he settled would later become a portion of northeast Limestone County, Alabama.

In the 1830 Limestone County, Alabama Census, Joseph H. Bradley is listed on page 12 of the census. On April 10, 1838, a J. Bradley entered 40 acres in Section 4 of Township 1 South and Range 4 West which is in the same area Joseph Bradley entered his land in 1812.

On October 26, 1843, Joseph H. Bradley married Elzira Crabb in Limestone County, Alabama; she was born about 1818 in Tennessee. Elzira was born to Stephen Crabb (1778-1858), and Mary Smith Crabb (1788-1866). Mary Smith Crabb was the daughter of William Smith (1760-1836); William Smith was one of the original Sims Settlers who signed the petition on September 5, 1810 (Find A Grave Memorial# 109062229).

According to land records, both the Bradley and Crabb families lived in the northern part of Limestone County not far from the Tennessee state line.

Several of the Crabb family are buried in Giles County, Tennessee, just a short distance from where they lived in Limestone County.

On February 22, 1844, Joseph H. Bradley and Elzira Crabb Bradley had their only child, Angeline Permelia (Palmyra) Bradley. Angeline was born in Limestone County, Alabama.

The 1850 Limestone County, Alabama United States Census, House Number 396 listed the following: Joseph H. Bradley, Male, 38, White, North Carolina; Susanna Bradley, Female, 56, North Carolina; and Rebecca Haldem, Female, 77, Virginia.

According to the 1850 Limestone County, Alabama, Slave Schedules, Joseph H. Bradley owned 115 black slaves. Angeline probably inherited some of the slaves of her father.

According to the 1850 Limestone County, Alabama, Agricultural Census, Joseph H. Bradley owned 900 acres of improved land and 1,100 acres of unimproved land worth $15,000. He also had $1,620 worth of farming equipment and livestock valued at 3,100.

Elzira Crabb Bradley, who died at Lester in Limestone County, Alabama, was not mentioned in the 1850 census with her husband Joseph H. Bradley; therefore, she was probably deceased. At the time, it also appears that Angeline, daughter of Joseph H. Bradley, was not living in his household; she would have been six years old. Angeline was probably living with her Crabb grandparents.

Angeline Permelia Bradley Powers Kennedy

On February 22, 1844, Angeline Permelia "Palmyra" Bradley was born, in Limestone County, Alabama. She was the daughter of Joseph H. Bradley and Elzira Crabb Bradley.

In 1850, Angeline was living with her grandparents, Stephen and Mary Smith Crabb in Limestone County. Her mother Elzira Crabb Bradley died before 1850 when Angeline was very young, perhaps during childbirth. By 1860, her father had died, and Angeline was left an orphan.

In the 1860, Limestone County, Alabama, Slave Schedules, Angeline Permelia (Palmyra) Bradley is listed as owning 33 black slaves. Angeline was a slave owner at 16 years of age, and being an only child, she probably inherited the estate of her father.

In 1865, Angeline married Richard Louis H. "Dick" Powers, who was the son of Ransom H. Powers and Martha A. York. The Powers family had arrived in Giles County, Tennessee, from Johnston County, North Carolina, about 1817. Ransom's father, Roadham Powers, served in the Virginia militia during the War of 1812. Ransom's mother, Lucy Snipes Powers, was the daughter of John Snipes. Lucy died in Giles County, Tennessee, at the age of 107.

Angeline Permelia "Palmyra" Bradley Powers and Richard Louis H. "Dick" Powers had the following children:
1. Samuel Powers, died young
2. Lewis Powers, died young
3. John Powers
4. Henderson Powers
5. Joseph Powers was born on April 8, 1870, in Limestone County. He died on July 28, 1943, at Lavaca in Sebastian County, Arkansas.
6. Lee Powers, died young
7. Mandy Elizabeth Frances Alnita Alice Diana Powers (1874-1931).

About 1878, after living in Limestone County, Alabama, for about a decade or longer after their marriage, Angeline and Richard moved to Lauderdale County, Alabama.

Between 1880 and 1889, Richard Powers died. He was probably buried in the old Butler Cemetery at Lock I in Lauderdale County.

In 1890, Angeline married Simpson A. Kennedy (1841-1902). In 1891, Angeline and Simpson had one son, Johnnie Lee. Simpson Kennedy was considered a country doctor, and he would tend to and sit with sick folks.

In 1892, Tom Kennedy, Simpson's son, married Angeline's daughter, Danie. Dani and her husband Tom Kennedy remained in Alabama when her mother moved to Arkansas.

In 1895, Angeline left Alabama because she was scared Simpson was going to bring a disease home. Angeline took Johnnie Lee with her to Sebastian County, Arkansas, where her sons were living along with other Powers relatives.

On May 22, 1900, Angeline Permelia Bradley Powers Kennedy died in Arkansas. She is buried Lavaca City Cemetery at Lavaca in Sebastian County, Arkansas (Find A Grave Memorial# 10171290).

In 1902 while tending a patient who had contracted smallpox, Simpson, who still lived in Alabama, died from the disease; however, his patient lived.

Brown, William

On February 3, 1813, William L. Brown entered 158.75 acres in section 2 of Township 2 South and Range 1 West in Madison County of Mississippi Territory. The land record stated that William Brown was from Lincoln County, Tennessee. On October 23, 1815, Samuel Brown entered 161.15 acres adjacent to William Brown. William entered two additional tracts in Madison County on January 25, 1815, and on September 25, 1818 (Cowart, 1979).

On February 11, 1818, William Brown entered 513.84 acres in Sections 1 and 3 of Township 1 South and Range 5 West in Limestone County, Alabama. On September 6, 1839, he also entered 214 acres in Section 2 and 3 of Township 1 South and Range 5 West in Limestone County, Alabama (Cowart, 1984).

On December 10, 1850, William L. Brown entered 157 acres in Section 33 of Township 2 South and Range 4 West in Limestone County, Alabama (Cowart, 1984).

In 1860, William L. Brown owned 147 black slaves. He was a successful cotton planter until the Civil War ravaged his estate. After the death of William

L. Brown, his possessions and considerable property in agricultural products was destroyed, run off, or consumed during the war. Both Union and Confederate forces occupied the land of William Brown. The Confederate Army conscripted some of his slaves to be teamsters. In addition, court records claim the Federal forces accompanied by his former slaves, who followed the Union Army, occupied the lands of William Brown for a period of time.

In 1862, Mary Brown, the widow of William L. Brown, was appointed administrator of his estate. Around 1864 or 1865, William H. Walker replaced Mary Brown as administrator. Walker asked permission of the court to sell the real estate of William L. Brown.

In January 1866, according to Limestone County, Alabama, Chancery Court records, Thomas J. Brown, an heir to the estate, purchased the interest in the estate of William L. Brown and Mary Brown. As owner of the land, Thomas sought an injunction to prevent William H. Walker, administrator of the estate of William Brown, from selling the real property to settle the debts.

On December 8, 1866, Thomas Brown filed petition number 20186609 in the Chancery Court of Limestone County. Thomas asserted that shortly after the death of William L. Brown, there was approximately $60,000 of personal property that would settle all the outstanding debts, excluding the 147 slaves.

Judge William Harrison Walker House

According to Limestone County, Alabama, court records accession number 20186434, there was not enough personal property to satisfy the debts of the estate. Therefore, William H. Walker asked the permission of the Chancery Court of Limestone County to sell real property belonging to the estate William L. Brown.

William H. Walker was born on March 2, 1822, at Mooresville; he was the son of John F. and Eliza Walker. He was a lawyer and probate judge for many years in Athens of Limestone County, Alabama. He married Sally E. Ryan, and they had the following children: Mary Eloise Walker Richardson, William Ryan Walker, Ada Walker, John Fortman Walker, Maria Walker Richardson, and Robert Henry Walker. William H. Walker died on March 4, 1876.

Cain, Allison Chappell

On September 16, 1800, Allison Chappell Cain was born in Sussex County, Virginia. His parents were Thomas Joseph Cain (1768-1803) and Mary Malone Cain (10/18/1777-1/2/1835); Thomas Cain and Mary Malone were married on October 17, 1799, in Sussex, Virginia.

In February 1818, it appears that Mary Malone Cain's family and her brothers, William E. Malone and Thomas Chappell Malone, came to Limestone County, Alabama. By 1818, they were entering land and cotton farming in Limestone County with their black slaves.

On February 9, 1818, Thomas Chappell Malone first entered land in Limestone County, Alabama. According to the Limestone County census, Thomas C. Malone owned 27 black slaves in 1830 and 21 black slaves in 1840. According to the 1820 Limestone County census, his brother William E. Malone owned 20 slaves, and by 1840, William owned 44 slaves.

On February 9, 1818, Mary Malone Cain entered 160 acres in Section 27 of Township 3 South and Range 4 West in Limestone County, Alabama. Mary Malone Cain's land was adjacent to three tracts of property entered by her son, Allison Chappell Cain, and four adjacent tracts of property were entered by her brother Thomas Chappell Malone.

In 1827, Allison Chappell Cain first married Mary Green Malone in Limestone County, Alabama. Mary Green Malone was born on June 6, 1808. Mary's parents were George Malone (1781-1847) and Martha "Patsy" Chambliss

(1796-1814); George and Martha were married on December 3, 1807, in Sussex, Virginia.

In 1830, George Malone, father of Mary Green Malone Cain, owned 28 black slaves, and in 1840, he owned 42 black slaves according to Limestone County census records. Two brothers of George also owned slaves in Limestone County: Booth Malone owned 48 black slaves in 1830; Thomas Hill Malone owned 50 slaves in 1820, 35 slaves in 1830, and 30 slaves in 1840.

Allison Chappell Cain and Mary Green Malone Cain had the following children:
1. Thomas Jefferson Cain was born on February 22, 1830; he died in 1896.
2. Martha Elizabeth Cain was born on August 24, 1831; she died in 1885.
3. George William Cain was born on May 28, 1833; he died in 1892.
4. Louisa (Loueza) Summerfield Cain was born on September 13, 1835; she died in1883.
5. James Henry Cain was born on April 12, 1838.
6. Mary Eugenia Cain was born on May 13, 1840.
7. Lucretia Tucker Cain was born on March 19, 1842.

On April 20, 1830, Allison Chappell Cain entered two 79-acre tracts, and on December 18, 1830, he entered an additional 79.75 acres all in Section 26 of Township 3 South and Range 4 West. Thomas Chappell Malone owned the other half of each ¼ section which was adjacent to his nephew Allison C. Cain. On January 12, 1848, Allison entered another 40 acres in Section23 of Township 3 South and Range 4 West.

On April 24, 1847, Mary Green Malone Cain, first wife of Allison Chappell Cain, died in Limestone County. On October 19, 1848, after the death of Mary, Allison C. Cain married Martha Ann Parham according to the marriage records in Limestone County, Alabama.

After Allison Chappell Cain and Martha E. Parham married, they had the following children:
1. John Parham Cain was born on November 18, 1849.

2. Martha Elizabeth Cain was born on August 24, 1851.
3. Theophelus C. Cain was born on January 15, 1852.

The 1850 Limestone County, Alabama, United States Census, House Number 460 gave the following: Allison C. Cain, Male, 30 (50), White, Virginia; Martha A. Cain, Female, 30, Virginia; Thomas J. Cain, Male, 29, Alabama; Martha E. Cain, Female, 19, Alabama; George M. Cain, Male, 17, Alabama; Louisa L. Cain, Female, 15, Alabama; James H. Cain, Male, 12, Alabama; Lucretia J. Cain, Female, 8, Alabama; and John P. Cain, Male, 0, Alabama.

According to the 1850 Limestone County, Alabama, Slave Schedule, Allison C. Cain owned 51 black slaves. According to the 1850 Limestone County, Alabama, Agricultural Census, Allison C. Cain owned 500 acres of improved land and 1,000 acres of unimproved land worth $6,000. He also owned $410 worth of farming equipment and livestock valued at $905.

The 1860 Limestone County, Alabama, United States Census, Household 492 listed the following: Allison C. Cain, Male, 39 (59), White, Virginia; Martha A. E. Cain, Female, 40, Virginia; and Theophilus Cain, Male, 9, Alabama.

According to the 1860 Limestone County, Alabama, Largest Slave Owners, Allison C. Cain is not listed. But in 1860, his son James H. Cain had 53 black slaves, and Thomas Jefferson Cain was listed with 13 slaves.

On May 22, 1862, during the Civil War, Allison Chappell Cain died in Limestone County, Alabama. Allison Chappell Cain was listed in United States Civil War Confederate Papers of Citizens or Businesses 1861-1865.

The 1880 Limestone County, Alabama, Beat 1, United States Census listed the following: Martha A. Cain, Female, 60, Widowed, White, Farmer, Virginia, Father's Birthplace Virginia, Mother's Birthplace Virginia; Theophilas Cain, Son, Male, 29, Alabama.

Carroll/Carrell, Grief

Grief Carroll was the son of Molly Douglass, daughter of David Douglass. His paternal grandfather was probably Daniel Carroll of North Carolina, who served at one point as a local Constable. Daniel also had a brother, William Carroll.

Douglass Carroll (1760-1827), a brother of Grief, was born in North Carolina and served in the American Revolution. After the Revolutionary War, he moved to Hancock County, Georgia. Douglass married Elizabeth Vinson, daughter of David Vinson, and they had four sons: Richmond, David, Harwell and Alfred Allison "Allen" Carroll.

By 1809, the Carroll family had migrated to Mississippi Territory. They came from North Carolina to South Carolina after the Revolution, then to Hancock County, Georgia, then to Madison County.

On September 18, 1809, William Carroll, brother of Grief, entered 160 acres in Section 7 of Township 2 South and Range 2 West in the original Madison County of Mississippi Territory. On March 21, 1812, William Carroll entered 80 acres in Section 12 of Township 2 South and Range 3 West the original Madison County of Mississippi Territory that became Limestone County, Alabama.

On May 10, 1813, Grief Carrell entered 156.86 acres in Section 15 of Township 2 South and Range 1 West in Madison County of Mississippi Territory that became the State of Alabama. On August 8, 1813, he entered another 156.86 acres in Section 15 of Township 2 South and Range 1 West in Madison County. On October 15, 1815, Grief entered 161.79 acres in Section 22 of Township 2 South and Range 1 West in Madison County.

Grief Carroll married Martha (last name unknown), and they had the following children:
1. Jacob Carroll
2. James Georgia Carroll who married Rachel Edwards in Madison County, Alabama in 1820.

3. Richmond Carroll, M.D. married Mildred McGee, and he died before January 29, 1834.
4. William W. Carroll married Sarah. On September 1, 1848, William W. Carroll entered 40.22 acres in Section 28 of Township 6 South and Range 9 West in Harrison County, Mississippi. The 1850 census of Harrison County, Mississippi, lists the following: William W. Carroll, 56, Male, Blacksmith, North Carolina; Sarah Carroll, 54, Female, Georgia; Samuel Carroll, 25, Male Wood Cutter, Alabama; Elizabeth Carroll, 20, Female, Tennessee; Grief Carroll, 19, Male, Blacksmith, Tennessee, Catharine, 15, Female, Alabama. William W. Carroll was living in Tennessee when his sons Grief and Samuel were born. They later moved to Mississippi and then to Louisiana.
5. Joseph S. Carroll.
6. Catherine Carroll.
7. Elizabeth "Betsy" Carroll married William Williams in Madison County, Alabama, in December 1821.

The 1820 Limestone County, Alabama Census listed the following for the household of Grief Carrell: White Males over 21: 1, White Males under 21: 1, White Females over 21: 1, White Females under 21: 2, Total Whites: 5, Total Slaves: 16, Total Cultivated Acres: 30, Number of Hands: 5, Total Bales: 12, Average Weight of Bales: 350 pounds.

In the 1830 Madison County, Alabama Census, the sons of Grief Carrell were enumerated and included Jacob, James, Richmond, and William. At this time, Grief was living either in Limestone or Lauderdale counties.

On October 31, 1832, Grief Carrell entered 40 acres in Section 34 of Township 2 South and Range 8 West in Lauderdale County, Alabama (Cowart, 1996). The area Grief settled was near Second Creek and just north of the Tennessee River.

On January 29, 1834, the following was found in the Limestone County, Alabama, Deed Book 4, page 484, "Grief Carriel of Lauderdale County, Alabama, deed of gift to granddaughter, Elizabeth H. Carriel, daughter of my late son, Richmond Carriel, Slave."

On August 20, 1834, the Will of Grief Carriel was given and recorded in the Lauderdale County, Alabama, Will Book A, 11. On March 5, 1836, the following Will of Grief Carrell was recorded at the courthouse in Lauderdale County, Alabama.

"Will of Grief Carroll, State of Alabama, Lauderdale County, I Grief Carroll of the County aforementioned being of sound mind and memory do ordain and constitute this my last Will and Testament by these presence revolking all former Wills by me make to date.
1. Item 1 My body to be decently interred without incurring any unnecessary expense, I bequeath to mother earth and my spirit to God who gave it.
2. Item 2 Should my beloved wife, Martha Carroll, survive me, unto her I give and bequeath six Negroes, Frerdrick, for a life of age about 48 years, Edinborough male slave for life of the age of about 24 years, Jenny female slave for life about the age of 55 years, Lerides (?) female slave for life about the age of 42 years, Charity Mulatto girl slave for life of the age of about 17 years, and Betty female slave for life of the age of about 14 years, and further to my beloved wife, I further give and bequeath the following personal property--one horse to be worth $75, tow beds and furniture, one yoke of oxen and one cart, one half of all the household and kitchen furniture except the beds, one year's provisions for her and family, two cows and calves, and further unto the land and promises of herein, i now give and bequeath with all the apportions to my beloved wife, and should she not be disposed to continue to live through my ancestors herein after named are requested and authorized to give the said promises at auction or other ways as they may think proper, and the proceeds arriving from such sales of goods placed in the hands of my son James G. Carroll with which to purchase another place of land for my said wife wherever she may want to move. All the above described property is given and bequeathed to my dearly beloved wife during her natural life, but it is my express wish and bequest that should my wife survive me that due to the property to her above willed and bequeathed share immediately upon my death bed in the hands of and possession of my son, James G. Carroll, who I do hereby ordain and consititue the Trustee of my beloved wife, who is

hereby empowered to use the said property in any manner he may think proper for the use and benefit of my said wife, and of the porceeds arising from the work and labor of land, six Negroes with the personal property of aforesaid and tallies of said land after first and annually providing my dearly beloved wife with everything she may desire or may be necessary for her ease and comfort. The balance, he, my said son, James, is authorized to apply to his own undertakings and use.

3. Item 3 Should my wife survive me of the six Negroes to her above bequest with the land and promises and personal property at her death, I wish disposed of in the following manner: Fredrick and Leudes (?) slaves of aforesaid with the beds aforesaid and personal property of aforesaid, I wish my Executor hereinafter named to sell at public auction on such time as they may think proper and the proceeds of such sale, I wish my Executors to divide equally between James G. Carroll, William W. Carroll, and the heirs of Katherine Matthews, and Joseph S. Carroll should said Joseph apply for his dividend in two years of my wife's death, but said Joseph not apply for said two years, I wish his dividend to be equally divided between James G. Carroll, William W. Carroll, and the heirs of Katherine Matthews.
4. Item 4 After death of my wife, the aforementioned and said premises whereon she may reside, I give and bequeath to John C. Matthews.
5. Item 5 At the death of my wife, to my son James G. Carroll, I give and bequeath four Negroes named Edinborough, Jenny, Charity, and Betty.
6. Item 6 At the death of my wife, I give and bequeath to William W. Carroll one Negro boy named Caleb.
7. Item 7 At the death of my wife unto John C. Matthews, I give and bequeath one Negro boy called Gebtatha.
8. Item 8 At my death, all the property herein I may possess of, I wish disposed of at public auction and out of the proceeds of such sale, I wish all my honorable debts paid off and discharged, and the balance remaining from such sale (disregarding $100 for Katherine Douglass) I give and bequeath to Joseph S. Carroll should he apply for the dividends in two years from and after my death, but should said Joseph not make such application, in two years, I wish said balance equally divided between James G. Carroll, William W. Carroll, and the heirs of Katherine Matthews.

9. Item 9 At the death of my wife, James G. Carroll will be indebted to the heirs of Katherine Matthews for him and the heirs, I wish my executors to take his notes for the same without interest to be said in five equal payments of $100 cash such notes with good and sufficient security are to be plced in the hands of the guardian of such heirs.
10. Item 10 At my death and out of the provision of the sale of my property not disposed of by the Will, I give and bequeath to Katherine Douglass $100.
11. Item 11 Provided Charles B. Matthews permits John C. Matthews to remain with his grandmother and Katherine Douglass.
12. Item 12 I do hereby appoint my son James G. Carroll and my trusty friend William Gambal my executors to this my last Will and Testament and also request that William Gambal to act as guardian to the heirs of Katherine Matthews.

In testimony whereof I have hereunto subscribed my hand and seal this 20th day of August, 1824.

Signed: Grief "X" Carroll

Witnesses: D. McNeal, James Cunningham, J. P. Cunningham, Robert Shane.

Before August 26, 1834, Grief Carrell died in Lauderdale County, Alabama. He lived between Rogersville and Elgin near Second Creek in Lauderdale County.

Cheatham, Christopher - Alba Wood

In the early 1800s, there were definitely two and maybe three Christopher Cheathams in North Alabama. The oldest Christopher was probably the son of Archer Cheatham and Mary Bass from Amelia County, Virginia. In1799, Archer died in Robertson County, Tennessee. Christopher probably had a son and grandson named Christopher.

Christopher Cheatham I

Around 1809, Christopher Cheatham I was among the earliest hotel keepers in Huntsville. He operated the Twickenham Hotel at Huntsville in Mississippi Territory, and he was part owner of that city's historic Bell Tavern. When he erected his hotel, Christopher needed a street on the south side of the hotel square; therefore, when his friend Colonel Leroy Pope sold the lots around the Big Spring, he provided for a street fifty feet wide that was called Pendleton Row.

Sometime in the 1810s, tradition holds that Christopher Cheatham of Scottish ancestry built the first structure at the location of present-day Florence as an inn and stagecoach stop. He constructed the facility at the request of political leaders Leroy Pope, founder of Huntsville, and Thomas Bibb, who would become Alabama's second governor. In 1811 according to legend, Christopher built and operated Pope's Tavern in Florence for Leroy Pope which was seven years before the founding of Florence in 1818.

In order to establish the stagecoach, stop and tavern in Indian Territory, Christopher Cheatham must have made arrangements with the local Cherokees and Chickasaws who owned and controlled the area. Many of the Cherokees had left the area according to passports issued in January and February 1810. Irishman John Melton, who was married to Doublehead's sister, was still living in the area, and he appeared to be on friendly terms with the white settlers leasing Doublehead's Reserve.

According to the History of Lauderdale County, Alabama: "Cheatham's Ferry was established by Christopher Cheatham at Smithsonia. He was in the county as early as 1811, but at what time he began his ferry is not known. The ferry was located 13 miles west of Florence.

Columbus Smith later operated this ferry. He had come to the county as a boy and began to work here as a young ferryman. This site was being called Smith's Ferry as early as 1832. During the Civil War, Smith at his ferry site was an eyewitness to all the marching and counter marching of the Confederate and Federal troops, as both forces used his ferry to cross the river." Smithsonia was named for Columbus Smith, who operated a steamboat landing and a gin at the ferry site.

On January 10, 1816, it appears that the oldest Christopher Cheatham I died in Lauderdale County, Alabama (Find A Grave Memorial# 94198543). The old Christopher is buried in the Rowell Cemetery at Smithsonia. If the death date is correct date, Christopher Cheatham I had a son Christopher Cheatham II that was probably the father of Martha Ann Cheatham Rowell who was born on February 25, 1811, in Hertford County, North Carolina.

Christopher Cheatham II

If Christopher Cheatham I died on January 10, 1816, Christopher Cheatham II was entering land in Limestone and Lawrence Counties during 1818. Christopher Cheatham II and his family were listed in the 1820 census of Limestone County, Alabama. In 1823, Christopher Cheatham II was documented as entering land in Colbert's Reserve in the Bend of the River in West Lauderdale County, Alabama, where Christopher Cheatham I was buried in 1816.

On February 10, 1818, Christopher Cheatham entered 79.62 acres in Section 2 of Township 4 South and Range 4 West in Limestone County, Alabama. On February 11, 1818, he entered 160.16 acres in Section 2 of Township 3 South and Range 4 West in Limestone County, Alabama (Cowart, 1984). On September 8, 1818, Christopher Cheatham entered 160 acres in Section 3 of Township 5 South and Range 6 West in Lawrence County, Alabama (Cowart, 1991).

The 1820 Limestone County, Alabama Census listed the following for the household of Christopher Cheatham: White Males over 21: 1, White Females over 21: 1, White Females under 21: 2, Total Whites: 4, Free Persons of Color: 20, Slaves: 28, Acres Cultivated: 40, Number of Bales of Cotton: 13, Average Weight of Bales: 350 pounds. It is believed that the 20 persons of color were black, since in 1830, he is listed as owning 49 black slaves.

In 1823, Christopher Cheatham II moved to Lauderdale County, Alabama, and entered land near the ferry that crossed the Tennessee River at Smithsonia.

Cheatham's Ferry was supposedly established in George Colbert's Reserve by Christopher Cheatham I sometime around 1811.

On May 27, 1823, Christopher Cheatham II and others entered 124.7 acres in Section 25 of Township 3 South and Range 13 West in Lauderdale County, Alabama (Cowart, 1996). Christopher eventually owned a 1,000-acre plantation in the Big Bend area that he called Alba Wood. He lived in a simple log house which he constructed on his Alba Wood Plantation.

Since Christopher Cheatham was a descendant of natives of Scotland, he called his place "Alba Wood," an ancient Celtic name meaning "Wood of Scotland." The Alba Wood Plantation was one of the largest antebellum cotton farms located in Colbert's Reserve in West Lauderdale County, Alabama.

According to the 1830 Lauderdale County, Alabama Census, Christopher Cheatham owned 49 black slaves. From his time in Limestone County, he had added 12 additional slaves within the ten-year period.

In 1839, Christopher Cheatham II, who owned Alba Wood Plantation and 49 slaves in 1830, died at his cotton farm in West Lauderdale County, Alabama. It should also be noted that in the 1830 Census, Will Cheatham was the only Cheatham listed in Limestone County, Alabama.

Also, according to the 1840 Lauderdale County, Alabama Census, Kit Cheatham owned 45 black slaves. Will Cheatham and Kit Cheatham are not in the land records of Limestone or Lauderdale Counties, and a direct relationship to Christopher Cheatham was not established for either Will or Kit.

Christopher Cheatham lies buried in the abandoned Rowell Cemetery on the former grounds of his Alba Wood Plantation near Smithsonia. The cemetery is on County Road 6 (Gunwaleford Road) in Lauderdale County, Alabama. The graveyard is on the north side of the road about 100 yards east of Smithsonia Church of Christ. The cemetery is about 75 yards from the main road and is surrounded by hand cut stone wall four feet in height.

Christopher Cheatham III

On October 4, 1843, Lauderdale County, Alabama, Grand Jury approved an indictment of Christopher Cheatham for carrying concealed weapon. The relationship of the three people identified as Christopher Cheatham in Lauderdale County, Alabama, was not established.

Martha Ann Cheatham Rowell

On February 25, 1811, Martha Ann Cheatham Rowell was born to Christopher Cheatham in Hertford County, North Carolina. Sometimes in 1811, it appears that Martha came with her father Christopher Cheatham as a small child to North Alabama.

In 1832, Dr. Neal Rowell married Martha Ann Cheatham, and she was the daughter of Christopher Cheatham, one of the earliest white settlers of Lauderdale County, Alabama. Neal Rowell was born in 1796 in what is now Wood County, West Virginia. He was a prominent physician in Lauderdale County, and practiced medicine in early Florence for a few years. Neal and Martha had the following children:
 1. Elizabeth Clifton Rowell b. 1833,
 2. Captain Christopher C. Rowell b.1836,
 3. Ann Rowell b. 1838,
 4. Virginia Rowell b. 1846

In 1839 after the death of her father, Martha Ann Cheatham Rowell inherited the original 1,000 acres of Alba Wood Plantation and some of the black slaves of Christopher Cheatham. After his wife inherited Alba Wood Plantation in West Lauderdale County, Dr. Neal Rowell retired from medicine and moved to the farm.

In the 1840 Lauderdale County, Alabama, United States Census, Neal Rowell owned 27 black slaves. Prior to 1840, known records of Rowell owning slaves did not exist until his wife inherited some of the slaves of her father Christopher; in 1830, her father owned 49 slaves.

In the early 1840s, Dr. Neal Rowell built his wife a plantation home at Alba Wood. His wife, Martha Ann Cheatham Rowell, had inherited the original 1,000 acres of Alba Wood Plantation from her father, Christopher Cheatham, following his death in 1839.

The old manor house at Alba Wood was on a knoll overlooking its surrounding cotton and corn lands. Its solid brick walls were laid in English bond design with a cross foundation of yellow poplar logs. The most unique architectural features of the home were its crow-step gables with double chimneys at both ends that were an intrinsic part of the wall design.

In the 1850, Lauderdale County, Alabama, Slave Schedule, Neal Rowell owned 72 black slaves. According to the 1850 Lauderdale County, Alabama, Agricultural Census, Neal Rowell owned 750 acres of improved land and 1,890 acres of unimproved land worth $35,000.00.

In the 1860 Lauderdale County, Alabama, Slave Schedule, Neal Rowell owned 89 black slaves. The 1860 census shows the cash value of Alba Wood in excess of $100,000.00 to make its owner one of the four wealthiest planters in the county. There were 90 black slaves living in a community of 21 small cabins on the plantation. In 1860, Alba Wood produced 269 bales of cotton, 6,000 bushels of corn, 500 bushels of wheat, 150 pounds of wool, and 400 pounds of butter.

In December 1886, Neal Rowell died after devoting himself to his farming interests for many years. Mrs. Martha Cheatham Rowell, an invalid for forty years, lived to see her husband pass away, at the age of ninety.

On July 13, 1890, Mrs. Martha Cheatham Rowell died at Alba Wood, near Florence. She was buried in Florence Cemetery at Florence, Lauderdale County, Alabama (Find A Grave Memorial# 54970233).

Clark, William Robert

In 1792, William Robert Clark was born in Mecklenburg County, Virginia. William married Sarah Blackbourn (1797-1860); in 1797, she was born in Mecklenburg County, Virginia. Sarah was the daughter of Clement Blackbourn (1760-1843) and Mary Ann Lewis (1768-1842). In the 1830 Madison County, Alabama Census, Clement Blackbourn owned 30 black slaves.

William Robert Clark and Sarah Blackbourn Clark had the following children:
1. Antoinette "Nettie" Blackbourn Clark Davis was born on February 4, 1822, in Limestone County, Alabama. In 1846 in Limestone County, Nettie married Robert Ruffin Davis (1819-1885), and they moved to Shelby County, Tennessee, to the home of Robert's father, Tinsley Davis. On February 2, 1914, Nettie died at the age of 91 at Plum Point in DeSoto County, Mississippi, and she was buried in the Davis-McCargo-Bowe Cemetery in Shelby County, Tennessee (Find A Grave Memorial# 151017061).
2. Mary Lewis Clark McCargo was born on August 10, 1825, in Limestone County, Alabama. She married Robert F. McCargo who was a cotton planter in Limestone County. Robert owned 26 slaves in 1840 and 37 slaves in 1850. Mary died on November 30, 1893, in Desoto County, Mississippi, and she is buried in the Davis-McCargo-Bowe Cemetery in Shelby County, Tennessee (Find A Grave Memorial# 151135490).
3. Mary Ann Clark Davis was born on June 20, 1833, in Limestone County, Alabama. In 1856, she married Watson Dabney Davis (1833-1902), son of Tinsley Davis and Virginia Emily Key. On September 26, 1878, at the age of 45, Mary along with two of her sons died of yellow fever. She died at Horn Lake in DeSoto County, Mississippi, and she is buried in the Davis-McCargo-Bowe Cemetery in Shelby County, Tennessee (Find A Grave Memorial# 151133837). The Davis-McCargo-Bowe Cemetery was destroyed by farmers with tombstones piled up along a fence; therefore, none of the graves are identifiable.

On December 14, 1811, William Clark entered 162 acres in Section 19 of Township 2 South and Range 2 East in Madison County, Alabama. From April 15, 1830, through November 15, 1841, William Clark entered an additional 630 acres in Township 5 South and Range 2 West in Madison County, Alabama.

The 1820 Limestone County, Alabama Census listed the following for William Clark: White Males over 21: 1, White Males under 21: 1, White Females over 21: 1, White Females under 21: 2, Total Whites: 5, Free Persons of Color: 15, Slaves: 35, Acres Cultivated Land: 10, Either Hands or Bales: 11, Approximate Weight per Bale: 350 Pounds.

In 1820, the census indicates that William Clark has 15 people of color and 35 black slaves. If the people of color are black, the household of Clark has a total of 50 black folks listed in his household.

In the 1830 Limestone County, Alabama Census, William Clark had some 23 slaves. In the 1830 Madison County, Alabama Census, William Clark had 39 slaves; therefore, he owned a total of 62 slaves in 1830.

In the 1840 Limestone County, Alabama Census, William was listed with 11 slaves. In 1850, William Clark owned 10 slaves.

In the 1850 Limestone County, Alabama, Agricultural Census, William Clark owned 75 acres of improved land and 145 acres of unimproved land valued at $1,000. He also had $60 worth of farming equipment and $355 worth of livestock.

The 1850 Limestone County, Alabama, United States Census, House Number 90 gave the following: William Clark, Male, 58, White, Virginia; Sarah Clark, Female, 56, Virginia; Maria Clark, Female, 16, Alabama; and, Mary J. Lewis, Female, 22, Alabama.

On February 3, 1852, William Clark entered 39.74 in Section 35 of Township 2 South and Range 3 West in Limestone County, Alabama. Before 1860, the William Clark family moved to an area south of Memphis, Tennessee.

In 1860, Sarah Blackbourn Clark died in DeSoto County, Mississippi, at the age of 62 or 63. She was buried in the Davis-McCargo-Bowe Cemetery at Memphis in Shelby County, Tennessee (Find A Grave Memorial# 151135061).

On December 9, 1876, William Robert Clark died at age 83 to 84 in DeSoto County, Mississippi. He was buried in the Davis-McCargo-Bowe Cemetery in Shelby County, Tennessee (Find A Grave Memorial# 151134986).

Clement and Mary Lewis Blackbourn

On October 21, 1784, Mary Ann Lewis married Clement Blackbourn in Mecklenburg County, Virginia. Mary Ann Lewis Blackbourn was the daughter of Revolutionary War soldier Edward Lewis and Mary Bressie.

Clement Blackbourn and Mary Ann Lewis Blackbourn were the in-laws of William Robert Clark. Clement and Mary Lewis Blackbourn had twelve children, but only three are listed below.
1. Sarah Blackbourn Clark (1797-1860) married William Robert Clark (1792-1876)
2. Maria A. Blackbourn Vaughan (1802-1862) married Edward Bressie Vaughan (1798-1868)
3. Frank Blackbourn

Clement and Mary died within months of each other at the home of their son-in-law William Robert Clark in Limestone County, Alabama. They were laid side by side in the orchard of their son Frank Blackbourn in District 3 of Madison County, Alabama.

In the 1830 Madison County, Alabama Census, Clement Blackbourn owned 39 black slaves. He had 15 male slaves and 15 female slaves.

In June 1842, Mary Ann Lewis Blackbourn, the mother-in-law of William Clark, died in Limestone County, Alabama. She was buried in the orchard of her son Frank Blackbourn in District 3 of Madison County, Alabama (Find A Grave Memorial# 168089095).

In 1843, Clement Blackbourn, who was born on February 11, 1760, in Lisbon, Portugal, died at the residence of son-in-law William Clark in Limestone County, Alabama.

On February 18, 1843, the obituary of Clement Blackbourn was given in the Huntsville Democrat: "Blackbourn, Clement-Died on Tuesday, 7th inst., about 12 o'clock, M., at the residence of Mr. William Clark, in Limestone, Mr. Clement Blackbourn, in his eighty-fifth year. Mr. B. was early in and continued thro' the entire war of the Revolution; his services were rendered chiefly in the Southern States. He removed from the County of Mecklenburg, Va., to Madison, Ala., in the year 1816, where he continued to reside, beloved and respected by these neighbours and acquaintances, until about two months ago. In June last, his old and beloved wife, with whom he had lived in the happiest state of matrimony for upwards of sixty years, was taken from him, by the ruthless hand of death; and left him, as he remarked to the writer of this notice, without one single motive or desire to remain here; and he only waited the call of his God, that he might be laid by her side in the orchard of his son Frank. Mr. Blackbourn was a man of fine sense-was well versed in history, ancient and modern; his kindness and benevolence knew no bounds, whilst upon these subjects he never let his right hand know what his left hand did. Mr. B. has left a large number of children, grandchildren, and great-grandchildren, to mourn his loss: whose tears were freely shed and mingled with those of his old neighbors-whilst the writer could but notice at the closing scene the deep distress and grief of his slaves, who were about him on that trying occasion. He is gone-he has paid the only debt he owed upon this earth and died, as he lived, an honest man, the noblest work of God."

Samuel D. White

Mary Clark, daughter of William Clark, married Samuel D. White. Samuel and Mary Clark White had the following children:
1. Cornelia White married Napoleon Beaty.
2. Jane White married a Ward.
3. William White
4. Maria White
5. Samuel White who lived in Limestone County.

In the 1830 Limestone County, Alabama Census, Samuel D. White, the son-in-law of William Clark, owned 22 black slaves. In 1840, he owned 61 slaves.

In the 1850 Limestone County, Alabama, Agricultural Census, Samuel D. White owned 800 acres of improved land and 1,140 acres of unimproved land valued at $40,000. He also had $950 worth of farming equipment and $4,269 worth of livestock. In 1850, Samuel D. White owned 118 slaves.

Coe, Jesse

On February 4, 1782, Jesse Coe was born on a plantation known as Coe's Addition at Bishopville in Worcester County, Maryland. His parents were Captain John Coe (1744-10/28/1807) and Sarah Hatton (1746-10/23/1822); his father served as captain of the Sinapuxent Battalion during the American Revolution. Jesse was two years old when his father moved the family to Guilford County, North Carolina, where he spent his childhood.

In April 1800, Jesse Coe entered the Virginia Conference of the Methodist Church, and four years later, he was ordained at the Methodist Conference at Salem, Virginia. In 1805, Jesse was stationed at Norfolk, Virginia; there he built the first Methodist church in the town.

On November 1, 1806, Jesse Coe first married Selah Drew Gilliam in Brunswick County, Virginia. Selah of Sussex County, Virginia, was the daughter of Charles and Elizabeth Gilliam. Jesse and Selah had the following children:
1. Elizabeth Figures Coe was born on May 30, 1809, in Sussex County, Virginia.
2. Sarah Selah Gilliam Coe was born on July 26, 1812, in Limestone County, Alabama. She married Dr. William F. Booth
3. Mary Drew Gilliam Coe Harris was born on January 20, 1821, in Limestone County, Alabama. She first married Charles Sanders Sibley (1810-1854); her father also deeded Charles Sanders Sibley the Rocky Comfort Plantation of 1,440 acres but returned to her on the death Sibley. On February 9, 1860, Mary married Isaac Ross Harris (1813-1887); at the time, she owned 125 slaves given to her by her father Jesse Coe. On March 28, 1885, she died at Quincy in Gadsden County, Florida, and she is buried in the Western Cemetery (Find A Grave Memorial# 113755368).

On June 17, 1807, Jesse Coe was paid the balance of $3,080.00 for 440 acres of land his wife had inherited from her father Charles Gilham. Jesse had sold the property of his wife that lay on the north side of Cumberland River in Davidson County, Tennessee, to John Camp of Greenville County, Virginia. John Camp was married to widowed mother-in-law of Jesse.

On July 1, 1813, Jesse Coe enlisted and served in the War of 1812 with Nicholas Massenburg's Company of Light Infantry Militia, 15th Regiment, and with Allen's Company, 1st Regiment of Virginia Militia. On September 13, 1813, at Norfolk, Virginia, Jesse Coe was discharged after providing William Buckston as his substitute.

On January 8, 1815, Major Jesse Coe served as staff officer under General Andrew Jackson at the Battle of New Orleans. In 1818 while serving with General Jackson, he saw much of southern Alabama and northern Florida.

On February 11, 1818, after his military service ended, Jesse Coe bought 640.95 acres from the State of Alabama in Limestone County, Alabama. From February 13, 1818, through December 18, 1818, Jesse Coe bought an additional 1,240 acres along the Tennessee River in Limestone County, Alabama.

On May 18, 1819, Joseph D. Smith was indebted to William Banks by bond assigned to Smith by John D. Erwin and Company for $5000 which was due in seven months after July 1, 1818. Joseph D. Smith was paid $1.00 by Jesse Coe to assume the debt for land totaling 960 acres. The witnesses were Richard Moore, Nicholas Davis, Joseph D. Smith, William Banks, and Jesse Coe. All together Jesse Coe was granted about 3,000 acres of land, all located on the banks of the Tennessee River in southern Limestone County.

The 1820 Limestone County, Alabama Census had the following for the household of Jesse Coe: White Males over 21: 1, White Females over 21: 2, White Females under 21: 2, Total Whites: 5, People of Color: 43, Total Slaves: 40, Cultivated Acres: 15, Number of Hands: 15, Number of Bales of Cotton: 300. If the 43 folks of color were black, Jesse Coe had 83 black people listed in his household in 1820.

On July 19, 1826, after the death of his first wife Selah Drew Gilliam Coe in the same year, Jesse Coe married the second time to Elizabeth Booth in Lawrence County, Alabama. Jesse and Elizabeth had the following children:
1. Jesse Coe Jr. was born on August 9, 1828, in Limestone County, Alabama. He died on August 18, 1859, at Quincy in Gadsden County, Florida.
2. William "Will" Booth Coe was born on September 18, 1830, in Limestone County, Alabama. He died in 1869 at Quincy in Gadsden County, Florida.

Elizabeth Booth Coe was born in 1806, and she was the daughter of William Fitzgerald and Mary Ann Fitzgerald Booth of Courtland, Alabama. Through marriage to Elizabeth Booth, Jesse became the brother-in-law to the following: Colonel Samuel Barron Stephens, a member of the Florida Territorial House of Representatives from 1841 through1842; Arthur J. Forman of the noted tobacco firm of Forman & Muse; Forman's partner Mr. Muse; Reverend Dr. David L. White; and Dr. John W. Malone.

Two uncles of Elizabeth Booth Coe, Reverend Freeman Fitzgerald and Littleberry Jones, moved from Lawrence County, Alabama, to Quincy in Gadsden County, Florida. Littleberry Jones was married to Elizabeth Fitzgerald that was a sister to Mary AnnBooth, the mother of Elizabeth Booth Coe.In 1861, Littleberry was buried in Eastern Cemetery at Quincy in Gadsden County, Florida (Find A Grave Memorial# 179743678). Sometime after 1830, Freeman Fitzgerald left Lawrence County, Alabama, with his family and 107 black slaves. At Quincy in Gadsden County, Florida, Reverend Freeman Fitzgerald was listed as a Methodist preacher owning 62 slaves and 3,360 acres on one plantation. On another plantation, Reverend Freeman Fitzgerald listed 60 slaves and 1,920 acres of land.

On February 11, 1830, Jesse Coe was granted a tract of 160 acres in Limestone County, Alabama. The 1830 Limestone County, Alabama Census had the following for Jesse Coe: 1 White Male 40-50; 1 White Male under 5; 1 White Female 20-30; 1 White Female 5-10; Slaves 114. In 1820, 43 folks of color and 40 slaves were in the household; however, only 114 slaves were listed in 1830.

Major Jesse Coe is mentioned in numerous court records of Limestone County, Alabama, in some of the following:

1. In 1822, Jesse Coe, Joshua L. Martin (twelfth governor of Alabama), and William Edmondson were commissioned to receive claims against the estate of John B. Chandler, deceased.
2. In 1822, Jesse Coe appears on record when letters of administration were issued to him, George Abel, John Young, and Edward Smith on the estate of John Abel.
3. On March 18, 1822, Jesse Coe, George Abel and Edward Smith were appointed appraisers of the estate of Henry Pike.
4. In 1827, Jesse, Silas Hine, Henry Yarborough, and John P. Malone were accepted as securities to $16,000 for Jane Malone, who applied for letters of administration on the estate of William Malone, her deceased husband. Jesse, Silas Hine and James P. Malone were appointed appraisers of Malone's estate.
5. On April 1, 1828, as ordained a Minister of the Methodist Episcopal Church, the Court of Limestone County authorized Jesse Coe to perform the rites of matrimony.
6. On October 18, 1830, Jesse Coe, Zacheus T. Wingfield, and Henry Smith were appointed by the county court to appraise the estate of Thomas Tinsley.
7. On August 9, 1831, Jesse Coe, Asa Allen, Gabriel Smith, Edward Wood, and Sampson Lane were appointed by the court to appraise and divide the estate Martha Hobbs. They filed the final dispersal report August 19, 1833.
8. On April 12, 1834, Jesse Coe was granted a tract of 159 acres in Limestone County
9. On August 11, 1834, in the will of David H. Mason, nephew of Governor Martin, dated, Mason mentioned undivided half of tract bought by my brother, John R. Mason from Major Jesse Coe.

In 1830, Jesse Coe purchased land in Gadsden County, Florida. In 1831, Jesse moved from Alabama to the land he purchased in Florida, an area he had campaigned in as one of Jackson's officers in 1818.

On April 8, 1833, he performed the marriage ceremony of Dr. H.H. Brown and Mary Dearborn in Quincy, Florida. In May 1833, Jesse purchased 479 acres in Jackson County, Florida, from Hardy and Bryan Croom for $5,045. The same year, he purchased 479.5 acres in the same area from Thomas Robinson of Leon

County, Florida, for $3,175. In June 1835, he and David G. Raney purchased the south reservation of the Apalachicola Indians on the Apalachicola River in Jackson County from Chief Yellow Hair for $3,250; Raney sold his portion to Jesse the following January for $2,500. The tract consisted of nearly a thousand acres and joined the Coe plantation on the south. On June 13, 1835, Jesse purchased 1,120 acres in Gadsden County for $3,000. On January 31, 1840, he purchased from William Toney of Randolph County, Georgia, 980 acres in Jackson County for $12,000.

In 1833, Jesse Coe was active in public affairs, and he was one of the founding shareholders of the Union Bank when it was formed in Gadsden County, Florida. During an 1837 investigation he was found to be the second largest shareholder with 329 shares, valued at $100 per share.

On May 14, 1836, at the first indications of Indian trouble in the area, the citizens of Gadsden County called a meeting held at the courthouse at Quincy. Jesse was called to chair the meeting with R.H.M. Davidson as secretary. Among resolutions made was a decision to form a committee of eight men including Jesse to report measures necessary for the safety of the country. At the time, Jim Henry's band of Creeks was rumored to be moving down the Chattahoochee into Florida. Richard Keith Call wrote the military commander at Pensacola that hostilities had begun, and he called on the governors of Alabama and Georgia seeking cooperation. After considering potential destruction along the Chattahoochee and Apalachicola Rivers, Call appointed Jesse Coe, with whom he had served with under Jackson, as a special agent to address the issue should problems occur.

In 1839, Major Jesse Coe, reverend of the Centenary Methodist Church, was listed as owning 36 slaves and 2,128 acres of land. At one time, Jesse Coe owned some 4,500 acres and at least three cotton plantations in Florida: Rocky Comfort Plantation, Toney Plantation, and Mount Pleasant Plantation. Jesse made his home on the Toney Plantation in a modest two-story house 1.5 miles north of Ocheesee Landing. The Apalachicola land he owned was known as Mount Pleasant Plantation. His daughter, Mary Drew Gilliam Coe Harris owned the Rocky Comfort Plantation.

In 1839 as founding member of Centenary Methodist Church in Gadsden County, Jesse Coe presented the church with a marble memorial marker which bore the inscription, "Centenary Monument of the Methodist Church Erected 25th of October, A.D. 1839."

In the years of 1834 to 1847 as a member of Washington Lodge Number 2, F&AM, Jesse is most celebrated mason for having served a total of ten years as Grand Master of the Grand Lodge of Florida. On July 21, 1849, when Gee Lodge Number 21, F&AM, Chattahoochee, Florida, was formed, Jesse Coe was appointed Worshipful Master. Coe Lodge Number 4 in Jackson County was named in his honor. Jesse Coe was esteemed for his long and distinguished record with the Florida Masons.

The 1840 census of Gadsden County, Florida, listed the following for the Jesse Coe household: one white male 50-60 years old with no wife; one son 10-15, one son 5-10, and two daughters 15-20. It appears that his wife Elizabeth Booth Coe had died between September 18, 1830, when her son Will was born and the 1840 census.

Between 1830 and 1840, Elizabeth Booth Coe died at Quincy in Gadsden County, Florida. As a blessing to Jesse Coe, Elizabeth was an affectionate stepmother to his daughters to whom they became endeared by the loveliness of her character and the kindness of her treatment. She was a most devoted mother, and her memory was cherished by her two sons, Jesse Jr. and Will, as a precious legacy.

On June 23, 1845, Jesse Coe gave the invocation for Tallahassee citizens of the new state of Florida. They had gathered at the new statehouse to inaugurate a new governor and a new government.

In 1848 when the Florida and Georgia Railroad Company was chartered with authorized capital stock of one million dollars, Major Jesse Coe, Charles S. Sibley, William Booth, and others were listed as incorporators. Jesse was a trustee of St. Andrew's College which was located on the Bay of St. Andrew in Washington County, Florida, where he had a two-story summer residence. Jesse also owned lots 163 and 164 with a home in Quincy.

By 1850, the plantations of Jesse Coe consisted of 3,200 acres and stretched from south of Port Jackson five miles along the Apalachicola River, which forms the Jackson-Gadsden County boundary, to the Calhoun County line. On his bay horse Bob, Jesse would ride over his property each morning; it was said that at one time he owned 600 black slaves.

In 1850, Jesse Coe was listed as one of the largest slave owners in Jackson County, Florida. He had gained considerable wealth from his extensive cotton plantations and provided for the education of several of his nephews. He owned land in Gadsden, Jackson, Washington, and Liberty Counties, Florida.

In 1852, Jesse was a delegate to the Democratic National Convention in Baltimore. After the fall election victory, local Democrats staged a rousing celebration march through Marianna, the seat of Jackson County, Florida. They heard the old Democratic regular Major Jesse Coe admonish them against too much jubilation for Whig friends who are already sufficiently distressed by their misfortunes.

On January 16, 1859, Major Jesse Coe died on Sunday afternoon at his home in Jackson County; the next day, he was scheduled to preach at a funeral. His body was taken to the Methodist church in Quincy where the funeral service was conducted by friends Reverend Dr. David L. White and Josephus Anderson. He was buried at the Rocky Comfort Plantation house of his daughter Mary Drew Gilliam Coe Harris of Quincy in Gadsden County, Florida.

Jesse Coe was a minister in the Methodist church for nearly sixty years. After his death the <u>Tallahassee Floridian</u> declared: "…his life, his character as a man, a husband, a father, a master, a citizen, a friend and a Christian is a beautiful commentary on the moral law, a striking and forcible exhibition of the excellency of religion, an example of practical goodness worthy of imitation. Highly esteemed by the whole community, repeatedly honored by the Masonic fraternity with the first offices at their disposal, greatly beloved by a great circle of warm friends, and almost idolized by his children and servants, he lived a patriarch among us. Full of Christian peace and hope, the evening of his life was beautifully calm and serene. Cheerful, benevolent, courteous to all…he is remembered as the highest style of man, a Christian gentleman, the poor man's friend, and the holy man of God."

At his death, Jesse Coe left 144 slaves which were appraised at $114,000. On June 22, 1866, the cotton plantation of Jesse Coe consisting of 4,485 acres was sold by the heirs. Edward P. Hudson of Jackson County, Florida, and F.M. Gilbreath of Washington, DC, paid $43,400.00 for the Coe property.

Coleman, Daniel - Coleman Hill

On August 2, 1801, Daniel Coleman II was born in Caroline County, Virginia. His parents were Daniel Coleman I, an officer in the Revolutionary War, and his mother was Martha Cocke (9/5/1761-3/1842), a descendant of Colonel Richard Cocke. Martha Cocke Coleman is buried in the Coleman Family Cemetery at Athens in Limestone County, Alabama (Find A Grave Memorial# 126119766).

In 1817 at sixteen years old, Daniel left his home to make his way in the world. His father had died and the family went from well off to poverty. For a year, he taught school at the Kanawha Salt Works, and he used the money he earned to graduate at the Transylvania University. He then obtained employment at a court in Frankfort, Kentucky, and he studied law under Judge Bledsoe.

In 1819, Daniel Coleman came to Mooresville in Limestone County, Alabama. In 1820 at only 19 years old, he was chosen by the legislature as judge of the county court through the influence of Nicholas Davis, and he held the office several years.

In 1822, Daniel and his brother Ruffin (1798-1849) were incorporators of Athens Female Academy. The school was one of the oldest in the State of Alabama, and later, it became Athens State University. In the 1830 Limestone County, Alabama Census, Ruffin was listed as owning 20 black slaves. On March 23, 1816, Ruffin had first owned 40 acres of land in Section 6 of Township 2 South and Range 2 West in Madison County, Alabama. On December 27, 1849, Ruffin died and was buried in the Coleman Family Cemetery at Athens in Limestone County, Alabama (Find A Grave Memorial# 126118747).

In 1827, Daniel Coleman II married Elizabeth Lockhart Peterson of Limestone County; she was born on May 22, 1811, in Northampton, North Carolina. Between 1830 and 1849, they had eight sons and two daughters.
1. John Heartwell Coleman was born on May 5, 1828, in Limestone County, Alabama. He died on September 19, 1829 and was buried in the Coleman Family Cemetery (Find A Grave Memorial# 126119633).
2. Reverend James L. Coleman was a graduate of La Grange College.
3. Eliza Lockhart Coleman Thach was born April 10, 1836, and on June 22, 1859, she married Robert Henry Thach (1837-1866), son of Thomas Harmon Thach and Frances Ann Sandifer; in 1840, Thomas H. Thach owned 40 slaves. Elizabeth died on April 25, 1918, at age 82 at Auburn in Lee County, Alabama. She had move to Auburn to be with her son Dr. Charles Coleman who was a member of the faculty. Elizabeth was buried at Pine Hill Cemetery at Auburn (Find A Grave Memorial# 29213390).
4. Captain Daniel Coleman III was born on September 7, 1838, at Athens in Limestone County, Alabama. He was a graduate of Wesleyan College, Florence, and the Law Department of the University of Virginia. He was a captain during the Civil War. After the war, he was the founder of the Athens, Alabama, Ku Klux Klan. Daniel III moved to Huntsville where he died on June 26, 1906; he is buried in Maple Hill Cemetery at Huntsville in Madison County, Alabama (Find A Grave Memorial# 8798452).

5. Captain John Hartwell Coleman was born on August 12, 1840, and he graduated at Florence and law courses at the University of Virginia. On December 31, 1862, he was killed at the Battle of Murfreesboro in the Civil War in Rutherford County, Tennessee. John is buried in Athens City Cemetery (Find A Grave Memorial# 40709460).
6. Richard Heartwell Coleman attended high school in Virginia, and during the Civil War, he joined the army at about seventeen years of age.
7. Lieutenant Richard Vasser Coleman was born on November 30, 1843. Richard was killed on September 20, 1863, at the Battle of Chickamauga in Walker County, Georgia. He is buried in Athens City Cemetery and shares a tombstone with his brother Captain John Hartwell Coleman (Find A Grave Memorial# 40724546).
8. Dr. Ruffin Coleman was born on October 1, 1846, in Limestone County, Alabama. Ruffin obtained his collegiate training at the Southern University, Greensboro, and studied medicine at the University of Nashville, Tennessee. During the Civil War, Ruffin was a Private, Company A, 11th Alabama Cavalry, Confederate States Army. At age 62, Ruffian died on September 24, 1909, at Mountain Creek in Chilton County, Alabama. He was buried in the Athens City Cemetery at Athens in Limestone County, Alabama (Find A Grave Memorial# 40709423).

Captain John H. Coleman

In 1829, Daniel Coleman was elected as an Alabama State Representative from Limestone County, Alabama. In 1835, he was selected by the legislature as a circuit court judge which he served for 12 years. Judge Daniel Coleman was slender and tall with a light complexion and a member of the Methodist Episcopal Church, South.

Between January 23, 1832, and October 30, 1854, Daniel Coleman entered some 320 acres in Townships 3, 4 South and Range 4, 5 West in Limestone County, Alabama (Cowart, 1984).

In the 1850 Limestone County, Alabama, Agricultural Census, Daniel Coleman owned 75 acres of improved land and 225 acres of unimproved land valued at $2,000. He also had $75 worth of farming equipment and $475 worth of livestock.

In June 1851, Governor Henry Watkins Collier selected him to fill a vacancy on the Supreme Court of Alabama. Due to health reasons, he declined the seat the following year.

On November 4, 1857, Daniel Coleman died at age 56 at Athens in Limestone County, Alabama. He was buried in Athens City Cemetery in Section 1, Lot# 33 (Find A Grave Memorial# 40724677).

In the 1860 Limestone County, Alabama, Slave Schedules, the Daniel Coleman estate owned 140 black slaves. In 1862 at the beginning of the Civil War, the Coleman estate was worth $152,733.

On February 14, 1885, Elizabeth Lockhart Peterson Coleman, wife of Daniel Coleman Sr. died at age 73 at Athens in Limestone County, Alabama. She is buried in the Athens City Cemetery, Section 1, Lot# 33 (Find A Grave Memorial# 40724604). Elizabeth survived her husband many years. She was a native of South Carolina and noted for her beauty of face and character.

Collier, James - Myrtle Grove

On October 13, 1757, Colonel James Collier was born in Lunenburg County, Virginia; he was the son of Cornelius Collier (11/12/1720-5/9/1810) and Elizabeth Wyatt (9/15/1730-2/23/1803). On April 18, 1753, Cornelius Collier, a

Revolutionary War soldier, married Elizabeth Wyatt in Gloucester County, Virginia; they died and were buried in Abbeville County, South Carolina.

On September 8, 1771, James Collier, a 13-year-old soldier in the American Revolution, was wounded at the Battle of Eutaw Springs by a saber cut across his cheek. James received the facial scar, which he carried to the grave, in hand-to-hand combat with a British soldier whom he killed. Wyatt Collier, the little brother of James, was killed in the same battle when only a boy.

On July 3, 1788, after the death of his first wife Elizabeth Littlepage, James Collier married Elizabeth Bouldin, daughter of James Bouldin and Sally Watkins of Charlotte County, Virginia. James Bouldin was the oldest son of Colonel Thomas Bouldin of Pennsylvania, who settled in Lunenburg County, Virginia, in 1744.

James Collier and Elizabeth Bouldin had the following children:
1. Bouldin Carter Collier was born on July 8, 1789, in Lunenburg County, Virginia. He married Sarah Slaughter from Limestone County, Alabama. On March 11, 1811, Bouldin and Wyatt Collier entered 161.4 acres in Section 8 of Township 4 South and Range 1 West in Madison County, Alabama (Cowart, 1979). On February 7, 1818, Bouldin entered 240.8 acres in Townships 4, 5 South and Range 3 West in Limestone County, Alabama (Cowart, 1984).
2. Wyatt Collier was born on August 19, 1791, in Lunenburg County, Virginia. In 1828, he married Janet Jane Walker, who was born in Elect, Scotland on May 17, 1805. She died on August 8, 1869 and is buried in the Florence Cemetery in Lauderdale County, Alabama (Find A Grave Memorial# 38552126). Wyatt owned The Oaks Plantation, 64 black slaves, and 1,453 acres on the Tennessee River in West Lauderdale County, Alabama. He died on October 6, 1856, and is buried in the Florence Cemetery in Florence, Alabama. (Find A Grave Memorial# 38552165).
3. Martha Watkins Collier was born on August 29, 1793, in Lunenburg County, Virginia; she died on February 4, 1867. On June 15, 1812, Martha married William Alexander Slaughter. He was born in 1792 in Culpeper County, Virginia. In 1879, William died and was buried in Neshobo County, Mississippi.

4. Dr. James Bouldin Collier Jr. was born on June 16, 1795; he married Sarah Ladd on June 03, 1819, and married Frances Slaughter on June 05, 1828. James died on May 09, 1839.
5. Eliza Wyatt Collier was born on May 1, 1797, in Lunenburg County, Virginia. On December 19, 1817, she married William Henry Blackwell in Madison County, Alabama; he was born on November 27, 1790, and died November 26, 1846. William Henry Blackwell owned 60 black slaves in 1840, and he was buried in the Blackwell-Collier Cemetery in Limestone County, Alabama (Find A Grave Memorial# 70347693). Eliza died on July 25, 1856, in Madison County, Alabama. She was buried in the Blackwell-Collier Cemetery in Limestone County, Alabama (Find A Grave Memorial# 70347757).
6. William Edward Collier was born on August 10, 1799, in Lunenburg County, Virginia. He first married Rosalie Stewart. On December 08, 1829, he married Jane Ophelia Stewart Slaughter Collier, 2/11/1805-12/11/1830; Jane was buried in the Blackwell-Collier Cemetery in Limestone County, Alabama (Find A Grave Memorial# 81980136). On February 7, 1818, William E. Collier entered 160.5 acres in Section 21 of Township 5 South and Range 2 West; and, on July 2, 1831, he entered 160.5 in Section 11 of Township 5 South and Range 2 West in Limestone County, Alabama (Cowart, 1984). On June 7, 1830, he entered 78.5 acres in Section 30 of Township 5 South and Range 2 West in Madison County, Alabama (Cowart, 1979). William died in 1833 in Madison County, Alabama.
7. Governor Henry Watkins Collier was born on January 17, 1801, in Charlotte County, Virginia. On April 26, 1826, he married Mary Ann Williams Battle in Tuscaloosa, Alabama; she was born on May 16, 1803, in Nash, North Carolina, and died on April 09, 1867, in Tuscaloosa, Alabama (Find A Grave Memorial# 68719731). Henry Watkins Collier served

Governor Henry Watkins Collier

as Chief Justice of the Alabama State Supreme Court from 1828 to 1849. From 1849-1853, Henry Watkins Collier was the 14th Governor of Alabama. Henry died on August 28, 1855, at Bailey Springs, Alabama. He is buried in Evergreen Cemetery in Tuscaloosa County, Alabama (Find A Grave Memorial# 7365985).
8. Thomas Bouldin Collier was born on January 08, 1803, in Abbeville, South Carolina. In 1824, he married Mary Dent in Madison County, Alabama. In the 1850 Limestone County, Alabama, Agricultural Census, Thomas B. Collier owned 980 acres of improved land and 1,200 acres of unimproved land worth $32,715. He also had $600 worth of farming equipment and livestock valued at $3,524.
9. Charles Ephraim Collier was born on January 10, 1805, in Abbeville, South Carolina. On June 19, 1828, Charles married Elizabeth Goowyne Stewart of Madison County, Alabama. Elizabeth was born on December 6, 1812, and she died on May 21, 1878. She is buried in the Blackwell-Collier Cemetery in Limestone County, Alabama (Find A Grave Memorial# 70347828). On December 25, 1830, Charles Ephraim Collier entered 75.5 acres in Section 20 of Township 5 South and Range 2 West. On July 12, 1837, he entered 162.18 acres in Section 28 of Township 4 South and Range 2 West in Madison County, Alabama (Cowart, 1979). He died on March 7, 1888 and is buried in the Blackwell-Collier Cemetery in Limestone County, Alabama (Find A Grave Memorial# 70532090).
10. Alfred A. Collier was born on August 05, 1807, in Abbeville, South Carolina, and he died on July 10, 1808, in Charlotte County, Virginia.

Until 1802, James was a large landowner in Lunenburg County, Virginia. In 1803, James and Elizabeth had a son, Thomas Bouldin Collier, who was born in Abbeville District, South Carolina. James had followed his father and other relatives to South Carolina where he became a large cotton planter.

On March 11, 1811, Bouldin and Wyatt Collier, the two oldest sons of James and Elizabeth, entered land in Madison County of Mississippi Territory. James followed his sons to Madison County in Mississippi Territory which became Alabama. James entered land and settled on his Myrtle Grove Plantation near Triana.

On February 4, 1818, James Collier entered some 1,308 acres of land in Sections 29 and 30 of Township 5 South and Range 2 West in Madison County, Alabama (Cowart, 1979). The land James entered was in the southwest part of Madison County. One 150-acre tract was entered with his son Charles Ephraim Collier.

From February 7, 1818, through June 2, 1831, James E. Collier entered some 478 acres in Townships 2, 5 South and Ranges 3, 5, 6 West in Limestone County, Alabama (Cowart, 1984). Some of the Limestone County land was on the Tennessee River and some was along Elk River.

On February 23, 1828, Elizabeth Bouldin Collier died at age 65. She is buried in the Collier Cemetery at Triana in Madison County, Alabama (Find A Grave Memorial# 39774355).

On August 20, 1832, James Collier died at age 74. He is buried in Collier Cemetery at Triana in Madison County, Alabama, on his Myrtle Grove Plantation near the Tennessee River about 20 miles southwest of Huntsville (Find A Grave Memorial# 17954217). His obituary reads: "Died at his residence near the village, on Monday the 20th instant, after a severe illness of two weeks, Mr. James Collier, in the 77th year of his age. Mr. Collier was a native of Virginia, and at an early period of his life entered the Revolutionary Army."

James and Elizabeth Collier are buried beside each other, and their monument inscriptions read: "To the memory of JAMES COLLIER who was born in Lunenburg County, Virginia Oct 13th, A. D. 1757, and died the 20th of August A. D. 1832. And though after my skin worms destroy this body, yet in my flesh shall I see God: whom I shall see for myself, and my eyes shall behold and not another. To the memory of ELIZABETH BOULDIN of Charlotte Co., VA., wife of James Collier, who was born the 13th of Feb., A. D. 1763, and died the 23rd of Feb., A. D. 1828. All flesh is grass, and all the goodliness thereof is as a flower of the field, for the wind passeth over it and it is gone, and the place thereof shall know it no more."

Thomas Bouldin Collier

Thomas Bouldin Collier was the son of James E. Collier and Elizabeth Bouldin Collier of the Myrtle Grove Plantation near Triana, in Madison County, Alabama. In the 1840 Limestone County, Alabama Census, Thomas B. Collier owned 30 black slaves.

The 1850 Limestone County, Alabama, United States Census, Household 344 listed the following: Thomas B. Collier, Male, 47, White, South Carolina; Mary H Collier, Female, 35, Georgia; James H. Collier, Male, 18, Alabama; Charles H. Collier, Male, 15 Alabama; Elenor M. H. Collier, Female, 13, Alabama; Edward B. Collier, Male, 6, Alabama; Powhattan Collier, Male, 4, Alabama; Percy D. Collier, Male, 1, Alabama; William H. Fogg, Male, 23, Virginia.

In the 1850 Limestone County, Alabama, Agricultural Census, Thomas Bouldin Collier owned 980 acres of improved land and 1,200 acres of unimproved land valued at $32,715. He also had $600 worth of farming equipment and $3,524 worth of livestock. According to the 1850 Limestone County, Alabama Slave Schedule, Thomas B. Collier owned 81 black slaves.

The 1860 Limestone County, Alabama, United States Census Household 361 listed the following: Thomas B. Collier, Male, 57, White, South Carolina; Charles H. Collier, Male, 25, Alabama; Elenor H. Collier, Female, 22, Alabama; Edward D. Collier, Male, 16, Alabama; Mollie H. Collier, Female, 7, Alabama. In the 1860 Limestone County, Alabama, Slave Schedules, Thomas B. Collier owned 49 slaves. In 1866, Thomas B Collier was listed in the Limestone, Alabama State Census.

Critz, George F.

In the 1820 Lawrence County, Alabama Census, George F. Critz household had one white male over 21, two white males under 21, one white female over 21, and one white female under 21.

In 1820, George owned 22 black slaves. According to the Lawrence County marriage records, George F. Critz married Elisa Carter on December 13, 1822. He left Lawrence County by 1830 and moved to Limestone County, Alabama.

On April 20, 1830, George F. Critz entered 80 acres in Section 17 of Township 4 South and Range 5 West in Limestone County, Alabama. From September 15, 1835, through October 14, 1836, George entered an additional 120 acres in Township 3 South and Range 5 West in Limestone County (Cowart, 1984).

According to the 1860 Limestone County, Alabama, Slave Schedules, George F. Critz owned only 13 black slaves. Information on his slave ownership from 1830 through 1850 was not available.

Davis, Captain Nicholas - Walnut Grove

On April 23, 1781, Nicholas Davis Sr. was born in Hanover County, Virginia. His parents were John Dabney Davis (1743-1817) and Catherine Anne Ragland Tinsley Davis.

In 1806, Nicholas Davis married Martha Hargrave of a wealthy Quaker family. On September 7, 1791, Martha Hargrave Davis was born in Caroline County Virginia; she was the daughter of Jesse Hargrave and Mary Pleasants.

Nicholas and Martha Hargrave Davis had the following children that were born in Virginia, Kentucky, and Alabama:
1. Edwin Rodney Davis was born about 1807.
2. Ann Maria Davis Richardson was born on March 23, 1810, in Hanover County, Virginia. She married William S. Richardson (12/21/1797-12/15/1866). In 1827, William Richardson, an attorney from Virginia, built a home for his wife on South Clinton Street in Athens. In the 1860 Limestone County, Alabama, Slave Schedules, William owned 23 black slaves. He was buried in the Athens City Cemetery at Athens in Limestone County, Alabama

(Find A Grave Memorial# 39575793). On May 3, 1861, Ann Maria died at age 51, and was buried in the Athens City Cemetery at Athens in Limestone County, Alabama (Find A Grave Memorial# 39575813).

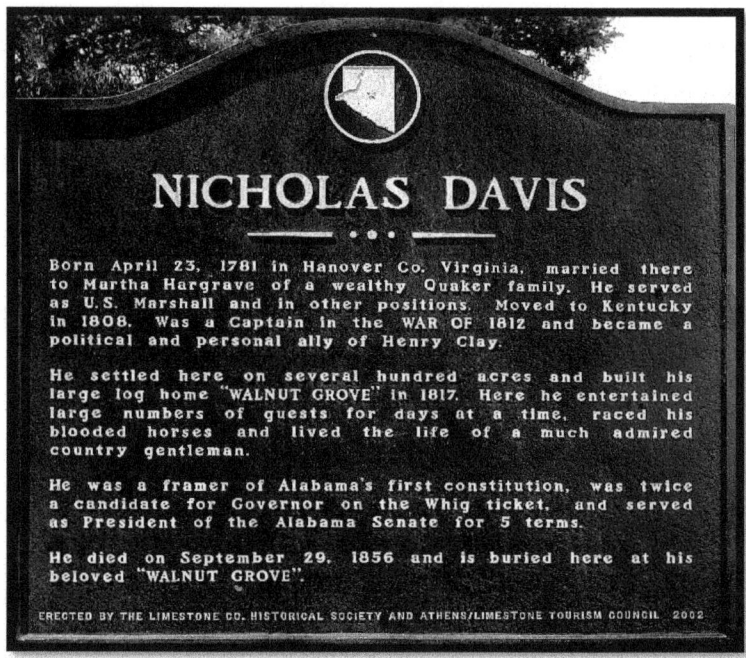

3. Philip Davis was born about 1812.
4. Martha Nichols Davis Lane was born in Virginia on November 23, 1814. In 1834, she married Judge George Washington Lane (6/14/1808-11/12/1863); he is buried in Cave Hill Cemetery at Louisville in Jefferson County, Kentucky (Find A Grave Memorial# 139997270). In the 1840, Limestone County, Alabama Census, George Washington Lane owned 44 black slaves. On May 16, 1896, Martha Nichols Davis Lane died at the age of 81 in Huntsville, Alabama. She is buried in Maple Hill Cemetery in Huntsville, Alabama (Find A Grave Memorial# 8807339).
5. Colonel Zebulon "Zeb" Pike Davis Sr. was on January 16, 1816, at Lexington in Fayette County, Kentucky. On December 20, 1840, Zeb married Williametta "Etta" D. Eason (8/17/1822-4/4/1889) in Huntsville, Alabama. On January 3, 1882, Colonel Zebulon Pike Davis Sr. died at age 65 at Huntsville in Madison County,

Alabama, and he was buried in Maple Hill Cemetery (Find A Grave Memorial# 94292003).

6. Lawrence Ripley Davis was born on February 27, 1819, in Limestone County, Alabama. In 1849, he ran and was elected to the House of Representatives in the Alabama. On March 27, 1851, Lawrence Ripley Davis first married Mary Abercrombie in Russell County, Alabama; she died in 1859. In1859, he was again elected as representative. In 1861, Lawrence married Sarah A. McClellan (1/24/1831-7/15/1891); she was buried in Athens City Cemetery (Find A Grave Memorial# 39524688). In 1873, he started the Limestone News in Athens for one year and sold out. In 1874, he was appointed private secretary to Governor George Smith Houston. In 1876, Lawrence Davis was appointed Register in Chancery. In October 1885, he was appointed postmaster by President Grover Cleveland; he served as postmaster at Athens. On August 20, 1892, Lawrence Ripley Davis died at Athens and is buried in the Athens City Cemetery (Find A Grave Memorial# 39524657).

7. Eliza James Lockard Davis was born about 1823, and she died in 1849.

8. Colonel Nicholas Davis Jr. was born on January 14, 1825, in Limestone County, Alabama. In 1851, he served as a member of

the Alabama State legislature. In 1854, he married Sophie Lowe Davis; her parents were General Bartley Martin Lowe (1802-1868) and Sophia Manning (1811-1844) of The Grove Plantation in Madison County, Alabama. On October 28, 1896, Sophie Lowe Davis died at Huntsville and is buried in the Maple Hill Cemetery (Find A Grave Memorial# 8806050). In 1861, Nicholas Jr. was a delegate to Alabama secession convention. He was then elected to represent Alabama in the Confederate Provisional Congress, serving from 1861 to 1862. He served in the Confederate Army as the Lieutenant Colonel of the 5th Alabama Battalion. On November 3, 1875, Nicholas Davis Jr. died at age

50 at Huntsville in Madison County, Alabama, and is buried at Maple Hill Cemetery (Find A Grave Memorial# 6420418).
9. Hector Davis.
10. Mary Pleasants Davis.
11. Dr. Dewitt Clinton Davis was born on January 14, 1830. On June 28, 1858, he married Susan Lowe; she was born in Huntsville in June 1833. Nicholas Davis Jr. and his brother Dewitt married sisters, Sophia and Susan Lowe; daughter of General Bartley M. Lowe. While living in Huntsville, General Lowe was in the mercantile business, and he was the first president of the Huntsville Bank. In 1838, Lowe lived in New Orleans, where he was a leading cotton merchant until his death. On May 2, 1908, Susan Lowe Davis died at age 74 at Meridianville in Madison County, Alabama; she was buried in Athens City Cemetery in Limestone County, Alabama (Find A Grave Memorial# 87816258). On October 18, 1904, Dewitt Clinton Davis died in Limestone County, Alabama, and was buried in the Athens City Cemetery (Find A Grave Memorial# 75240719).
12. Virginia Dudley Davis was born about 1836.

On November 23, 1814, the daughter of Nicholas Davis, Martha Nichols Davis, was born in Virginia, and on January 16, 1816, his son, Zebulon "Zeb" Pike Davis, was born at Lexington in Fayette County, Kentucky. Based on the birth of his children, Nicholas Davis Sr. probably moved to Kentucky in 1815. On February 27, 1819, his son, Lawrence Ripley Davis, was born in Limestone County, Alabama; therefore, between 1816 and 1819, the Nicholas Davis family moved to Limestone County, Alabama.

In 1817, it appears Nicholas Davis owned 159.85 acres in Section 11 of Township 3 South and Range 2 West in Madison County, Alabama. The records show that the land was originally owned by William Renick in 1811, then to James Titus in 1812, and then assigned to Nicholas Davis in 1817, and finally to Freeman Pettus (Cowart, 1979).

On February 5, 1818, Nicholas Davis first entered land in Limestone County, Alabama adjacent to the Madison County property. Between February 5, 1818, and July 9, 1855, Nicholas Davis entered approximately 2,380 acres of land in Townships 3, 4 South and Range 3 West in Limestone County, Alabama (Cowart, 1984). A large antebellum cotton farm called Walnut Grove Plantation was established on the land of Nicholas Davis in Limestone County, Alabama.

According to Old Land Records of Limestone County, Alabama by Margaret Matthews Cowart (1984), Nicholas Davis entered the following tracts of land in Limestone County:
1. February 5, 1818, 93 acres, S. 1, T3S R3W,
2. February 5, 1818, 40 acres, S. 20, T3S R3W,
3. February 5, 1818, 185.5 acres, S. 12, T3S R3W,
4. February 6, 1818, 159.8 acres, S. 20, T4S R3W,
5. February 6, 1818, 160.7 acres, S. 21, T4S R3W,
6. February 6, 1818, 160.8 acres, S. 21, T4S R3W,
7. February 23, 1818, 158.6 acres, S. 10, T3S R3W,
8. April 20, 1830, 80 acres, S. 18, T4S R3W,
9. May 10, 1831, 158.6 acres, S. 10, T3S R3W,
10. May 12, 1831, 159.7 acres, S. 2, T3S R3W,
11. May 12, 1831, 159.75 acres, S. 20, T4S R3W,
12. February 25, 1835, 160.8 acres, S. 21, T4S R3W,
13. October 6, 1837, 185.5 acres, S. 12, T3S R3W,
14. January 1, 1851, 39.7 acres, S. 10, T3S R3W,
15. November 8, 1854, 39.7 acres, S. 10, T3S R3W,
16. November 8, 1854, 158.9 acres, S. 11, T3S R3W,
17. November 8, 1854, 79.3 acres, S. 10, T3S R3W,
18. July 9, 1855, 159.8 acres, S. 3, T3S R3W.

Nicholas Davis settled on Limestone Creek on over 2,000 acres of land in the Capshaw Community of Limestone County, Alabama. He built his large log home on his Walnut Grove Plantation some two years before Alabama became a state. At his home, he entertained large numbers of guests for days at a time, raced his blooded horses, and lived the life of a much-admired country gentleman. Nicholas became a political and personal ally of Henry Clay.

The following is a timeline for Captain Nicholas Davis Sr. from his birth until his death:

1. On April 23, 1781, Nicholas Davis was born in Hanover County, Virginia.
2. In 1806, Nicholas Davis married Martha Hargrave.
3. In the War of 1812, Nicholas Davis was a captain in the military.
4. Prior to 1814, Davis was a United States marshal in Virginia.
5. About 1815, Nicholas Davis and family moved to Kentucky.
6. In 1817, Nicholas Davis entered land in Madison County and built large old log house in Limestone County, Alabama.
7. In May 1819, Nicholas Davis was elected to the first Constitutional Convention, and a member of the House of Representatives of the first legislature of Alabama.
8. In 1820, according to the Limestone County, Alabama Census, Nicholas Davis was a cotton planter with 21 black slaves.
9. From 1820 to 1828, Nicholas Davis was a member of the Alabama Senate, and he served as president of the senate for five sessions.
10. In 1829, he ran for United States Congress against C. C. Clay and was defeated by only eighty votes.
11. In 1830, based on the Limestone County, Alabama Census, Nicholas Davis was a cotton planter with 55 black slaves.
12. In the 1840 Limestone County, Alabama Census, Nicholas Davis was a cotton planter who owned 81 black slaves.
13. In 1844, Nicholas Davis was placed at the head of the Whig electoral ticket.
14. In 1847, Nicholas Davis was the Whig candidate for governor of the State of Alabama.

15. In 1850, noted historian Albert James Pickett visited Senator Nicholas Davis at his prosperous Walnut Grove plantation in Limestone County.
16. Prior to 1856, Nicholas Davis lived with the family of his daughter, Ann Richardson, before his death.
17. In 1856, he died at the age of seventy-six years.

In the 1850 Limestone County, Alabama, Agricultural Census, Nicholas Davis Sr. owned 1,491 acres of improved land and 829 acres of unimproved land valued at $31,840. He also had $2,600 worth of farming equipment and $6,110 worth of livestock. In the 1850 Limestone County, Alabama Census, Nicholas Davis, a cotton planter, owned 114 black slaves.

On March 18, 1853, Martha Hargrave Davis died at age 61. Prior to her death, Mrs. Martha Hargrave Davis lived in Huntsville with her son Nichols Davis Jr. and his wife Sophie Lowe Davis. Martha Hargrave Davis was buried at the Davis Cemetery at Capshaw in Limestone County, Alabama (Find A Grave Memorial# 54933606).

On September 29, 1856, Nicholas Davis Sr. died and was buried at his beloved Walnut Grove Plantation at Capshaw in Limestone County, Alabama, and he is buried in Davis Cemetery. His tombstone monument was erected by his children with the inscription: "In memory of Nicholas Davis; Born in Hanover County Va., April 23, A.D. 1781. Died Sept. 19, 1856."

Willis Brewer writes about Nicholas Davis Sr. in <u>Alabama, Her History, Resources, War Record, and Public Men</u>: "He was fluent and eloquent as an orator, with a large fund of practical knowledge. He was exceedingly candid and hospitable and swayed opinions of men as much by his large-heartedness as by his strong magnetism. He was a patron of the turf and carried out in his Alabama home all the other attributes of a Virginia gentleman of the approved school" (Find A Grave Memorial# 54933368).

Davis, Tinsley

In 1788, Tinsley Davis was born to John Dabney Davis and Anne Ragland Tinsley Davis. John D. Davis was a Revolutionary War veteran, and his wife Anne was his second cousin. Tinsley was born in Hanover County, Virginia.

In 1813, Tinsley married Frances Bowe Ragland in Virginia; she was born in 1796 in Hanover County, Virginia. On February 22, 1822, at age 25 or 26, Frances died and was buried in Limestone County, Alabama (Find A Grave Memorial# 161346750). She was the daughter of Beverly and Rebecca Bowe Ragland, sister of Dr. Nathaniel Ragland.

Tinsley and Frances Bowe Ragland Davis had the following children:
1. Maria Ann Ragland Davis Pettus was born on February 23, 1814, in Fayette County, Kentucky. She first married William T. Key, brother of the third wife of her father; her second marriage was to Anthony Winston Pettus. In January 1888, Maria died at age 73 near Memphis in Shelby County, Tennessee, and is buried in the Davis-McCargo-Bowe Cemetery (Find A Grave Memorial# 151363945).
2. Lycurgus Davis was born on May 20, 1817, in Fayette County, Kentucky. In April 1862, he died at age 44 and was buried in the Davis-McCargo-Bowe Cemetery in Shelby County, Tennessee (Find A Grave Memorial# 151372518).
3. Robert Ruffin Davis was born on August 23, 1819, in Limestone County, Alabama. In 1846, in Limestone County, Robert Ruffin Davis married Antoinette "Nettie" Blackbourn Clark Davis (February 4, 1822-February 2, 1914); Nettie died at Plum Point in DeSoto County, Mississippi, and buried in Shelby County, Tennessee (Find A Grave Memorial# 151017061). On April 18, 1885, Robert Ruffin Davis died at Plum Point, Mississippi and was buried in Shelby County, Tennessee Find A Grave Memorial# 151016996)
4. Beverly Samuel Davis was born on August 13, 1821, in Limestone County, Alabama. Beverly married his first cousin Mary Elizabeth Davis, daughter of Nathaniel Bowe Davis and Martha Davis Bowe

Davis. Mary Elizabeth Davis was born in Madison County on March 9, 1831 and died on March 4, 1882. She was buried next to her husband (Find A Grave Memorial# 151370224). On April 2, 1878, Beverly Samuel Davis died and was buried in the Davis-McCargo-Bowe Cemetery in Shelby County, Tennessee (Find A Grave Memorial# 151362041).

About 1814, Tinsley moved with family from Virginia to Fayette County, Kentucky. In 1817, Tinsley Davis along with other family members moved to Limestone County, Alabama. This is the same move made by Nicholas Davis.

The 1820 Limestone County, Alabama Census listed the following for Tinsley Davis: White Males over 21: 2; White Males under 21: 2 ; White Females over 21: 1; White Females under 21: 2; Total Whites: 7; Free Persons of Color; 7; Slaves: 32. Number of Acres Cultivated: 6, Either Number of Hands or number of bales of cotton: 12, Average Weight per bale: 320 pounds.

About 1824, after of his first wife France died in Alabama, Tinsley Davis returned to Virginia and married Elvira Cross. Tinsley and Elvira had a son John Hector Davis who was born on August 25, 1825. In 1839, John died in Shelby County, Tennessee, and he was buried in the family cemetery (Find A Grave Memorial# 151328186). Elvira was buried in Limestone County, Alabama.

In 1832, Tinlsey Davis married the third time to Virginia Emily Key; she was born in Virginia on February 8, 1813. In 1846, she died near Memphis, Tennessee, and is buried in the Tinsley Davis Cemetery or Davis-Bowe-McCargo Cemetery in Shelby County, Tennessee (Find A Grave Memorial# 151040891). Tinlsey Davis and Virginia Emily Key Davis had the following children.
1. Watson "Watt" Dabney Davis was born on April 5, 1833, in Limestone County, Alabama. In 1856, he married Maria Ann Clark (1833-1878). In1878, Maria and two sons died of the yellow fever epidemic. After the death of Maria, Watt married Sarah E. Baldwin. On February 23, 1902, Watt died at age 68 at Horn Lake in DeSoto County, Mississippi, and he was buried in the family cemetery in Shelby County, Tennessee (Find A Grave Memorial# 151133116).

2. Laura Emily Davis was born in 1835 in Limestone County, Alabama. In 1841, she died at age five or six and is buried in the family cemetery in Shelby County, Mississippi (Find A Grave Memorial# 151176021).
3. Angelina Harriet Davis Edmondson was born on April 2, 1837, in Limestone County, Alabama. She was the wife of Eumenes A. Edmondson; she sued her half-brother Robert R. Davis over the estate of her father Tinsley Davis. In October 1878, she died at the age of 41 and was buried in the family cemetery in Shelby County, Tennessee (Find A Grave Memorial# 151176164).
4. Cornelia Davis was born on October 3, 1839, in Shelby County, Tennessee, and died in 1840 (Find A Grave Memorial# 151176164).
5. Tinsley Davis Jr. was born on April 15, 1844, in Shelby County, Tennessee. He married Mollie E. King (11/20/1850-6/24/1928); she is buried in Oak Grove Cemetery at Searcy in White County, Arkansas (Find A Grave Memorial# 70981862). On August 2, 1897, Tinsley Jr. died at age 53 at Searcy in White County, Arkansas; he was buried in the Oak Grove Cemetery (Find A Grave Memorial# 70981949).
6. Hugh Davis was born on October 25, 1845, in Shelby County, Tennessee; in October1878, he died of yellow fever and was buried in the Davis-McCargo-Bowe Cemetery in Shelby County, Tennessee (Find A Grave Memorial# 151176246).

On May 28, 1838, while living in Limestone County, Tinsley Davis purchased 640 acres at Memphis in Shelby County, Tennessee. On October 3, 1839, Cornelia Davis, the daughter of Tinsley Davis, was the first child of Tinsley Davis born in Shelby County, Tennessee.

In 1839, after the death of his son John Hector Davis, Tinsley Davis Sr. set aside an acre on a rise surrounded by tall trees for a family burial ground and cemetery on his farm outside of Memphis. Over some 90 years, at least 67 Davis family members and their relatives were buried in the Davis family cemetery.

The 1840 Shelby County, Tennessee Census listed the following for the Tinsley Davis household: White Males: 5-10: 1, 15-20: 2, 20-30: 3, 50-60: 1, White Females: Under 5: 2, 20-30: 1, Slaves: 48 Total.

On November 25, 1842, Nathaniel Bowe Davis, cousin of Tinsley, migrated to the area where the Tinsley Davis family settled. From the Forks of Horn Lake Creek in DeSoto County, Mississippi, Nathaniel wrote the following to his lawyer son Nathaniel Hart Davis in Montgomery, Texas: "Memphis grows rapidly, is soon destined to be a large city. About three miles out south of Memphis, the Central Jockey Club racetrack was opened; more than 100 fine racehorses have been stationed there. Tinsley Davis had a racehorse stable. Willy Wiley and Tom Breckenridge, old Kentucky turf men, friends of 1/4 century ago are visiting us."

On February 23, 1850, Tinsley Davis died of pleurisy at the age of 62 in Shelby County, Tennessee. Tinsley Davis Sr. was buried in the Tinsley Davis Cemetery or Davis-McCargo-Bowe Cemetery in Shelby County, Tennessee (Find A Grave Memorial# 151039832). Tinsley Davis Sr. left a large estate and four young children by his third wife Virginia Emily Key Davis. Robert Ruffin Davis, son of Tinsley, and his wife Antoinette Blackbourne Clarke Davis reared Watson, Angelina, Tinsley Jr., and Hugh that were the young half-siblings, Robert.

In 1929, John Hector Davis, a grandson Tinsley, was the last burial in the cemetery. The Davis-McCargo-Bowe Cemetery of the Davis family was destroyed by farmers and the graves can no longer be identified. The remains of the cemetery are located on the east side of Tchulahoma Road a little more than a half mile south of Shelby Drive inside a subdivision in southeast Memphis. In 1974, a subdivision known East Haven Park was built and destroyed most visible traces of the cemetery.

Dickerson (Dickinson), Bejamin

Benjamin Dickerson Sr. was the son of Daniel Dickerson II and Martha Turner Dickerson. Benjamin first married his cousin Priscilla Dickerson; he then married Mary Roundtree who died in 1828. His third marriage was to Mary Buchanan at Athens in Limestone County, Alabama.

On February 6, 1818, Benjamin Dickerson entered 401.5 acres in Sections 14 and 22 in Township 4 South and Range 3 West in the Limestone Creek drainage of Limestone County, Alabama. From March 29, 1830, through May 24, 1831, Benjamin entered an additional 220 acres in Sections 15 and 22 in Township 4 South and Range 3 West in the Limestone County, Alabama (Cowart, 1984).

The 1820 Limestone County, Alabama Census listed the following for Benjamin Dickerson: White Males over 21: 5; White Males under 21: 3; White Females over 21: 1; White females under 21: 6; Total of white population 15; total of free people of color 20; Total of slaves 150; Number of acres cultivated 11; Number of Hands 60; Number bales of cotton 114; Average Weights 300; Gins 2; Saws 0; Mills 0.

According to the 1830 Limestone County, Alabama Census, Benjamin Dickerson had seven males in his household. The oldest was 50-60 years old which was probably Benjamin. There were also three females in this household with the oldest 20 to 30 years old. In 1830, Benjamin Dickerson was listed with only 39 slaves.

In 1832, John Nelson Spotswood Jones paid Benjamin Dickerson $3.12 for the following blacksmithing work for the year 1831: August 4, 1831-new shoes and one old shoe repaired; August 11, 1831-four renewed; August 26, 1831-for repairing pump iron; and September 1831-repairing iron.

As did a lot of families, some of the Dickerson family moved west in search of better cotton ground. In 1840, Benjamin Dickerson Jr. was listed in the Federal Census of Caddo Township in Clark County, Arkansas.

According to the 1850 Caddo Township, Clark County, Arkansas, United States Census, Household 248, enumerated on November 27, 1850, Benjamin Dickinson was a 38-year-old white male farmer born in North Carolina, Sarah Dickinson was a 40-year-old white female born in North Carolina, and Thomas Dickinson was a 16-year-old white male born in Alabama.

Dillard, George H. - Oak Mount

George H. Dillard married Ann C. Jones. Ann was born on February 18, 1785. George Dillard and Ann C. Jones had a daughter Huldah Jones Dillard who was born May 25, 1802.
1. Huldah Jones Dillard married James Hurt Gamble. On July 7, 1845, Huldah Jones Dillard Gamble died, and she was buried in the Gamble Cemetery in Limestone County, Alabama (Find A Grave Memorial# 63704401).

On February 7, 1818, George H. Dillard entered 160.89 acres near Limestone Creek in Section 6 of Township 5 South and Range 3 West in Limestone County, Alabama (Cowart, 1984). The land was adjacent to James H. Gamble and approximately five miles north of the Tennessee River and five miles west of the Madison County line. On February 13, 1818, George H. Dillard entered 159.9 acres near Lucy's Branch in Section 27 of Township 3 South and Range 6 West. He entered an adjacent 159.9 acres on April 27, 1830 (Cowart, 1984).

The 1820 Limestone County, Alabama Census listed the following for the household of George Dillard: White Males over 21: 1; White Females over 21: 1; Total Whites: 2; Free Persons of Color: 17; Slaves: 30, Acres Cultivated: 10; Number of Bales: 13, Average Weight per Bale: 300 pounds. In 1820, it appears that 47 black folks lived at the household of George Dillard if those listed as free persons of color were black.

On April 23 and 27, 1830, George Dillard entered 160 acres in Sections 10, 13 of Township 5 South and Range 4 West. On June 29, 1831, George H. Dillard and William H. Moseley entered 161.37 acres in Section 7 of Township 5 South and Range 3 West. On June 1, 1835, George H. Dillard and James H. Gamble entered 160 acres in Section 13 of Township 5 South and Range 4 West in Limestone County, Alabama (Cowart, 1984). George H. Dillard entered a total of some 960 of land in Limestone County, Alabama.

The 1830 Limestone County, Alabama Census had the following for the household of George Dillard: White Males: 20-30: 1; 40-50: 1, White Females: 40-50: 1; Slaves: 25.

On August 1, 1838, George Dillard died in Limestone, Alabama. It appears that George Dillard owned an estate in Grenada County, Mississippi, or that he lived some of his time in Mississippi before he died. In order to administer the estates of George, James M. Duncan was obviously appointed to oversee the affairs. James was the son-in-law of Huldah Jones Dillard Gamble.

On May 12, 1851, Ann C. Jones, wife of George Dillard, died in Limestone County, Alabama. Her body was interred in the Gamble Cemetery at Oak Mount in Limestone County, Alabama. The inscription on her tombstone reads, "In Memory of ANN DILLARD, wife of George Dillard, Born Feb.18, 1785, Died the Christian's death on the 12th day of May A.D. 1851."

Donnell, Robert - Pleasant Hill

In April 1784, Robert Donnell was born in Guilford County, North Carolina. Robert was the son of William and Mary Bell Donnell, who were married about the year 1760, and resided in Guilford County, North Carolina.

In October 1789, William Donnell started a move toward Sumner County, Tennessee, and settled at Bell's Fort on Drake's Creek. In 1792, the family moved and settled about eight miles from Lebanon on Spring Creek in Wilson County, Tennessee. Robert Donnell was reared from a boy to a man in Wilson County, Tennessee. From 1775 through June 26, 1794, Doublehead and his Chickamauga warriors waged war on the Cumberland settlements.

According to Find A Grave: "The Donnell family, in its several generations, has furnished a large quota of ambassadors for Christ; and in this respect has been much honored of God. Reverend Robert Donnell's parents at an early day were members of that branch of the great Presbyterian family commonly called Secedes; but before 1794, joined, what is now called the Old Presbyterian Church. In the month of October 1789, when Father Donnell was in his sixth year, his parents started for the Cumberland country…expecting to join an emigrating party, which it seems was to rendezvous near, or at Abington, Virginia. But being too late to affect this object, they remained in the vicinity of Abington until the following October, when they joined another party, and proceeded to Sumner County, Tennessee. But owing to the hostilities of the Indians, they spent the first year after their arrival in Captain Bell's fort, situated about one mile from Smith's fort, afterward called Hendersonville, on Drake's creek, some seven or eight miles from Nashville, on the north side of Cumberland River. Sometime in the next year (1792) they settled on Spring Creek, in the adjoining county of Wilson, not many miles from where Lebanon now stands. Here they soon assisted in erecting a house of worship, and in organizing a church. Here their pilgrimage on earth was ended; and here sleep their bodies in the tomb, awaiting the resurrection morn."

Robert Donnell

In 1797, Robert was only 13 years old when his father died. Robert managed his family farm and took care of his mother and two sisters. At age 16, he constructed a horse powered grist mill to grind corn for the family and his neighbors. It was also said that Robert

Donnell could split more rails in a day than any man in the country.

In 1809, Robert Donnell made his first trip to Madison County in Mississippi Territory. On his journey to the Huntsville area, Robert crossed Elk River at Fayetteville, Tennessee. His crossing of Elk River was on a flatboat ferry run by an old man he called Mr. Norris.

On September 18, 1809, Robert Donnell entered 157.75 acres in Section 10 of Township 2 South and Range 1 West in Madison County of Mississippi Territory, now Alabama (Cowart, 1984). The land was originally assigned to George Smith of Sumner County, Tennessee, who was probably an uncle to Ann Eliza Smith Donnell.

On March 21, 1811, Robert Donnell was licensed by the Cumberland Presbytery as a minister of the gospel. Not only did he preach, but Robert also built churches in Tennessee and North Alabama.

On March 17, 1817, Robert Donnell first married Ann Eliza Smith who was born in September 1795, in Granville County, North Carolina. Ann Eliza was the daughter of Colonel James Webb Smith and Mary Downey Smith of Jackson County, Tennessee.

Robert Donnell Ann Eliza Smith Donnell had five children, and all died in infancy except one; Samuel Robert Bell Donnell (1824-1825) and Frances Jane Donnell (1826-1826) died as infants. Robert and Ann Eliza Donnell had only one child to live to adulthood, and he was James Webb Smith Donnell (1820-1876).

On February 6, 1818, Robert Donnell entered 79.39 acres in Section 5 of Township 4 South and Range 3 West in Limestone County, Alabama. On the same date, he entered 158.85 acres in Section 17 of Township 4 South and Range 3 West in Limestone County, Alabama (Cowart, 1984).

Around 1818, it appears that Robert Donnell moved from Madison County to Limestone County when he entered land in the area. The first home of Robert and his family in Limestone County was about ten miles southeast of Athens. He settled on a section of land that became the property of Luke Matthews.

According to the 1820 Limestone County, Alabama Census, Robert Donnell owned 11 black slaves. In addition, James Donnell owned 12 black slaves in 1820.

On November 3, 1828, Ann Eliza Smith Donnell died at their home, and she was buried in the Athens City Cemetery in Limestone County, Alabama (Find A Grave Memorial# 39524322). After the death of his wife, Robert moved and built the Pleasant Hill home where he lived until his death.

According to the 1830 Limestone County, Alabama Census, Robert Donnell owned 26 black slaves. On June 25, 1831, Robert Donnell entered about 320 acres in Sections 5 and 20 of Township 4 South and Range 3 West in Limestone County, Alabama (Cowart, 1984).

On June 21, 1832, the second marriage of Robert Donnell was to Clarissa "Clara" Whipple Lindley; she was born on April 15, 1806. Her parents were Reverend Jacob Lindley (1774-1857), President of Ohio University, and Hannah Dickey (1782-1848).

In 1835, Robert Donnell moved his family to Mooresville for about two years. In about 1837, he his family moved back to his home and continued farming and preaching in Limestone and Madison Counties.

According to the 1840 Limestone County, Alabama Census, Robert Donnell owned 34 black slaves. Robert, as was his son James Webb Smith Donnell, were cotton farmers utilizing black slave labor.

On January 3, 1845, Robert Donnell entered a little over 320 acres in Sections 18 and 19 of Township 4 South and Range 3 West in Limestone County, Alabama (Cowart, 1984). Some of this land was adjacent to Nicholas Davis and Thomas Bibb. In 1845, Robert spent a few months at Memphis, Tennessee, to organize and build a church. During the same year, he accepted a preaching job at Lebanon, Tennessee. In 1849, he returned from Lebanon to Athens, Alabama, where he spent his final days.

According to the 1850 Limestone County, Alabama, Slave Schedules, Robert Donnell owned 29 black slaves; he was farming cotton and preaching the gospel. In 1850, he supposedly completed his Pleasant Hill home in Athens.

Pleasant Hill

About 1850, Reverend Robert Donnell, an influential Presbyterian Minister, completed his Pleasant Hill Plantation house in Athens, Alabama. According to Wikipedia: "The house was built in 1840 by Robert Donnell, a minister who had come to Athens in the 1820s to establish a Presbyterian church. After his death in 1855, the house passed to his son, James. It was purchased in 1869 by Joshua P. Coman in order to establish the Athens Male College, beginning the house's association with education. In 1879, it was purchased by the city and became part of the public-school campus and sold ten years later to the North Alabama Experiment Station an Agricultural School. The house returned to city ownership in 1936 and is today part of the campus of Athens Middle School. The house is a two-story frame structure clad in clapboard. A double-height portico with paired square columns covers the entry. The main block has a center-hall plan with a two-story, gable roofed wing off the rear. The house was listed on the National Register of Historic Places on September 19, 1973."

In the 1850 Limestone County, Alabama, Agricultural Census, Robert Donnell owned 80 acres of improved land and 80 acres of unimproved land valued at $3,000. He also had $45 worth of farming equipment and $180 worth of livestock.

On May 25, 1855, at after preaching the gospel with almost unparalleled success for near half a century, Reverend Robert Donnell died at his residence in Athens at 4:30 o'clock in the morning at the age of 72 years. He was buried at Athens in the Athens City Cemetery in Limestone County, Alabama (Find A Grave Memorial# 30141955).

On June 30, 1883, Clara died at age 77 at Athens. She was buried in the Athens City Cemetery in Limestone County, Alabama (Find A Grave Memorial# 39524355)

James Webb Smith Donnell

On July 13, 1820, James Webb Smith Donnell, son of Robert and Ann Eliza Donnell, was born in Limestone County, Alabama. He owned the Seclusion Plantation in Lawrence County, Alabama. James married Maria Louisa Jones (1824-1894).

James Webb Smith Donnell and Maria Louisa Jones Donnell had the following children:
1. Robert Smith Donnell 1842-1916.
2. Eliza Haywood Donnell 1843-1846.
3. Nannie Smith Donnell 1846-1862.

4. Spotswood Jones Donnell 1848-1876.
5. John Haywood Donnell 1850-1912.
6. Webb Ridley Donnell 1851-1852.
7. Marcella Donell Carney 1852-1877.
8. Alexander Donnell 1854-1857.
9. Octavia Donnell Carney 1855-1936.
10. James Webb Smith Donnell 1859-1920.
11. Susie Owen Donnell Peck 1862-1898.
12. Nannie Donnell Hundley 1863-1937.
13. Pauline Walter Donnell Harrison 1866-1915.
14. Maria Louise Donnell Moore 1868-1919.

In the 1850 Lawrence County, Alabama, Agricultural Census, James Webb Smith Donnell owned 700 acres of improved land and 600 acres of unimproved land valued at $15,000. He also had $1,035 worth of farming equipment and $2,549 worth of livestock. In the 1850 Lawrence County, Alabama, Slave Schedules, James Webb Smith Donnell owned 56 black slaves.

On May 25, 1855, James Webb Smith Donnell inherited the Pleasant Hill Plantation home and land of his father, Robert Donnell. On November 5, 1855, Thomas Hubbard Hobbs recorded in his diary that James Donnell was elected vice president of the Board of Trustees of the Tennessee Conference Female Institute.

Poplar Mount or Pleasant Hill

In the 1860 Lawrence County, Alabama, Slave Schedules, James Webb Smith Donnell owned 85 black slaves. After the Civil War, James Webb Smith Donnell fell into financial ruin. James lost both the Seclusion Plantation and the Pleasant Hill Plantation.

On January 8, 1876, James Webb Smith Donnell died in Limestone County, Alabama. He was buried in the Athens City Cemetery (Find A Grave Memorial# 39524014).

Fisher, Jacob

On December 19, 1785, Jacob Fisher was born at Leacock in Lancaster County, Pennsylvania. His parents were Peter and Barbara Souder Fisher (1759-1831), and they were 26 years old when Jacob was born.

On February 2, 1815, Jacob Fisher married Martha Blanton Alexander (1796-1865) in Rutherford County, North Carolina. The following is the 14 children that they had in 29 years.

1. Oliver Hazard Perry Fisher was born November 18, 1815, in Rutherford County, North Carolina. On October 23, 1843, he died at age 27 in Limestone County, Alabama (Find A Grave Memorial# 161137899)
2. William Decatur Fisher was born May 13, 1817 and died on October 3, 1888; he married Martha D. Young (9/25/1837-12/9/1917). William and Martha are buried in the Fisher Cemetery in Gregg County, Texas, (Find A Grave Memorial# 5398819 & 5398821).
3. Henry Peter Fisher was born January 5, 1819, and he died April 10, 1901. Henry was buried in Fisher Cemetery in Gregg County, Texas (Find A Grave Memorial# 6263443).
4. Julia Agnes Fisher English was born on November 23, 1822, at Athens in Limestone County, Alabama. On September 30, 1840, in Limestone County, she married Elbert Hartwell English; he was born on Capshaw Mountain in Madison County in 1816. On June 7, 1871, Julia died at age 48 at Little Rock in Pulaski County, Arkansas. On September 1, 1884, Elbert died at Asheville in Buncombe County, North Carolina. Julia and Elbert are buried at Mount Holley Cemetery at Little Rock in Pulaski County, Arkansas (Find A Grave Memorial# 7573550 & 7573549).

5. Martha Margaret Fisher Chadick was born on April 21, 1824. On December 26, 1847, she married Reverend Stokely R. Chadick (3/27/1818-2/12/1909) in Limestone County, Alabama, by Cumberland Presbyterian Minister Reverend James Kirkland. On December 14, 1882, Martha died in Gregg County, Texas. Both Martha and Stokley are buried in Fisher Cemetery in Gregg County, Texas (Find A Grave Memorial# 5398849 & 5398856).

Stokley R. Chadick

6. Malinda Jane Fisher Montgomery was born on December 15, 1825, in Limestone County, Alabama. On July 6, 1843, Malinda married Andrew Jackson Montgomery (3/31816-4/21/1874), and they moved to Texas. On February 2, 1901, Malinda died at age 75 at Whitewright in Grayson County, Texas. Malinda and Andew are buried in Oak Hill Cemetery at Whitewright in Fannin County, Texas (Find A Grave Memorial# 19227093 & 19226939).
7. Silas McBee Fisher was born on September 23, 1827; he died on January 25, 1892. Silas married Martha Killingsworth (7/4/1829-7/8/1906); they are buried in the Fisher Cemetery in Gregg County, Texas (Find A Grave Memorial#5398902 & 5398900).
8. Ann Elizabeth Fisher Fisher was born on July 3, 1829, in Limestone County, Alabama. She married George W. Fisher, and Ann died July 16, 1868. They are buried in Fisher Cemetery in Gregg County, Texas (Find A Grave Memorial# 161138215 & 5397940).
9. Robert Donnell Fisher was born on March 12, 1831, in Limestone County, Alabama; he died November 16, 1833, in Limestone County, Alabama (Find A Grave Memorial# 161138351).
10. Jacob Lindley Fisher was born on May 8, 1833, in Limestone County, Alabama. On August 24, 1851, Jacob married Josephine Howell (1834-Unknown) in Upshur, Texas. Jacob was a soldier in the Civil War, and he died in1876. Jacob and Josephine are buried in the Fisher Cemetery in Gregg Texas (Find A Grave Memorial# 161138609 & 161138638).

11. Barbara S. Fisher was born on June 30, 1835, at Philadelphia in Philadelphia County, Pennsylvania; she died on July 16, 1835, in Limestone County, Alabama (Find A Grave Memorial# 161138770).
12. Mary Blanton Fisher Zimmerman (1839-1926). She married William Woodward Reyburn (1803-1863) and Jesse Vinter Zimmerman (1834-1907) (Find A Grave Memorial# 103936744).
13. George Alexander Fisher July 29, 1842, in Limestone County, Alabama; he married Fannie Awalt. They are buried in the Fisher Cemetery in Gregg County, Texas (Find A Grave Memorial# 161138856 & 161138878).
14. Joan Reinhardt Fisher Allison was born on February 27, 1844; she married Dr. Jonathan N. Allison (1828-11/11/1884). Joan died February 14, 1889. Joan and Jonathan are buried in the Greenwood Cemetery at Longview in Gregg County, Texas (Find A Grave Memorial# 5704178 &5704181).

On February 6, 1818, Jacob Fisher entered 80 acres of land in Section 7 of Township 4 South and Range 3 West in Limestone County, Alabama. On February 10, 1818, William Fisher, probably the brother of Jacob, entered 160.9 acres in Section 35 of Township 4 South and Range 4 West in Limestone County (Cowart, 1984). William also owned 13 slaves in 1830 and 14 slaves in 1840.

The 1820 Limestone County, Alabama Census listed the following for Jacob Fisher: White Males over 21: 2; White Males under 21: 3; White Females over 21: 1; Total Whites: 6; Free Persons of Color: 13; Slaves: 26; Acres Cultivated: 3; Bales: 7; Average Weight per bale: 350 pounds. If the 13 free persons of color were black, 39 black folks were listed in the household of Jacob Fisher in 1820.

On February 24, 1830, Jacob Fisher entered 80 acres in Section 7 of Township 4 South and Range 3 West in Limestone County, Alabama. On June 28, 1831, Jacob entered an additional 160 acres in the same area (Cowart, 1984).

The 1830 Limestone County, Alabama United States Census listed the following for Jacob Fisher: White Males: under 5: 1, 10-15: 3, 15-20: 1, 40-50: 1; White Females: under 5: 2, 5-10: 1, 30-40: 1, 70-80: 1; Total Slaves: 31.

The 1840 Limestone County, Alabama, United States Census listed the following for Jacob Fisher: White males: 5-10: 1, 10-15: 1, 20-30: 3, 50-60: 1; White Females: under 5: 1, 10-15: 2, 15-20: 2, 40-50: 1; Slaves: 37, Number involved in agriculture: 18.

According to the 1850 Limestone County, Alabama, United States Census, House Number 279, Jacob Fisher was a 65-year-old white male born in North Carolina. Also in his household the following were listed: Martha Fisher, Female, 53, North Carolina; William Fisher, Male, 30, Alabama; Henry Fisher, Male, 28, Alabama; Luke Fisher, Male, 22, Alabama; Jacob Fisher, Male, 16, Alabama; Mary Fisher, Female, 10, Alabama; George Fisher, Male, 12, Alabama; Lovinna Fisher, Female, 8, Alabama; Stephen Chadich, Male, 32, Alabama; Martha Chadich, Female, 26, Alabama; Lina M. Chadich, Female, 1, Alabama; and John Fisher, Male, 80, North Carolina.

In the 1850 Limestone County, Alabama, Agricultural Census, Jacob Fisher does not have land listed but his farm value was $3,724. He also had $250 worth of farming equipment and livestock worth $2,215. According to the 1850 Limestone County Alabama, Slave Schedules, District 3, Jacob Fisher owned 20 black slaves, and Jonathan Fisher owned five slaves.

On December 15, 1876, Jacob Fisher died at the impressive age of 90 in Gregg County, Texas. The inscription on his tombstone reads, "Erected in 1966 by their Descendants." Jacob was the husband of Martha Fisher, and he was buried in Fisher Cemetery, Gregg County, Texas (Find A Grave Memorial# 5398827).

Fletcher Family

All the members of the Fletcher family (John, Richard, William, and Rebecca) that moved to North Alabama originally lived in Brunswick County,

Virginia. By 1810, they moved together to live in Madison County of Mississippi Territory. By 1818, it appears that most of the Fletchers were living in Limestone County, Alabama.

By 1809 based on land records, John, Richard, William, and Rebecca Fletcher Moore were family that migrated from Brunswick County, Virginia, to Madison County of Mississippi Territory. By 1818, most of their families had settled in Limestone County, Alabama. All of them except Richard have family listed in the 1809 land records of Madison County of Mississippi Territory. On March 1, 1817, Madison County would officially become a part of Alabama Territory.

John Jacob Fletcher

About 1761, John Jacob Fletcher was born in Brunswick County, Virginia. From 1784 through 1795, based on census and tax records, John lived in Surry County, North Carolina, before moving to Greenville County, South Carolina.

In 1801 while living in Greenville County, John Fletcher sold his property in Surry County, North Carolina. Two members of the family of Matthew Stewart, son-in-law of John, witnessed the deed.

In 1804, Matthew Stewart and Nathaniel Fletcher were together on the insolvent taxpayers list of Buncombe County, North Carolina. Later, members of the Stewart family were listed as the neighbors of John Fletcher in Greenville, South Carolina.

In 1809, John and his family moved to Madison County in Mississippi Territory which would later become Alabama in 1817. It is thought that part of the journey into Mississippi Territory by John Jacob Fletcher was by way of the French Broad River to the Tennessee River to Madison County.

On January 15, 1810, John Jacob Fletcher entered 160.4 acres in Section 3 and 161.4 in Section 32 of Township 3 South and Range 1 West in Madison County of Mississippi Territory. On January 9, 1816, John entered 39.75 acres in Section 10 of Township 3 South and Range 1 West in Madison County (Cowart, 1979).

On February 10, 1818, John Fletcher entered 158.64 acres in Section 9 of Township 4 South and Range 4West in Limestone County, Alabama. On May 25, 1831, John entered 158.2 acres in Section 17 of Township 4 South and Range 4West in Limestone County, Alabama (Cowart, 1984).

It appears that John Fletcher was married first to Rachel Middleton Myrick and later to Susannah Lowry; all were from Brunswick County, Virginia. John Jacob Fletcher had the following children:
1. Richard Fletcher was the son of John Fletcher and Rachel Middleton Myrick. On December 18, 1800, Richard Fletcher married Elizabeth Jones at Brunswick County, Virginia. The children of Richard and Elizabeth Jones Fletcher were Lucy C. Binns Fletcher (1801-2/20/1842) and Matthew M. Fletcher (1803-?). About 1833, Elizabeth Jones Fletcher died in Madison County, Alabama.
2. Nancy Fletcher (1785-1875) was the daughter of John and Susannah Fletcher; about 1801, Nancy married Matthew Stewart. In 1810, John Fletcher along with Nancy and Matthew Stewart, son-in-law of John Fletcher, were listed with taxable property in Madison County of Mississippi Territory. By 1818, John and Susannah Fletcher were neighbors to Matthew and Nancy Fletcher Stewart in Limestone County, Alabama. In 1822, Matthew died in Limestone County, Alabama. The children of Matthew and Nancy Stewart were in Orphans Court at Athens; Nancy was made guardian of her children. According to probate court records, the estate of Matthew was sold with his wife Nancy as executor. On May 23, 1831, Nancy Stewart (Stuart) owned 158.69 acres in Section 8 of Township 4 South and Range 4 West in Limestone County, Alabama. The land of Nancy was adjacent to her father John Jacob Fletcher and her uncle William Fletcher; both her father and uncle owned land in Section 9 of Township 4 South and Range 4 West. About 1875, Nancy died in Limestone County, Alabama
3. William Fletcher
4. Edward Fletcher
5. Nathaniel Fletcher

According to the 1820 Limestone County, Alabama Census, John Fletcher owned seven black slaves. On December 11, 1831, John Jacob Fletcher died in Limestone County, Alabama.

Richard Fletcher

Richard Fletcher married Nancy Ann Fletcher. Richard Fletcher moved to North Alabama with family members including John Jacob Fletcher, William Fletcher, and Rebecca Fletcher Moore. Richard did not live long after moving to Madison County in Mississippi Territory.

Fletcher, James Nicholas - Aspen Dell

On September 1, 1786, James Nicholas Fletcher was born to Richard and Nancy Ann Fletcher in Brunswick County, Virginia. In the 1810 Brunswick County, Virginia, United States Census, James Nicholas Fletcher was living in the Meherrin Parish.

James Nicholas Fletcher (1785-1869) and his first wife had the following children:
1. John James Fletcher (1806-1884)
2. Edward A. Fletcher (1808-after 1870)

In March 1826, James Nicholas Fletcher married Matilda G. Golden Cheatham in Chesterfield County, Virginia. Matilda was born on January 10, 1808, in Chesterfield County, Virginia. James Nicholas Fletcher (1786-1869) and Matilda Golden Cheatham Fletcher (1808-1883) had the following children:

1. Dr. Richard Matthew Fletcher was born on April 1, 1830, and he married Martha Rebecka Mason (1832-1910). According to the 1860 Limestone County, Alabama, Slave Schedules, Richard M. Fletcher owned 14 black slaves. Richard died on June 17, 1906, and he was buried in Maple Hill Cemetery (Find A Grave Memorial# 86333931).
2. Mary Branch Fletcher was born in 1831, and she died in 1858.
3. Captain Algernon Sydenham Fletcher was born on April 8, 1833, in Chesterfield County, Virginia; in 1867, he married Matilda Holding

(1838-1931). Algernon died on October 8, 1908, and he is buried at Maple Hill Cemetery (Find A Grave Memorial# 62047587)
4. William Edward Fletcher was born in 1837.
5. Peter Beasley Fletcher was born in Limestone County, Alabama on March 19, 1840. On May 6, 1920, Peter died in Birmingham, Alabama, and he is buried at Maple Hill Cemetery (Find A Grave Memorial# 86360018).
6. James Lockhart Fletcher Sr. was born on June 25, 1845, in Limestone County, and in 1873, he married Elizabeth G. Howard (1853-1933). On May 18, 1927, James died in Birmingham, and he is buried in the Elmwood Cemetery (Find A Grave Memorial# 189459846).
7. Walter Scott Fletcher was born on June 1, 1849, and in 1883, he married Mary E. Beasley (1847-1919) and Alexander Allardyce (Unknown-1944). Walter died on November 29, 1927, and he is buried in Maple Hill Cemetery (Find A Grave Memorial# 13894859).

Between 1835 and 1836, James Nicholas Fletcher and his two older sons, John James Fletcher and Edward A. Fletcher, arrived in Limestone County, Alabama, from their home State of Virginia. James and his family moved to North Alabama, to be near his extensive family many of whom arrived in Mississippi Territory by 1809.

James Nicholas Fletcher and his family settled on a place near the Limestone-Madison County lines that he initially called Aspen Dell. Later, the place was referred to as Nubbin Ridge because the land was so poor that corn would only produce nubbins.

On April 8, 1833, his son Algernon Sydenham Fletcher was born in Chesterfield County, Virginia, and on March 19, 1840, his son Peter Beasley Fletcher was born in Limestone County, Alabama. Based on birth records of the children of James Nicholas Fletcher, John James Fletcher, and Edward A. Fletcher, the James Nicholas Fletcher family arrived in Limestone County by 1836.

The 1840 Limestone County, Alabama, United States Census listed James N. Fletcher with 30 black slaves. Prior to 1840, James was not listed in Limestone County census records.

According to the 1850 Limestone County, Alabama, United States Census, House Number 302, James Nicholas Fletcher was a 62-year-old white male born in Virginia. Also listed in his household were: Matilda G. Fletcher, Female, 38, Virginia; Richard M. Fletcher, Male, 19, Virginia; Algernon L. Fletcher, Male, 17, Virginia; William E. Fletcher, Male, 13, Alabama; Peter B. Fletcher, Male, 10, Alabama; James L. Fletcher, Male, 6, Alabama; and Walter S. Fletcher, Male, 1, Alabama.

According to the 1850 Limestone County, Alabama, Slave Schedule, James N. Fletcher owned 78 black slaves. In 1850, the two older sons of James N. Fletcher, John James Fletcher and Edward A. Fletcher, combined owned 80 slaves; therefore, the father and his two sons owned a total of 158 black slaves in 1850.

In the 1850 Limestone County, Alabama, Agricultural Census, James Nicholas Fletcher owned 100 acres of improved land and 420 acres of unimproved land valued at $17,000. He also had $500 worth of farming equipment and livestock worth $2,600.

According to the 1860 Limestone County, Alabama United States Census, James N. Fletcher was a 73-year-old white male born in Virginia. Also listed in his household were: Matilda Fletcher, Female, 52, Virginia; William E. Fletcher, Male, 22, Alabama; James L. Fletcher, Male, 15, Alabama; Walter S. Fletcher, Male, 10 Alabama, (illegible) Fletcher, Female, 10, Alabama; (illegible) Fletcher, Female, 8 Alabama.

In the 1860 Limestone County, Alabama, Slave Schedule: James N. Fletcher owned 103 black slaves. In 1860, the father and his two older sons owned 191 black slaves. They were farmers that used black slave labor to plow, cultivate, and harvest their cotton and other crops.

James N. Fletcher was listed in the United States Civil War Confederate Papers of Citizens or Businesses. Many times, during the Civil War, which lasted from April 12, 1861, through May 13, 1865, the Fletcher family had Union troops passing or staying nearby.

Octavia Fletcher Frazieruring in her book <u>Dr. Richard Matthew Fletcher, 1830-1906, A Sketch of his Life and Works</u> describes an account of her father and grandfather Fletcher during the war as follows. "During the last year of the Civil War, Richard was sitting on the porch at Aspen Dell (name of the plantation to "Nubbin Ridge") with his father. James told his son to get a ladder and see if he could work out a knot from the top of one of the eight wooden columns of the porch by putting a small nail partially into it. Richard was able to do the job, and then his father disappeared for a while and came back with a sack containing $10,000 in gold coins. He told Richard to drop the gold into the knothole, from which the coins fell to the bottom of the inside of the column. Then Richard removed the nail and glued the knot back into the hole. Every time thereafter that the Union troops came to search for money and other valuables, James would take his rocking chair and lean back against that column while talking with the searchers. After the war, a hole was cut into the bottom of the column, and the money saved many local Confederates from starvation and foreclosure."

On August 13, 1869, James Nicholas Fletcher died. He was buried in the Maple Hill Cemetery at Huntsville in Madison County, Alabama (Find A Grave Memorial# 86359937).

On April 1, 1883, Matilda G. Golden Cheatham Fletcher died in Limestone County. She was buried at Maple Hill Cemetery in Section 9 and Row 8 at Huntsville in Madison County, Alabama (Find A Grave Memorial# 86359965). The following is the inscription on the tombstone of Matilda G. Golden Cheatham Fletcher: "Wife of James N. Fletcher. Our Mother. Her children rise up and call her blessed."

The Fletcher family plot includes James N. Fletcher, Dr. Richard M. Fletcher, Rebecca M. Fletcher, Matilda G. Fletcher, P. B. Fletcher, James Nicholson Fletcher, and "Little Howard" Fletcher.

Fletcher, John James

About 1806, John James Fletcher was born to James Nicholas Fletcher and his first wife (1786-1825) in Virginia. Based on census records, it appears that John James Fletcher had several children by his first wife:
1. Susan Fletcher, born 1831.

2. Delia C. Fletcher, born 1831.
3. Ann M. Fletcher, born 1833.
4. Eliza N. Fletcher, born 1836.
5. Mary E. Fletcher, born 1838.
6. Lucy C. Fletcher, born 1840.

Between 1833 and 1836, based on birth records given in the census of Ann and Eliza Fletcher, John James Fletcher moved from Virginia to Limestone County, Alabama. In 1840, John James Fletcher was first listed in the census of Limestone County, Alabama.

According to the 1840 Limestone County, Alabama, United States Census, John J. Fletcher owned 20 black slaves. He appears to have a relative named John Jacob Fletcher who entered land in 1810 in Madison County and 1818 in Limestone County.

On July 18, 1844, John James Fletcher married the second time to Fidelia S. Cheatham in Limestone County, Alabama. John James Fletcher and Fidelia Cheatham Fletcher had the following children:
7. John J. Fletcher, born 1846.
8. James Fletcher, born 1854.
9. Mattie Fletcher, born 1857.

According to the 1850 Limestone County, Alabama, United States Census, Household 538, John James Fletcher was a 44-year-old white male born in Virginia. Also listed in his household was Delia C. Fletcher, Female, 19, Virginia; Ann M. Fletcher, Female, 17, Virginia; Eliza N. Fletcher, Female, 14, Alabama; Mary E. Fletcher, Female, 12, Alabama; Lucy C. Fletcher, Female, 10, Alabama; and John J. Fletcher, Male, 4, Alabama.

In the 1850 Limestone County, Alabama, Slave Schedules, John James Fletcher owned 39 black slaves. Together, John James Fletcher, his brother, and father owned 158 black slaves in 1850.

In the 1860 Limestone County, Alabama, Slave Schedules, John James Fletcher owned 27 black slaves. John James Fletcher combined with his father and brother owned 191 black slaves in 1860.

In 1866, John James Fletcher is listed in the Alabama State Census as living in Limestone County, Alabama. After the Civil War, John J. Fletcher felt the hardships of cotton farming without the assistance of his black slaves.

According to the 1870 Limestone County, Alabama, United States Census, John James Fletcher was a 63-year-old white male born in Virginia. Also living in his household was the following: Ann M. Fletcher, Female, 34, Virginia; Eliza N. Fletcher, Female, 32, Virginia; Mary E. Fletcher, Female, 29, Alabama; Susan Fletcher, Female, 39, Alabama; James Fletcher, Male, 16, Alabama; and Mattie Fletcher, Female, 13, Alabama.

According to the 1880 Limestone County, Alabama, United States Census, John James Fletcher was a 74-year-old widowed white male farmer born in Virginia. The census indicates that his father and mother were born in Virginia. Also in his household was S. F. Moore, Daughter, Female, 42, Alabama; John M. Fletcher, Husband, Male, 59, Alabama; and John R. Fletcher, Son, Male, 1, Alabama.

About 1884, John James Fletcher died in Limestone County, Alabama. The location of his grave is not known.

Fletcher, Edward A.

About 1808, Edward A. Fletcher was born to James Nicholas Fletcher and his first wife (1786-1825) in Brunswick County, Virginia. Based on census records, Edward A. Fletcher and his first wife had the following children:
1. John R. Fletcher, born 1833.
2. Nathan Fletcher, born 1835.
3. James E. Fletcher, born 1838.

Between 1835 and 1838, based on birth records given in the census of Nathan and James E. Fletcher, Edward A. Fletcher moved from Virginia to Limestone County, Alabama. By 1836, Edward's family appears to be in Limestone County. In 1840, Edward A. Fletcher was first listed in the census of Limestone County, Alabama.

In 1840 Limestone County, Alabama, United States Census, Edward A. Fletcher owned 18 black slaves. His father owned 30 slaves and his brother owned 20 slaves. Together, they had 68 black slaves in 1840.

On November 16, 1842, Edward A. Fletcher married Rebecca J. Fletcher Moore in Limestone County, Alabama. Based on census records, Edward and Rebecca had the following children.
4. Milton Fletcher, born 1845.
5. Ann R. Fletcher, born 1846.
6. Ernest (Emmett) Fletcher, born 1850.
7. Lucy Fletcher, born 1852.
8. Milton Fletcher, born 1856.
9. Eliza Fletcher, born 1860.

According to the 1850 Limestone County, Alabama, United States Census, Household 537, Edward A. Fletcher is a 42-year-old white male from Virginia. The following were living in his household: Rebecca J. Fletcher, Female, 28, Alabama; John R. Fletcher, Male, 17, North Carolina; Nathan Fletcher, Male, 15, North Carolina; James E. Fletcher, Male, 12, Alabama; Milton Fletcher, Male, 5, Alabama; Ann R. Fletcher, Female, 4, Alabama; Ernest Fletcher, Male, 0, Alabama.

In the 1850 Limestone County, Alabama, Slave Schedules, Edward A. Fletcher owned 41 black slaves. Combined with his father and brother, they owned 158 black slaves in 1850.

In the 1850 Limestone County, Alabama, Agricultural Census, Edward A. Fletcher owned 500 acres of improved land and 500 acres of unimproved land valued at $600. He also had $670 worth of farming equipment and livestock worth $1,969.

The 1860 Limestone County, Alabama, United States Census, Household 304 listed the following: Edward A. Fletcher, Male, 52, White, Kentucky; Rebecca J. Fletcher, Female, 38, Alabama; John R. Fletcher, Male, 27, North Carolina; Ann R. Fletcher, Female, 13, Alabama; Emmet Fletcher, Male, 10, Alabama; Lucy Fletcher, Female, 8, Alabama; Milton Fletcher, Male, 4, Alabama; Eliza Fletcher, Female, 0 Alabama.

According to the 1860 Limestone County, Alabama, Largest Slave Owners, Edward A. Fletcher owned 61 slaves. Combined with his father and brother, they owned 191 black slaves in 1860.

The 1870 Limestone County, Alabama United States Census had the following: Edward A. Fletcher, Male, 62, White, Virginia; Rebecca Fletcher, Female, 40, Alabama; John R. Fletcher, Male, 37, North Carolina; Ann R Fletcher, Female, 20 Alabama; Eliza Bradley, Female, 32, Alabama; Lucy Fletcher, Female, 17, Alabama.

William Fletcher

On July 30, 1771, William Fletcher was born in Brunswick County, Virginia. William married Sarah Burcham; Sarah was born in August 1780 in Surrey County, North Carolina. The parents of Sarah Burcham were John Henry Burcham who was born in 1736 in Surrey County, North Carolina, and Roseanne Swearingen who was born in 1738 in Frederick County, Virginia.

On August 10, 1811, William Fletcher entered 164.5 acres in Section 27 of Township 1 South and Range 1 East in Madison County of Mississippi Territory. On October 25, 1814, William entered 82.25 acres in Section 27 of Township 1 South and Range 1 East in Madison County of Mississippi Territory (Cowart, 1979).

On October 24, 1829, Susannah Fletcher married William Gray Buchanan in Madison County, Alabama. Susannah Fletcher, who was born about 1799, was the daughter of William and Sarah Burcham Fletcher.

On October 10, 1843, William Fletcher died in Limestone County, Alabama. The location of his burial is not known.

Gamble, James Hurt - Oak Mount

On March 8, 1791, James Hurt Gamble was born near Nashville in Davidson County, Tennessee. He was the only child of Edmund (1759-1824) and Mary Hurt Gamble (1764-8/16/1828). Edmund was buried in Davidson County, Tennessee, and Mary Hurt Gamble was buried at Oak Mount Plantation in the Gamble Family Cemetery in Limestone County, Alabama (Find A Grave Memorial# 63704437).

James Hurt Gamble was a veteran of the War of 1812. He served under the command of General Andrew Jackson.

On February 10, 1818, James Hurt Gamble entered 159.97 acres in Section 1 of Township 5 South and Range 4 West in Limestone County, Alabama. The land James entered was adjacent to his future father-in-law George Dillard who entered the adjacent tract on February 7, 1818.

On January 12, 1819, James married Huldah Jones Dillard; she was born on May 25, 1802, in Tennessee. Huldah was the daughter of George Dillard and Ann C. Jones.

James was a cotton planter and slave owner at Oak Mount Plantation in Limestone County, Alabama, just west of Belle Mina Plantation. All the children of James Hurt Gamble and Huldah Jones Dillard were born at Oak Mount Plantation, and they are buried in the Gamble Family Cemetery in Limestone County, Alabama, west of Belle Mina:

1. Mary Hurt Gamble Duncan was born on February 12, 1821. On July 21, 1836, Mary married James Madison Duncan. On October 28, 1813, James was born in Greene County, Tennessee, and died on December 12, 1902 (Find A Grave Memorial# 32893560). Mary was a homemaker and mother of two children: Benjamin and Mary. On June 21, 1841, Mary Hurt Gamble Duncan died at 19 years of age (Find A Grave Memorial# 63522476).
2. Ann Eliza Gamble Kimbell was born on February 19, 1823. On October 27, 1840, she married Henry Warren Kimbell. They had three children: James G. Kimbell (1841-1847), Mary Ann Kimbell (1843-

1844), and Lawrence Dillard Kimbell (1846-1847). On November 19, 1858, Ann Eliza Gamble Kimbell died at 35 years of age (Find A Grave Memorial# 63704479). Henry owned 28 slaves in 1850 and 38 slaves in 1860. On July 6, 1878, Henry W. Kimbell died, and he was buried in the Gamble Cemetery (Find A Grave Memorial# 63704468).
3. James Edmund Gamble was born on March 29, 1825, and he died on September 29, 1826 (Find A Grave Memorial# 63704425).
4. George Dillard Gamble was born on July 9, 1827. He died December 17, 1831, at four years of age (Find A Grave Memorial# 63704327).
5. Ruffin Coleman Gamble was born on August 30, 1832. On November 27, 1855, Ruffin married Helen Perina Girault in Tallahatchie County, Mississippi. She was born at Elliot in Tallahatchie County, Mississippi, on March 20, 1835. Helen was the daughter of James Augustus Girault and Susan Dunbar. On August 13, 1914, Helen died at 79 years of age. She was buried alongside her husband in the Gamble Family Cemetery.
6. John Hicks Gamble was born on April 27, 1839. He married Fannie E. Smythe on September 27, 1860. John fought in Civil War and was wounded near Murphreesboro, Tennessee, while serving in Company B, 14th Alabama Cavalry in the Confederate States Army. He was captured, and on December 31, 1862, at 23 years of age, John Hicks Gamble died as prisoner of war at a prison camp in Alton, Illinois. His remains were returned home, and he was buried in the Gamble Family Cemetery (Find A Grave Memorial# 63704375).

From December 3, 1829, through February 10, 1837, James Hurt Gamble entered 1,036.16 acres of land in Townships 3, 5 South and Ranges 3, 4 West in Limestone County, Alabama. On June 1, 1835, James entered one 80-acre tract with his father-in-law George Dillard in Section 13 of Township 5 South and Range 4 West in Limestone County, Alabama (Cowart, 1984).

According to the 1830 Limestone County, Alabama Censuses, James Hurt Gamble owned 37 black slaves. In the 1840 Limestone County, Alabama Censuses, James H. Gamble was listed as owning 50 black slaves.

The 1850 Limestone County, Alabama, Slave Schedules had James H. Gamble owning 93 black slaves. In 1850, his son Ruffin owned 20 black slaves;

therefore, father and son owned a total of 113 black at Oak Mount Plantation in Limestone County, Alabama.

According to the 1850 Limestone County, Alabama, Agricultural Census, James H. Gamble owned 1,000 acres of improved land and 750 acres of unimproved land valued at$16,000. He also had $375 worth of farming equipment and livestock worth $3,230.

According to the 1850 Limestone County, Alabama, United States Census, House Number 363, James H. Gamble was a 59-year-old white male born in Tennessee. Also, living in his household was the following: Huldy J. Gamble, Female, 49, Virginia; Ruffin C. Gamble, Male, 17, Alabama; John H. Gamble, Male, 11, Alabama.

On July 7, 1854, Huldah Jones Gamble died at 52 years of age. Her body was interred in the family cemetery at Oak Mount Plantation in Limestone County, Alabama.

The tombstone of Huldah has the following inscription: "Wife of Jas. H. Gamble, Born May 25, 1802, and died in the full triumph of the Christian faith, Blesed are the dead that die in the Lord. Her flesh will slumber in the ground. Till the last trumpets joyful sound; Then burst the tomb with sweet surprise, And in her Saviours image rise. Huldah was buried in the Gamble Cemetery in Limestone County, Alabama (Find A Grave Memorial# 63704401).

On March 8, 1855, James Hurt Gamble died at Oak Mount Plantation in Limestone County, Alabama, at 64 years of age. His body was interred in the Gamble Family Cemetery at Oak Mount Plantation in Limestone County, Alabama (Find A Grave Memorial# 63704384).

According to the 1860 Limestone County, Alabama, Slave Schedule, the sons of the deceased James Hurt Gamble were slave owners. John Hicks Gamble owned 54 black slaves, and his brother Ruffin Coleman Gamble owned 50 black slaves. Together, the two brothers owned 104 slaves that they probably inherited from their father James Hurt Gamble.

James Madison Duncan

On October 28, 1813, James Madison Duncan was born in Greene County, Tennessee. His father was Benjamin Duncan of Botetourt County, Virginia. In 1812, Benjamin Duncan married Nancy Ross, daughter of William Ross, in East Tennessee.

In November 1822, Benjamin and Nancy Duncan moved to Limestone County, Alabama, from Greene County, Tennessee. James M. Duncan grew up in Limestone County, Alabama.

In 1834, as some other residents of Limestone County, Benjamin and Nancy moved to Shelby County, Tennessee, near Memphis. In 1836, Nancy Ross Duncan died in Shelby County, Tennessee. After his wife died, Benjamin married the second time. On June 1, 1860, Benjamin Duncan died in Shelby County, Tennessee.

On July 21, 1836, James M. Duncan first married Mary H. Gamble. In 1836, he started his career as a merchant at Mooresville in Limestone County, Alabama. In the spring of 1840, James M. Duncan went to Grenada County, Mississippi, to administer the estate of George Dillard, the grandfather of his wife Mary.

On June 21, 1840, Mary Gamble Duncan, wife of James M. Duncan, died leaving two children: Benjamin and Mary. Benjamin served in the Civil War as a member of the battery of Captain Stanford, and he died on April 6, 1880, in Grenada, Mississippi. Mary died young in Alabama.

In the 1840 Limestone County, Alabama Census, James M. Duncan was listed as owning eight black slaves. In the fall of 1840, James M. Duncan moved to Grenada, Mississippi, and settled near the old Town of Chocchuma. James become a wealthy Mississippi cotton planter owning some 2,300 acres of excellent farming land and 93 black slaves.

On July 26, 1849, James M. Duncan married Mrs. Susan Augusta Girault Sykes, widow of Dr. J. B. Sykes; she was born on October 19, 1832; the parents of Susan were James A. Girault and Susan Dunbar Girault, early settlers of

Limestone County, Alabama. On February 6, 1818, James A. Girault acquired 160 acres in Section 27 of Township 4 South and Range 3 West in Limestone County, Alabama. James and Susan Duncan had nine children.

The following was found in the Limestone County, Alabama, Orphans' Court Minutes, Book 1835-1843: "Aug. 20, 1838, George Dillard died intestate, James M. Dunkin admin, bond $80,000, security, James H. Gamble and Ann Dillard; appr. Thomas H. Thack, Robert Prebles, James Word, James Woodruff, Jonathan Fisher."

On December 12, 1902, James Madison Duncan died at Grenada in Grenada County, Mississippi. He was buried at Odd Fellows Cemetery (Find A Grave Memorial# 32893560).

Ruffin Coleman Gamble

The children of Ruffin Coleman Gamble and Helen Perina Girault Gamble were born at Oak Mount Plantation in Limestone County, Alabama, just west of Belle Mina:
1. James Augustus Gamble was born on October 15, 1856. He died December 22, 1875, at 19 years of age and was buried in the Gamble Family Cemetery.
2. Sue Huldah Gamble was born on August 14, 1858. She died September 27, 1863, at five years of age and was buried in the Gamble Family Cemetery.
3. John Girault Gamble was born on February 18, 1860. He married Kate Garrett on October 26, 1892. Kate was born in Limestone County, Alabama on July 2, 1871. She died August 20, 1908, at Tanner in Limestone County, at 37 years of age. John Girault Gamble died on March 17, 1917, at 57 years of age and was buried in the Gamble Family Cemetery.
4. Dunbar Thach Gamble was born on September 11, 1861. He died May 27, 1879, at 17 years of age and was buried in the Gamble Family Cemetery.
5. Ann Eliza Gamble was on November 2, 1863. She died July 12, 1868, at four years of age, and she was buried in the Gamble Family Cemetery.

6. Katie Gamble was born in 1864 and died the same year at less than one year of age. She was buried in the Gamble Family Cemetery.
7. Mary Gamble was born on December 30, 1866. She married William Edmond Nethery (1863-1910). On June 7, 1953, Mary Gamble Nethery died at Jonesboro in Craighead County, Arkansas, and was buried there at Oaklawn Cemetery.
8. Edmond Gamble was born on March 30, 1869. He died on October 29, 1871, at two years old and was buried in the Gamble Family Cemetery.
9. Robert Wade Gamble was born on April 13, 1871. Robert died on October 8, 1874, at three years of age, and he was buried in the Gamble Family Cemetery.
10. Francis Perine Gamble was born on October 15, 1873. He married Anna Tiffee Safford on February 7, 1924, and she died before 1930. About 1833, he married Pansy. On December 19, 1949, Francis died in California at 76 years of age, and he was buried at Willows in Glenn County, California.
11. Helen "Nell" Girault Gamble was born on June 15, 1876. On June 1, 1900, she married Harry Edgar Wheeler, a minister who was born in Pennsylvania, on May 18, 1874. On March 7, 1954, Helen died at 77 years of age.
12. Ruffin Coleman Gamble Jr. was born on March 15, 1878. He died on November 25, 1878, at less than one year of age, and was buried in the Gamble Family Cemetery.

During the Civil War, Ruffin was a private in Company C, 9th Alabama Cavalry of the Confederate States Army. After the war, Ruffin resumed life as a cotton farmer at Oak Mount Plantation just west of Belle Mina in Limestone County, Alabama.

On June 16, 1909, Ruffin Coleman Gamble Sr. died at Oak Mount at 76 years of age. He was buried in the Gamble Family Cemetery at Oak Mount Plantation.

Garrett, Jesse

In 1816, Jesse Garrett was born in Madison County of Mississippi Territory. His folks had migrated to Madison County of Mississippi Territory from North Carolina.

In the 1850, Limestone County, Alabama, Agricultural Census, Jesse Garrett owned 1,060 acres of improved land and 413 acres of unimproved land. His real estate was worth $2,600, and his farm equipment was valued at $620 and livestock at $3,635.

According to the 1850 Limestone County, Alabama, United States Census, House Number 275, Jesse Garrett was a 34-year-old white male born in Madison County, Alabama. Also living in his household was the following: C. E. Garrett, Female, 63, North Carolina; Lewis Garrett, Male, 33 Alabama; Nancy Garrett, Female, 21, Alabama; Joseph Garrett, Male, 11, Alabama; Mary Garrett, Female, 8, Alabama; John Garrett, Male, 4, Alabama.

According to the 1850 Limestone County, Alabama, Agricultural Census, Jesse Garrett owned 1,060 acres of improved land and 413 acres of unimproved land valued at $2,600. He also had $620 worth of farming equipment and livestock worth $3,635. According to the 1850 Limestone County, Alabama, Slave Schedule, Jesse Garrett owned 90 black slaves.

Garrett, Edmond

In 1786, Edmond Garrett was in Buckingham, Virginia, to Isaac Ayers Garrett and Mary Elizabeth Agee (1762-1803). In 1807, Edmond Garrett married Sarah "Sallie" Gough; in 1789, she was born in Buckingham, Virginia. They had the following children:
1. Isaac Garrett was born in 1806 in Buckingham County, Virginia.
2. Sarah Judith Garrett was born in 1808 in Buckingham County, Virginia; she died between 1854 and 1855 in Lawrence County, Alabama.

3. Peter Francisco Garrett was born April 25, 1810, in Buckingham County, Virginia.
4. Nicholas Garrett was born in 1813 in Buckingham County, Virginia. He died in 1869 in Galveston, Texas.
5. William H. Garrett was born on March 9, 1816, in Buckingham County, Virginia. According to the 1850 Limestone County, Alabama, Agricultural Census, William H. Garrett owned 500 acres of improved land and 220 acres of unimproved land valued at $7,920. He also had $275 worth of farming equipment and livestock worth $640. On February 22, 1875, he died in Limestone County, Alabama, and was buried in Athens City Cemetery (Find A Grave Memorial# 29061670).
6. Edmond Agee Garrett was born on March 3, 1818, in Buckingham County, Virginia. Edmond A. married Elizabeth Marie Greer (11/6/1826-6/7/1864); she was buried in Athens City Cemetery (Find A Grave Memorial# 39540474). On May 24, 1856. Edmond Agee Garrett died in Limestone County, Alabama, and was buried in the Athens City Cemetery (Find A Grave Memorial# 41584741).

In the 1810 Buckingham County, Virginia, United States Census, Edmond Garrett was the owner of 13 black slaves. The 1816 Turkey Town Treaty ceded Indian land claims in northwest Alabama and caused a mass migration of cotton farmers out of Virginia which became known as Alabama Fever. Edmond Garrett was one of those Virginia cotton planters who got the fever to move south; therefore, he began looking for better cotton land in Alabama

Sometime prior to February 1818, it appears that the Edmond Garrett made the trip from Buckingham County, Virginia, to Limestone County, Alabama, where he entered land. On February 10, 1818, Edmond Garrett entered 319.8 acres in Section 36 of Township 4 South and Range 4 West in Limestone County, Alabama (Cowart, 1984).

According to the 1820 Buckingham County, Virginia, United States Census, Edmond Garrett was listed with 23 black slaves. In 1830, Edmond was listed in the Limestone County, Alabama Census with 22 black slaves.

On March 8, 1830, Edmond Garrett entered an adjacent 159.9 acres in Section 36 of Township 4 South and Range 4 West in Limestone County, Alabama (Cowart, 1984). The land Edmond entered was adjacent to 160.9 acres that had been entered on February 10, 1818, by Benjamin Peete, who became the father-in-law of his son Peter F. Garrett. Edmond Garrett built his home on Piney Bluff high above the banks of Piney Creek in Limestone County, Alabama.

On October 18, 1834, Edmond Garrett entered two additional tracts of land in Limestone County, Alabama: 79 acres in Section 26 of Township 5 South and Range 3 West and 80.4 acres in Section 26 of Township 4 south and Range 4 West (Cowart, 1984).

According to the 1850 Limestone County, Alabama, United States Census, Edmond Garrett was a 64-year-old white from Virginia. Also living in his household were the following: Sarah Gough Garrett, Female, 62, Virginia; Edmond A. Garrett, Male, 32; Elizabeth Maria Greer Garrett, Female, 24, Tennessee; and Maria Garrett, Female, 11 months, Alabama. Also, in the census in adjacent households was the following: Peter F. Garrett, Male, 39, Virginia; and, William H. Garrett, Male, 34, Virginia.

According to the 1850 Limestone County, Alabama, Agricultural Census, Edmond Garrett owned 400 acres of improved land and 240 acres of unimproved land valued at $9,600. He also had $405 worth of farming equipment and livestock worth $1,614.

On August 17, 1850, Sarah Sallie Gough Garrett died in Limestone County, Alabama. Sarah was buried in the Athens City Cemetery (Find A Grave Memorial# 29061663).

On September 5, 1850, Edmond Garrett died at Belle Mina in Limestone County, Alabama. Edmond was buried in the Athens City Cemetery (Find A Grave Memorial# 29061656).

Garrett, Peter Francisco - The Cedars

Peter Francisco Garrett, son of Edmond and Sallie Gough Garrett, married Mary Goodson Peete (12/10/1832-7/10/1884). Mary was the daughter of

Benjamin Blount Peete and Darthula English. A crossroads two miles north of Belle Mina on the farm of Benjamin Peete became known as Peete's Corner.

Peter Francisco Garrett and Mary Goodson Peete Garrett had the following children:
1. Edmond Peete Garrett was born on August 21, 1859. He married Augusta Bibb, daughter of David Porter Bibb of Woodside; she was born on January 8, 1871 and died on July 30, 1949. Augusta is buried in the Athens City Cemetery (Find A Grave Memorial# 29797081). On June 18, 1918, Edmond Peete Garrett died and was buried in Athens City Cemetery (Find A Grave Memorial# 29061621).
2. Frank Garrett (1861-1862) died very young in Limestone County, Alabama.
3. Mary Orline Garrett Hine was born on February 24, 1864; she married Thomas E. Hine on January 9, 1897. Mary Orline Garrett Hine died on September 18, 1897, and she was buried in the Athens City Cemetery (Find A Grave Memorial# 41273406).
4. Thomas Thatch Garrett was born on March 10, 1866. Thomas Thatch Garrett died on March 23, 1945 and was buried in the Athens City Cemetery (Find A Grave Memorial# 29061648).
5. Kate W. Garrett Gamble was born on July 2, 1871; she married John Girault Gamble on October 26, 1892, in Limestone County, Alabama. Kate W. Garrett Gamble died on August 20, 1908 and was buried in the Athens City Cemetery (Find A Grave Memorial# 38841333).

In the 1850 Limestone County, Alabama, slave Schedules, Peter F. Garrett owned 19 black slaves, and his brother William H. Garrett owned 21 slaves. Their father, Edmond, owned 41 slaves; therefore, in 1850, the father and his two sons owned a total of 81 slaves.

According to the 1850 Limestone County, Alabama, Agricultural Census, Peter Francisco Garrett, son of Edmond Garrett, owned 220 acres of improved land and 400 acres of unimproved land valued at $7,536. He also had $550 worth of farming equipment and livestock worth $1,036.

In 1859 with the help of slave labour, Peter Francisco Garrett built a 5,000 square foot plantation house for his wife, Mary Goodson Peete Garrett. The house was built with slave made materials and bricks all of which came from the plantation. Because of the numerous cedar trees that had been planted in the area, the home became known as The Cedars and was located on Garrett Road a few miles west of Belle Mina. However, within four years, Union soldiers took over the home and farm during the Civil War; they destroyed some of the unique features of the house.

In the 1860 Limestone County, Alabama, Slave Schedules, Peter F. Garrett owned 34 black slaves. His father had died in 1850, and he controlled the large antebellum estate.

On July 10, 1884, Mary Goodson Peete Garrett died in Limestone County. Mary was buried in Athens City Cemetery (Find A Grave Memorial# 41273252).

The Cedars

On January 24, 1894, Peter Francisco Garrett died at The Cedars at Belle Mina in Limestone County, Alabama. Peter was buried in the Athens City Cemetery (Find A Grave Memorial# 41273202).

Harris, Captain John Henry - Flower Hill

On August 3, 1778, John Henry Harris was born in Albemarle County, Virginia. His parents were Matthew Harris and Elizabeth Tate of Albemarle County, Virginia. John Henry Harris was a captain in the War of 1812.

On March 18, 1805, John Henry Harris married Frances Rowzee in Madison, Virginia. On April 12, 1781, Frances Rowzee was born to John Rowzee and Isabella Miller of Essex County, Virginia.

John Henry Harris and Frances Rowzy Harris had the following children:
1. Sarah Ann Harris Roberts (1806-1871) (Find A Grave Memorial# 76005429).
2. Matthew Harris (1808-1824).
3. John R. Harris (1810-1863) (Find A Grave Memorial# 76006451).
4. Caroline "Carolyn" Harris Gamble (1815-1837).
5. Elizabeth Tate Harris Washington (1818-1893).
6. Benjamin M. Harris (1820-1837) (Find A Grave Memorial# 76005963).
7. Schuyler Harris (1823-1880) (Find A Grave Memorial# 76006317).
8. Isabella Virginia Harris Pryor (1826-1889) (Find A Grave Memorial# 39560184).

By 1818 based on land records, it appears that John Henry Harris came from Virginia to Limestone County, Alabama, in order to enter cotton land. From February 10, 1818, through September 1, 1818, John Henry Harris entered 1,515.53 acres in Township 4 South and Ranges 4, 5 West in Limestone County, Alabama. On May 23, 1828, he entered another 79.87 acres in Section 28 of Township 4 South and Range 4 West in Limestone County, Alabama (Cowart, 1984).

In February 1818, several members of the English family entered land in Limestone County, Alabama. Some of the English land was adjacent to the property owned by John Henry Harris.

According to the 1820 Limestone County, Alabama Census, James English owned 14 black slaves and Patrick English owned 12 slaves. The English Spring just east of the Flower Hill Plantation home of John Henry Harris; the spring was named in honor of the English family.

According to the Limestone County, Alabama Census records, John H. Harris owned 26 black slaves in 1820. John owned 47 slaves in 1830, and in 1840, he owned 66 slaves.

On September 10, 1843, John H. Harris of Flower Hill Plantation in Limestone County died. However, another John H. Harris in Limestone County was listed with 82 slaves in 1850 and 83 slaves in 1860; therefore, the following are three possible explanations:
1. The 1850-1860 slaves may have been identified as the estate of John Henry Harris.
2. The 1850-1860 slaves of John H. Harris in Limestone County may actually be John Hunter Harris from Lawrence County who married Susan Smith of Limestone County, the daughter of Gabriel and Mary Smith. In the Lawrence County records, John Hunter Harris owned 0 slaves in 1830, 13 slaves in 1840, 99 slaves in 1850, and 183 slaves in 1860.
3. The 1850-1860 slaves of John H. Harris may be those of John H. Harris of Mooresville in Limestone County, Alabama. On January 3, 1845, the Secretary of State tract book had John H. Harris entering 80.61 acres in Section 23 of Township 4 South and Range 4 West in Limestone County, Alabama (Cowart, 1984). From 1860 through 1861, John H. Harris of Mooresville in Limestone County, Alabama, attended LaGrange Military Academy in Franklin County. In 1863 during the Civil War, Captain John H. Harris was killed in Mississippi, and he was returned to Mooresville in Limestone County, Alabama, for burial.

On July 13, 1842, Frances Rowzy Harris, wife of John Henry Harris, died. She was buried in the Harris Cemetery in Limestone County, Alabama (Find A Grave Memorial# 76005861).

On September 10, 1843, John Henry Harris of Flower Hill Plantation died at Tanner. He was buried in the Harris Cemetery in Limestone County, Alabama (Find A Grave Memorial# 76005797).

John R. Harris

On September 4, 1810, John R. Harris was born to John Henry Harris and Frances Rowzy Harris in Albemarle County, Virginia. Since his father entered land in Limestone County, Alabama, in February 1818, John R. Harris probably came to Alabama with his father when he was seven years old.

John R. Harris married Elizabeth Jones Perkins; she was born on August 29, 1821. Elizabeth was the daughter of Frances Anna Mariah Jones, daughter of Llewellyn Jones, and Benjamin Perkins.

John R. Harris and Elizabeth Jones Perkins Harris had the following children:
1. John H. Harris.
2. Benjamin Perkins Harris (1844-1902).
3. Francis Maria Harris Floyd (1848-1910).
4. Sarah Elizabeth Harris (1849-1852).

According to the 1840 Limestone County, Alabama Census, John R. Harris owned 25 slaves. In the 1850 Limestone County, Alabama, Slave Schedules, John R. Harris owned 24 slaves.

According to the 1850 Limestone County, Alabama, Agricultural Census, John R. Harris, son of John Henry Harris, owned 920 acres of improved land and 1,197 acres of unimproved land valued at $21,170. He also had $750 worth of farming equipment and livestock worth $2,475.

On August 7, 1851, Elizabeth Jones Perkins Harris died in Limestone County, Alabama at age 29. She was buried in the Harris Cemetery (Find A Grave Memorial# 76006493).

In the 1860 Limestone County, Alabama, Slave Schedules, John R. Harris owned 23 slaves. John R. Harris was a wealthy cotton planter like his father.

On January 13, 1863, John R. Harris died in Limestone County, Alabama, at age 52. He was buried in the Harris Cemetery (Find A Grave Memorial# 76006451).

Schuyler Harris - Flower Hill

On March 28, 1823, Schuyler Harris was born in Albemarle County, Virginia, to John Henry Harris and Frances Rowzy Harris. Since John Henry Harris, father of Schuyler, was in the early 1818 land records and the 1820 census of Limestone County, Alabama, it is probable that Schuyler Harris was born in Limestone County, Alabama, instead of Albemarle County, Virginia.

On June 18, 1845, Schuyler Harris married Ann Eliza Dewoody; she was born on March 28, 1827, at Cottonport in Limestone County, Alabama. The parents of Ann were William Dewoody (7/10/1794-7/5/1862) and Ann Nelson Adams (3/30/1799-1/18/1860); William and Ann were married on January 10, 1822, at Cottonport in Limestone County, Alabama.

Schuyler Harris and Ann Eliza Dewoody Harris had the following children:
1. Frances Ann Harris was born on September 24, 1847, at Tanner in Limestone County. She died on September 6, 1848 and was buried in the Harris Cemetery in Limestone County, Alabama (Find A Grave Memorial# 76006066).
2. Ida Marie Harris Pryor was born on July 27, 1849. Ida married her first cousin William Richard Pryor. Ida Marie Harris Pryor died on August 9, 1915 and was buried in the Athens City Cemetery in Limestone County, Alabama (Find A Grave Memorial# 39560107).
3. William Dewoody Harris was born on July 10, 1851. He died on October 9, 1852, at Tanner and was buried in the Harris Cemetery in Limestone County (Find A Grave Memorial# 76006135).
4. Minnie Dora Harris Richardson was born on March 25, 1853. She married William Nicholas Richardson. Minnie Dora Harris Richardson died on December 31, 1910, at Huntsville in Madison County, Alabama.

5. Sally Bettie Harris was born on August 5, 1855. She died on December 10, 1855, at Tanner and was buried in the Harris Cemetery in Limestone County, Alabama (Find A Grave Memorial# 76006191).

According to the 1850 Limestone County, Alabama, Agricultural Census, Schuyler Harris, son of John Henry Harris, owned 500 acres of improved land and 400 acres of unimproved land valued at $18,000. He also had $570 worth of farming equipment and livestock worth $1,670.

Isabella Virginia Harris Pryor was a sister to Schuyler Harris. Isabella was born on January 7, 1826, in Limestone County, Alabama. On August 20, 1845, she married Luke Pryor; they were the parents of William Richard Pryor. On June 16, 1899, Isabella Virginia Harris Pryor died at Athens in Limestone County, Alabama (Find A Grave Memorial# 39560184).

According to the historic marker: "Harris-Pryor House (Flower Hill Farm) was built about 1858 by Schuyler Harris on land once owned by Henry Augustine Washington, a distant relative of the first U.S. president. Through purchases, marriages and inheritance between the Washington, Harris and Pryor families, all from Virginia, a large plantation of more than 3,000 acres was established. Long after the demise of slavery, approximately 60 tenant families lived on the land.

Schuyler Harris gave this house to his daughter, Ida Maria, and her husband, William Richard Pryor, son of Luke Pryor II and Isabella Virginia Harris Pryor. It is through this descent that this historic house and farm, known as Flower Hill, is owned and held in trust for future generations by Luke Pryor IV and wife Betty (Lamb) Pryor. It is managed through a family corporation and is not open to the public.

Flower Hill

Across the U.S. 31 is a large spring, known since early times as English's Spring. It produced enough water for a town, and the little settlement that formed around it was a contender for the site of the county seat. It was not chosen, however, and the settlement ceased to exist. This area for several miles around was known as Quid Nunc (Latin for what next) Beat and Post Office until about 1910, when it was changed to Harris Station, a community that had formed along the railroad tracks to the southwest. Time and progress brought about the demise of that community. Named for the prominent Harris family, the Harris Cemetery is among the trees across the highway."

On June 17, 1863, Ann Eliza Dewoody Harris died at age 36 at Tanner. She was buried in the Harris Cemetery in Limestone County, Alabama (Find A Grave Memorial# 76006273).

On September 22, 1880, Schuyler Harris died at age 57 at the Flower Hill Plantation at Tanner in Limestone County, Alabama. He was buried in the Harris Cemetery in Limestone County, Alabama (Find A Grave Memorial# 76006317).

Hine, Silas Jr.

On September 30, 1793, Silas Hine Jr. was born in Connecticut; he was the son of Silas Hine Sr. (1764-1841) and Elizabeth Tyrell (1767-1834). In 1790 United States Census, Silas Hine Sr. was listed at Cheshire in New Haven County, Connecticut. In 1800 United States Census, Silas Hine Sr. was listed at Wolcott in New Haven County, Connecticut. In 1810 United States Census, Silas Hine Sr. was at Wolcott in New Haven County, Connecticut.

Later, the Hine family moved to Virginia where Silas Hine Jr. married Temperance Harrison. Temperance was born on April 20, 1791, in Dinwiddie County, Virginia.

Silas and Temperance Harrison Hine had three sons and two daughters. They had the following children who lived in Limestone County, Alabama:
1. James Harrison Hine was born on September 4, 1814, in Dinwiddie County, Virginia. James married Elizabeth Oglesby Redus; she was born on April 6, 1817. Aaron Redus and Elizabeth Oglesby, parents of Elizabeth, came from White County, Indiana, and floated down the Ohio River and up the Tennessee River to Limestone County in 1820. Elizabeth Redus Hine died on April 16, 1897 and was buried in the Athens City Cemetery (Find A Grave Memorial# 41372358). According to the 1850 Limestone County, Alabama, Agricultural Census, James Harrison Hine owned 400 acres of improved land and 300 acres of unimproved land valued at $6,000. He also had $760 worth of farming equipment and livestock worth $1,101. On August 27, 1884, James Harrison Hine died at age 69 in Limestone County, and he is buried in the Athens City Cemetery (Find A Grave Memorial# 41372352).
2. Elizabeth Hine was born on January 24, 1819 and was the twin sister of Frances Ann Hine. Elizabeth died on June 16, 1831, and she was

buried in the Hine-Malone Cemetery in Limestone County, Alabama (Find A Grave Memorial# 52741529).
3. Frances "Fannie" Ann Hine was born on January 24, 1819; she married James M. Malone. Frances died on July 25, 1842, and she was buried in the Hine-Malone Cemetery in Limestone County, Alabama (Find A Grave Memorial# 52741475).
4. William Anson Hine was born on January 29, 1822; he married sisters- Leticia C. Sloss and Eveline Sloss. William died on January 31, 1894 and was buried in the Athens City Cemetery (Find A Grave Memorial# 39541966).

In 1818, Silas Hine Jr. moved to Alabama, where he became a cotton planter and merchant. On February 11, 1818, Silas Hine entered 160.62 acres in Section 3 of Township 4 South and Range 5 West in Limestone County, Alabama (Cowart, 1984). The land he entered was adjacent to 80.31 acres entered on February 11, 1818, by John Petway Malone.

On February 11, 1818, Silas Hine entered 160.02 acres in Section 10 of Township 4 South and Range 5 West in Limestone County, Alabama (Cowart, 1984). Section 3 and Section 10 are adjacent to each other in a north-south directions; therefore, the two 1818 tracts entered by Silas Hine were probably adjacent to each other. The land he entered was in the drainage of Round Island Creek in Limestone County.

The 1820 Limestone County, Alabama, United States Census listed the following for the household of Silas Hine: White Males over 21: 2; White Males under 21: 3; White Females over 21: 3; White Females under 21: 3; Total Whites: 11; People of Color: 16; Slaves: 50. If the people of color were black, the Silas Hine household actually had 66 black folks.

According to the 1830 Limestone County, Alabama Census, Silas Hine owned 42 black slaves. On September 3, 1830, Silas Hine entered another 160.62 acres in Section 3 of Township 4 South and Range 5 West in Limestone County, Alabama (Cowart, 1984). The land he entered was adjacent to his first entry on February 11, 1818. The 1830 entry by Silas was adjacent to 80.31 acres entered by John Petway Malone on January 20, 1830.

On May 20, 1838, Mary H. Malone, daughter of John Petway Malone, married Roswell Hine, brother of Silas. Mary was born on May 14, 1817, and she died on July 23, 1841. Roswell was born on February 5, 1838, and on March 9, 1878, he died and was buried in the Athens City Cemetery (Find A Grave Memorial# 39541207)

According to the 1840 Limestone County, Alabama Census, Silas Hine owned 34 black slaves. His sons James and William are not shown as owning any slaves until 1850. In 1850, James H. Hine, brother of William, owned 33 black slaves, and in 1860, James owned 47 black slaves.

In July 1830, Temperance Harrison Hine died and was buried in the Hine-Malone Cemetery in Limestone County, Alabama (Find A Grave Memorial# 52741463). On January 25, 1850, Silas Hine died, and he was buried in the Hine-Malone Cemetery in Limestone County, Alabama (Find A Grave Memorial# 132079017).

According to the 1860 Limestone County, Alabama, Slave Schedules, James H. Hine owned 47 black slaves. In 1860, James Hine, son of Silas Hine, was one of largest slave holders in Limestone County, Alabama.

William A. Hine

On January 29, 1822, William A. Hine was born in Limestone County, Alabama, to Silas and Temperance Harrison Hine. After receiving his education in the Athens schools, William became a merchant and planter.

In 1843, William A. Hine was engaged in the mercantile business as a hardware merchant in Athens, Alabama. He had learned about the business of merchandizing from his father Silas Hine who was a merchant in Athens.

In February 5, 1845, William A. Hine married Leticia C. Sloss in Lauderdale County, Alabama. On July 8, 1823, Leticia was born to Joseph Long Sloss (1789-1883) and Clarisa A. Wasson (1800-1882).

William Anson Hine and Leticia C. Sloss Hine had the following four children:

1. Cornelius Hine was born on November 7, 1845, and at age six, he died on December 9, 1851. Cornelius was buried in the Hine-Malone Cemetery in Limestone County (Find A Grave Memorial# 52741374).
2. Clara Hine married Dr. Borroum of Corinth, Mississippi.
3. William A. Hine Jr. was born in 1857, and he died in February, 1879, at the age of 22.
4. William Ernest Hine was born in Athens on December 3, 1858. The following excerpts was published on September 16, 1943, in the Limestone Democrat: "Ernest Hine...died at his home on West Washington Street....His body was interred in the Athens City Cemetery beside that of his wife, Mrs. Kate Anderson Hine (1862-1939)....He was the son of the late William Anson Hine and Letitia Sloss Hine....serving as mayor from 1916 to 1920, Mr. Hine was one of the organizers of the Limestone County Fair Association...an advocate of improved educational facilities and a lover of music... a member of the choir of the Athens First Methodist Church...Surviving Mr. Hine are three daughters, Mrs. J.E. Clem, Mrs. Robert S. Beattie and Miss Henrietta Hine, of Athens; one son, Butler P. A. Hine of Decatur." William Ernest Hine died on September 3, 1943 (Find A Grave Memorial# 41426302).

According to the 1850 Limestone County, Alabama, Slave Schedules, William A. Hine owned 11 black slaves. William directed more energy in his business than in that of cotton planting and farming.

During the Civil War, William Hine was commissioner of revenue and roads for Limestone County, Alabama. The only time that he was ever in politics was during the war. William devoted most of his time to being a successful merchant in Athens. He was a loyal member of the Methodist Episcopal Church. William was a Mason and one of the leading businessmen and religious leaders in Athens.

On October 2, 1865, Leticia C. Sloss Hine, the first wife of William Anson Hine, died at 42 years old. Leticia was buried in the Old City Cemetery at Athens, Alabama (Find A Grave Memorial# 24868407).

On December 11, 1866, William Hine married a second time in Corinth, Mississippi, to Eveline Sloss, a younger sister of his first wife. Eveline was born on June 12, 1833, and at age 58, she died on August 4, 1891. Eveline was buried in the Old City Cemetery in Athens, Alabama (Find A Grave Memorial# 24868455).

Hine-Malone Cemetery

The Hine-Malone Cemetery or Bethlehem Cemetery located in Limestone County, Alabama, has the following burials:

1. Hine, Mary H., 14 May 1817-23 July 1841, Consort of Roswell Hine, and d/o John Petway Malone, md. 20 May 1838. In memory of Mary H. Hine consort of Roswell Hine and daughter of John P. Malone, Born May 14, 1817, married May 20th, 1838, and died Jul 23rd, 1841.
2. Hine, Silas, b. New Haven County, Connecticut, 30 September 1793-25 Jan 1850, Aged 50 years 3 months & 28 days. Moved to this county 1818. In memory of Silas Hine, who was born in New Haven County Conn Sept 30, 1793, departed this life Jan 25, 1850, aged 56 years, 3 mos., 28 days. He moved to this county 1818.
3. Hine, Temperance Hine, Consort of Silas Hine, b. Dinwiddie Co., Va. 20 Apr 1791 - ?? Jul 1830. IN Memory of Temperance H., Consort of Silas Hine, born in Dinwiddie County, Va. April 20th, 1791. Died July 1830.
4. Hine, Elizabeth H.. d/o S. & T. H. Hine, 24 Jan 1819-16 Jun 1831. IN Memory of Elizabeth H. Daughter of S. & T. H. Hine, Born Jany 24th, 1819. Died 16th June 1831.
5. Hine, Cornelius, son of W.A. & L.C. Hine 7 Nov 1845-9 Dec 1851
6. Malone, Frances Ann, Consort of James M. Malone and d/o S. & T. H. Hine, 24 Jan 1819-25 Jul 1842; IN Memory of Frances Ann, Consort of James M Malone and daughter of S & T. H. Hine. Born 24th Jany 1819. Died 25th July 1842.

Horton, Rodah

In 1794, Rodah Horton was born in Staunton, Virginia. His parents are not known, but by 1818, he had moved from Virginia to Madison County, Alabama.

On February 2, 1818, Rodah Horton and Littleberry Robinson entered 586.97 acres in Section 19 of Township 5 South and Range 1 West in Madison County, Alabama (Cowart, 1979). Littleberry Robinson was obviously an acquaintance of Rodah; he was probably kin to one of the brother-in-laws of Rodah-John Robinson or James Berry Robinson. John Robinson married Caroline Louise Otey and James Berry Robinson married Mary Frances Otey; Caroline and Mary were sisters to the wife of Rodah, Lucy Ann Margaret Otey.

On November 9, 1824, Rodah Horton married Lucy Ann Margaret Otey at Huntsville in Madison County, Alabama; she was born on September 3, 1805. Lucy was the daughter of Walter Otey and Mary Walton. Lucy was the sister of John Walter Otey, Eliza S. Otey Hildreth, Christopher Clark Otey, Mary Frances Otey Robinson, Caroline Louise Otey Robinson, Armistead H. Otey, William Madison Otey, and Malinda Maria Otey Pruitt.

Rodah Horton and Lucy Ann Margaret Otey Horton had the following children:
1. William Walter Horton, August 27, 1825-September 15, 1865.
2. Mary Eliza Horton Branch, 1827-after 1870.
3. Josephine Horton Rhett, March 5, 1830-June 28, 1860.
4. Lucy Frances Horton Colcock, November 18, 1832-April 21, 1862.
5. James E. Horton, May 20, 1833-January 28, 1924.
6. Rodah Van Horton, November 14, 1835-March 21, 1895.

In the 1830 Madison County, Alabama Census, Rodah Horton owned 94 black slaves. According the census record, he had 43 black males and 51 black females.

On September 10, 1846, Rodah Horton died at the age of 52 years. He was an extensive cotton planter, and represented Madison County the Alabama

State Legislature. Rodah was buried in the Maple Hill Cemetery in Huntsville (Find A Grave Memorial# 98746668).

In the 1850 Madison County, Alabama, Agricultural Census, Lucy A. M. Horton owned 90 acres of improved land worth $7,500. She also had $150 worth of farming equipment and $750 worth of livestock. Lucy was listed just under John Robinson and only two names under James B. Robinson; therefore, it appears that she was living adjacent to her sisters, Caroline Otey Robinson and Mary Otey Robinson.

On November 30, 1861, Lucy Ann Margaret Otey Horton died at Huntsville in Madison County, Alabama. She is probably buried in the Maple Hill Cemetery in Huntsville near her husband.

Horton, James Edwin

On May 20, 1833, James Edwin Horton was born in Madison County, Alabama. His parents were Rodah Horton and Lucy Ann Margret Otey who were from Virginia. James E. Horton was educated at the University of Alabama, and University of Virginia.

In the 1850 Madison County, Alabama, Slave Schedules, James E. Horton owned nine black slaves. In the 1850 Madison County, Alabama, Agricultural Census, James Horton owned 100 acres of improved land and 50 acres of unimproved land worth $500. He also had $50 worth of farming equipment and $430 worth of livestock.

In 1857, James E. Horton settled on the Elk River, and engaged in cotton farming.

In the 1860 Limestone County, Alabama, Slave Schedules, James E. Horton owned 39 black slaves. In that same survey, his brother, Rodah V. Horton, owned 47 black slaves.

On October 16, 1860, James E. Horton married Emily Donelson in Sumner County, Tennessee, near the Hermitage Plantation of General Andrew Jackson. Emily was the daughter of Daniel S. Donelson, a nephew of Rachel

Donelson Jackson, the wife of General Andrew Jackson. Emily Donelson was born on February 19, 1838, at Nashville in Davidson County, Tennessee.

James Edwin Horton and Emily Donelson Horton had the following children:
1. Daniel D. Horton 1862-1863(Find A Grave Memorial# 31882561).
2. Margaret Donelson "Donna" Horton Lewis Estes 1867-1928(Find A Grave Memorial# 31882756).
3. Sarah B. Horton 1869-1885(Find A Grave Memorial# 31882481).
4. Maribee Horton Major 1872-1893 (Find A Grave Memorial# 31882572).
5. Emily Doneslon Horton McClellan 1874-1896(Find A Grave Memorial# 31882691).
6. Jessie Louise Horton Frost 1876-1935 (Find A Grave Memorial# 29854675).
7. James Edwin Horton Jr. 1878-1973 (Find A Grave Memorial# 31288404).

In the fall of 1862, at Bardstown, Kentucky, James E. Horton entered the Confederate service and was an aide to General Daniel S. Donelson. In the latter part of 1863, James E. Horton was with General Donelson until he died at Knoxville, Tennessee. From 1863 until the close of the war, Major Horton was Acting General Quartermaster, and was on the Florida coast when the war closed.

In 1865, at the end of the Civil War, James E. Horton returned to Limestone County and resumed his planting operations. In August 1886, James E. Horton was elected Judge of Probate of Limestone County, Alabama.

On January 28, 1924, James Edwin Horton died at age 90. He was buried in the Athens City Cemetery at Athens in Limestone County, Alabama (Find A Grave Memorial# 31811291).

On December 29, 1931, Emily Donelson Horton, wife of James E. Horton, died at age 93 at Athens. She was buried in the Athens City Cemetery in Limestone County, Alabama (Find A Grave Memorial# 31811318).

Houston, George Smith

On January 17, 1808, George Smith Houston Sr. was born at Franklin in Williamson County, Tennessee. He was the grandson of John Houston and Mary Ross, who migrated from County Tyrone in the north of Ireland and settled in Newbury District in North Carolina in 1760.

George was the son of David Houston and Hannah Pugh Reagan who moved from Virginia to Franklin in Williamson County, Tennessee. The Houston family settled twelve miles west of Florence, in Lauderdale County, Alabama, and engaged in agriculture as a cotton planter and slave owner.

George Smith Houston received an elementary education in an academy in Lauderdale County, Alabama. He read law under Judge Coalter, in Florence, and completed his studies in the law school at Harrodsburgh, Kentucky.

In1831, George Smith Houston was admitted to the bar. In 1832, he was elected to the Alabama State Legislature. He was there twice elected Circuit Solicitor, in which position he made a decided reputation, being considered one of the ablest prosecutors in the State.

In 1831, George Smith Houston first married Mary Jackson Beaty, daughter of Robert W. Beaty. She was born on April 16, 1815. George and Mary L. Beaty Houston had eight children, all of whom died before 1860, except the following children:
1. David Houston entered the service as captain of a company of the 9th Alabama Regiment, CSA. He was afterward a member of General Roddy's command. David never married, and he died on September 7, 1880.
2. George S. Houston Jr. birth is unknown. He entered the CSA Army as a private in Johnson's Regiment under the command of General Roddy. He was promoted to lieutenant of the escort of General Roddy. George married Maggie Irvine of Florence, Alabama, and lived on a farm near Mooresville in Limestone County, Alabama. George S. Houston Jr. died on September 30, 1934, and he was buried in the Athens City Cemetery (Find A Grave Memorial# 39541686).

3. John P. Houston was an attorney of law in Memphis, Tennessee.
4. Mary E. Houston was a resident of Athens, Alabama.

In 1832, George Smith Houston served as a Member of the Alabama State House of Representatives.

In 1835, George Smith Houston moved to Limestone County, Alabama. Athens was the home of Governor George S. Houston. During Reconstruction, Athens was the home of the Trinity School, a school founded for the children of former slaves by the American Missionary Association.

George Smith Houston

In 1840, George Smith Houston Sr. was listed in the Limestone County, Alabama, United States Census. According to the 1840 census, he owned 21 black slaves.

In 1841 George S. Houston was elected to Congress on the general ticket. He served in Congress until January 21, 1861.

According to the 1850 Limestone County, Alabama, United States Census, House Number 634, George Smith Houston was a 41-year-old white male born in Tennessee. Also listed in his household was Mary J Houston, Female, 32 Alabama; David Houston, Male, 13, Alabama; William P. Houston, Male, 4, Alabama; Mary J. Houston, Female, 1, Alabama; Morning Parrot, Female, 74, Virginia; and George L. Houston, Male, 8, Alabama.

The 1850 Limestone County, Alabama, Slave Schedule listed George S. Houston owning 49 black slaves. In the 1850 Limestone County, Alabama, Agricultural Census, George S. Houston owned 793 acres of improved land and

1,250 acres of unimproved land worth $15,000. He also had $500 worth of farming equipment and $1,726 worth of livestock.

From 1851 to 1861, George Smith Houston served in the United States House of Representatives from Limestone County.

On April 20, 1856, Mary Jackson Beaty Houston died and was buried in the Athens City Cemetery at Athens in Limestone County, Alabama (Find A Grave Memorial # 39541443).

According to the 1860 Limestone County, Alabama, United States Census, George Smith Houston was a 50-year-old white male born in Tennessee. Also listed in his household was George S. Houston, Male, 19, Alabama; John P. Houston, Male, 9, Alabama; and Mary E. Houston, Female, 7, Alabama.

According to the 1860 Limestone County, Alabama, Slave Schedules, George Smith Houston owned 78 black slaves. George was one of the wealthiest cotton planters of Limestone County.

In April, 1861, George Smith Houston married a second time to Ellen Irvine of Florence, Alabama. She was born in 1836 and was a daughter of James Irvine, one of the leading lawyers of the State. George and Ellen had two children:
1. Emma Houston lived with her mother at Athens.
2. Maggie Lou Houston died on November 24, 1877.

George Smith Houston served as chairman of Military Affairs, Ways and Means, and the Judiciary, and served several times as chairman of Ways and Means Committee. He was earnestly opposed to secession and became a member of the famous committee of 33 to devise means to save the Union.

In 1865 he was elected to the Senate of the United States, but not allowed a seat, because his State was denied representation. In 1866, he was again offered for the Senate, but was defeated by ex-Governor Winston, the vote being Winston 65 and Houston 61.

In the 1870 Limestone County, Alabama, United States Census, George Smith Houston was a 61-year-old white male born in Tennessee. Also in his household was Ellen Houston, Female, 36, Alabama; David Houston, Male, 33, Alabama; Mary E. Houston, Female, 15, Alabama; Emma Houston, Female, 7, Alabama; Maggy Houston, Female, 3, Alabama; Miles Houston, Male, 45, Alabama; Ann Houston, Female, 28, Alabama; Mary Cartwright, Female, 45, Alabama; Maggy Cartwright, Female, 15, Alabama; and Larrod Cartwright, Female, 15, Alabama.

George Smith Houston home

In 1876, George Smith Houston served another term as Governor of Alabama. At the expiration of his second term as governor, George Smith Houston was elected to the United States Senate. He served in the extra session of 1879 but did not return to Washington on account of ill health.

From 1874 through 1878, Governor George Smith Houston served as the first post-Reconstruction Democratic governor of the State of Alabama.

In 1879, George Smith Houston served as a United States Senator, but did not return to Washington on account of ill health. The Honorable Luke Pryor, his former law partner, was a great friend and successor in the Senate.

On December 31, 1879, George Smith Houston died at his home in Athens with burial in the Athens City Cemetery at Athens in Limestone County, Alabama (Find A Grave Memorial# 6421223).

On August 4, 1909, Ellen died at Athens. She was buried in the Athens City Cemetery at Athens in Limestone County, Alabama (Find A Grave Memorial # 39541463)

Jackson, James

From August 30, 1809, through February 4, 1818, James Jackson of the Forks of Cypress of Lauderdale County, Alabama, entered 3,442 acres in Madison County, Alabama (Cowart, 1979). The first land entries of James Jackson were in Madison County of Mississippi Territory after the county was organized on December 13, 1808. He was described in the land records as James Jackson of Nashville, James Jackson of Tennessee, or James Jackson of Madison County.

Forks of Cypress

Starting on February 6, 1818, James Jackson of the Forks of Cypress entered some 2,160 acres in Limestone County, Alabama (Cowart, 1984). James Jackson entered a total of some 20,242 acres in Limestone, Madison, Lauderdale, and Franklin Counties of North Alabama. He was not found in the land records of Morgan County, Alabama.

In 1820, the James Jackson, owner of the Forks of Cypress in Lauderdale County, Alabama, was listed as living in Limestone County, Alabama. The 1820 Limestone County, Alabama Census had the following for the household of James Jackson: White Males over 21: 1; Total Whites in Household: 1; Free Persons of Color: 48; Slaves: 100; Acres Cultivated: 20; Hands: 50. If the free persons of color were black, there were 148 blacks living in the household of James Jackson in Limestone County, Alabama, in 1820.

James Jackson Sr.

There was another James Jackson living in Limestone County, Alabama, but it appears that he was not a slave owner. James Jackson Sr. of Limestone County was born in South Carolina in 1784, and James Jackson of Forks of Cypress was born in Ireland in 1782.

On June 23, 1784, James Jackson Sr. was born in South Carolina. On January 11, 1845, James entered 76.84 acres of land in Section 7 of Township 1 South and Range 6 West. The land was northwest of Elk River near the corner of Limestone County, Alabama. On September 9, 1848, George W. Jackson entered 38.42 acres in Section 7 of Township 1 South and Range 6 West of Limestone County, Alabama in near his father James Jackson Sr.

James Jackson Sr. of Limestone County had children by three different wives. Martha "Patsy" Dobbins was probably his last wife. The children of James Jackson Sr. were:
1. Hezakiah Jackson who was born in 1814 and he died in 1866.
2. Hannah Jackson who was born on February 29, 1816, and in 1852, she married Claborn Palmore (1808-1884). She died on March 18, 1870 and is buried at Second Creek Cemetery in Lawrence County, Tennessee (Find A Grave Memorial# 17493609).

3. Mary Jackson was born in 1820. She married James Orr of South Carolina.
4. James Matthew Jackson was born on June 18, 1823, and in 1847, he Married Mary Consada Belue (1828-1890). James Matthew Jackson died on September 5, 1898 and was buried in the Oak Valley Cemetery in Sebastian County, Arkansas (Find A Grave Memorial# 49848543).
5. Aaron Jackson was born between 1821 and 1824.
6. George Winston Jackson was born on March 19, 1825, in South Carolina. He married Lucinda C. Belue Jackson (1826-1913). George died on March 4, 1897, and was buried in Mitchell Cemetery at Anderson, Alabama (Find A Grave Memorial# 49040142).
7. Martha Jackson was born in 1825.
8. William Jackson was born in 1831.
9. John Jackson was born in 1836.
10. Robert Jackson born in 1837; prior to 1860, he married Mary Nail/Neal of Lauderdale County, Alabama.
11. Rufus Jackson was born in 1840 in South Carolina. He was buried in the Second Creek Cemetery at Five Points in Lawrence County, Tennessee (Find A Grave Memorial# 17440920).
12. Samuel J. Jackson was born in 1851.
13. Nancy Jane Jackson Roper was born on August 10, 1854, in Alabama. Nancy was the daughter of Martha "Patsy" Dobbins, and she married Jacob Cyle Roper (1849-1921). Nancy Jane Jackson Roper died on August 9, 1914, and she was buried in the Minor Hill Cemetery in Giles County, Tennessee (Find A Grave Memorial# 18746685).
14. Clemmie J. Jackson Harvell was born on July 17, 1858. In 1880, she married Miles Harvell (1833-1916). Clemmie died on May 29, 1938, and was buried in the Liberty Cemetery at Rogersville, Alabama (Find A Grave Memorial# 47071300).
15. Rispia Ann Jackson was noted as in probate records of Limestone County, Alabama.

In the 1850, there were four families of James Jackson Sr. listed in the Limestone County, Alabama Census:
1. Family #714, James Orr, 31, South Carolina; Mary Jackson Orr, 30, South Carolina (daughter of James Jackson Sr.); Francis M. Orr, 10,

South Carolina; Charles A. Orr, 8, South Carolina; William T. Orr, 6, South Carolina; Mary E. Orr, 5, South Carolina; and Martha Orr, 3, South Carolina.
2. Family #715 George W. Jackson, 26, South Carolina (son of James Jackson Sr.); Lucinda C. Jackson, 24, South Carolina; Louisa Jackson, 1, South Carolina;
3. Family #721 District #4 Enumerated on December 18, 1850, James Jackson Sr., 67, South Carolina; Martha Jackson, 25, Alabama; William Jackson, 19, South Carolina; John Jackson, 14, South Carolina; Robert Jackson, 13 South Carolina; Rufus Jackson, 10, South Carolina; Alexander Jackson, 1, Alabama; Josiah Jackson, 22, South Carolina; Andrew J. Jackson, 24, South Carolina; and James D. Jackson, 43, South Carolina.
4. Family #722, James M. Jackson, 29, South Carolina, Mary Jackson, 21, Tennessee; Sarah E. Jackson, 2 Alabama; Martha Jackson, 3/12, Alabama.

In the 1850 Limestone County, Alabama, Agricultural census, James Jackson Sr. had 100 acres of improved land and 360 acres of unimproved land worth $2,500. He had $100 worth of farm implements and $330 of livestock. James M. Jackson and Aaron J. Jackson were listed under their father, but they do not have any recorded land. James Orr, son-in-law of James Jackson Sr., was listed above his father-in-law, but had no acreage.

On October 17, 1858, James Jackson died in Lawrence County, Tennessee. He was buried in the Second Creek Cemetery at Five Points in Lawrence County, Tennessee (Find A Grave Memorial# 17440920).

Rufus Jackson

In 1840, Rufus Jackson was born in South Carolina. He was the son of James Jackson of Limestone County, Alabama. In the 1850 Limestone County, Alabama Census, Rufus was living in the county with his family. By 1860 the parents of Rufus had died, and he was living with his older brother James and his family.

In 1868 after the Civil War, Rufus married Sarah Ann Grindle Cox in Lawrence County, Tennessee. Sarah was first married to Fulker Cox and had one child Maryetta "Mollie" Cox. Fulker had served in the Arkansas 33rd Infantry and died in August of 1863. In the early 1870's, Sarah and Rufus moved to Lafayette County, Arkansas with their two daughters Lizzy and Minda.

Rear: Eliza Maryetta "Mollie" Cox
Front: Sarah Ann Grindle Cox Jackson
Joanna Arminda "Minda" Jackson
Rufus Jackson
Elizabeth "Lizzie" Jackson
ca 1879

In 1880 United States Census, Rufus Jackson and his family are listed in the LaGrange Township of Lafayette County, Arkansas. Rufus and Sarah are not recorded in census records after 1880. In 1879, the oldest daughter of Sarah, Maryetta "Mollie" Cox, married Henry Hawkins Brown. Dora Elizabeth Ann "Lizzy" Jackson married a Burns and moves to Shelby County, Texas (Find A Grave Memorial# 22151516). Joanna Arminda "Minda" Jackson stayed in the Lafeyette County, Arkansas, and married A.C. "Bud" Quillin (Find A Grave Memorial#14845335). Rufus Jackson (1840-after1880) was buried in the Mount Nebo Cemetery at Patmos in Hempstead County, Arkansas (Find A Grave Memorial# 96208447).

Jones, John Nelson S. - Druid's Grove

On September 1, 1793, John Nelson Spottswood (Spot) Jones was born in Louisa, Virginia. His parents were Captain Llewellyn Jones of Campbell County, Virginia, and Mary Anderson Jones. In 1803, Llewellyn Jones(1760-1820) sold his land in Bedford County, Virginia, and the family moved to Rutherford County, Tennessee.

In 1809, Llewellyn moved his family from Tennessee to Madison County in Mississippi Territory. They settled and developed the Avalon Plantation at the present-day site of the University of Alabama at Huntsville.

From August 11, 1809, through September 19, 1809, Llewellyn Jones entered 1,279.15 acres in Madison County of Mississippi Territory (Cowart, 1979). In every land record, Llewellyn Jones was listed from Rutherford County, Tennessee. Llewellyn also entered land in Lawrence and Limestone Counties of North Alabama.

In 1814, John N. S. Jones went to Yale College, and he graduated under Dr. Timothy D. Wright. John had received his early education from the Reverend Gideon Blackburn at Murphreesboro, Tennessee, an eminent Presbyterian minister.

By October 1818, John N. S. Jones returned to Madison County, Alabama, and he established law practice in Huntsville, Alabama, after completing his study with Judge John Haywood. John N. S. Jones had worked with and continued his study of law with Judge John Haywood of Tennessee. While working with Judge Haywood, John fell in love with his daughter, Eliza Haywood.

John N. S. Jones married Eliza Haywood Jones, the youngest daughter Judge John Haywood of Tennessee. Eliza Ann Haywood Jones was born on March 8, 1807, in Franklin County, North Carolina. John and Eliza Jones had the following children:
1. Maria Louisa Jones (10/3/1822-7/1/1823).
2. Maria Louisa Jones Donnell (4/6/1824-8/16/1894).
3. John Haywood Jones (9/26/1826-8/13/1866).
4. Octavia Isabelle Jones Adair Mills Lewis (2/1/1829-11/20/1890).
5. Almira Marcella "Marcie" Jones Dearing (11/14/1831-5/1908)
6. Alexander "Zandy" Thompson Jones (1/29/1834-6/3/1857).
7. Caesaria Julia Jones (5/11/1836-8/17/1847).
8. Antominda Severa Jones (3/1838-9/1840).
9. Paul Llewellyn Jones (4/4/1840-4/11/1884).

10. Walter Blackstone Jones (4/27/1842-5/26/1887).
11. Antonina "Nina" Sabina Jones Hansell (11/27/1844-1/19/1917).
12. Spotswood Adair Jones (10/11/1850-12/21/1852).

In 1822, John N. S. Jones moved to Limestone County, Alabama, where he resided until his death. He developed a fine cotton plantation know as Druid's Grove near the community of Greenbrier. Druid's Grove derived its name came from the many ancient old growth oak trees that surrounded the home.

John Nelson Spottswood (Spot) Jones and Elizabeth (Eliza) Ann Haywood Jones lived on and farmed the Druid's Grove Plantation. The plantation was inherited from his father, Lewellen Jones (1760-1820), and covered some 3,000 acres of land at one time. In the1830 Limestone County, Alabama, United States Census, John N S Jones was a resident of the county.

Llewellyn Jones told his son, "I've no notion of the great bargain I purchased in this land. I give it to you. It is yours. Do whatever you please with it" (Jones-Donnell Papers, 1817-1994).

Llewellyn Jones also gives his daughter, Francis Ann Mariah Jones Perkins, a 2,500-acre plantation in Lawrence County that became known as Seclusion. He also gives her several slaves, but there was tremendous debt on the plantation. The land passed to her brother, John N. S. Jones, and he gives the plantation to his daughter Maria L. Jones Donnell and her husband James Webb Smith Donnell. About 1850, James W. S. Donnell built the beautiful plantation home at Seclusion and paid the debt owed on the property.

According to the 1850 Limestone County, Alabama, Slave Census, John N. S. Jones owned 115 black slaves. In the 1850 Limestone County, Alabama, Agricultural Census, John N. S. Jones owned 1,130 acres of improved land and 850 acres of unimproved land worth $40,000. His farm equipment was valued at $650, and his livestock was worth $3,520. The son of John N. S. Jones, John Haywood Jones, was listed just above his father in the agricultural census with $45,000 in land value.

In the 1850 Limestone County, Alabama, United States Census, House Number 384, John N. S. Jones was a 57-year-old white male born in Virginia. Also in his household was Eliza A. Jones, Female, 43, North Carolina; Paul Jones, Male, 10, Alabama; Walter Jones, Male, 8, Alabama; Antominda Jones, Female, 5, Alabama; and Alexander Jones, Male, 16, Alabama.

On May 30, 1853, just six months before his death, John N. S. Jones wrote to his daughter Maria Louisa Donnell. His letter opens with: "My dear child…I am anxious to see you and Mr. Donnell and the children, bring them all to my house, you could leave them with me….I have sent for Paul and Birket. They will return with Alexander on Friday or Saturday. So, you can see that I am all alone until they return. Walter is going to school every day with Mr. Green and learning well….Paul and Walter would delight to see Robert….I am in hopes that Mr. Donnell, yourself and family will come….Do you ever hear from Marcie or Octavia?....I am very anxious to hear from you. Write to me when you get this. Give my love to the children. Your affectionate father" (The Jones-Donnell Papers, 1817-1994).

On September 17, 1852, Eliza Ann Haywood Jones died in Limestone County, Alabama. She was buried in the Jones-Donnell Cemetery with her husband and children (Find A Grave Memorial# 22021384).

On November 17, 1853, John Nelson Spottswood (Spot) Jones died in Limestone County, Alabama. He was buried in the Jones-Donnell Cemetery or Hundley Cemetery at Greenbrier in Limestone County, Alabama (Find A Grave Memorial# 22021405). At his death in 1853, the land and slaves of John N. S. Jones were given to his children, but only seven of the 12 children lived beyond 1860.

According to the Limestone County, Alabama, Book D of Probate Court Minutes, James W. S. Donnell, son-in-law, and John Haywood Jones, son, were appointed as administrators of the estate of John N. S. Jones. The heirs of John N. S. Jones were notified, and his slaves and land were to be divided among the heirs.

The estimate of the estate of John N. S. Jones was $146,218.50. According to the Limestone County records, each of the children of John N. S. Jones was to receive over $10,000 in slaves and $7,000 in land.

Jones-Donnell Cemetery

The Jones-Donnell Cemetery is in Greenbrier on Old Highway 20 in Limestone County, Alabama. The following are those of the Jones-Donnell family buried in the cemetery.
1) Carney, Marcella, 9 Aug 1852-5 May 1877, wife of Ed. M. Carney, Daughter of J. W. S and Maria Louisa Donnell.
2) Carney, Octavia Donnell, 2 Jun 1855-30 Mar 1936.
3) Donnell, James Webb Smith, 12 May 1859-8 Feb 1920, son of James Webb Smith and Maria Louisa Jones Donnell.
4) Jones, Alexander Thomas, 29 Jan 1834-3 Jun 1857. Aged 28 yrs, 4 mo's, 4 days, "Be ye therefore ready also; for the son of man cometh at an hour when ye think not. Luke 12 c. 40 v., 2nd Son of J. N. S. and Eliza Jones."
5) Jones, Antominda Severa, Mar 1838-Sep 1840. Daughter of J N. S. and Eliza A. Jones, "Sweet child thou art bourn to many these immortals. Thou art gone to that Almighty being who animates the universe. Indignite wisdom, mercy and benevolence cannot place the wrong."
6) Jones, Bouldin Collier, 22 Sep 1849-8 Jan 1855. Eldest son of J. Haywood and Sallie M. Jones, "Suffer little children to come unto me and forbid them not, for of such is the kingdom of Heaven."
7) Jones, Caesaria Julia: 11 May 1836-17 Aug 1847. Daughter of J. N. S. and Eliza A. Jones, "Died in the 12 year of her age Full many a gem of purest lay serene. The dark unfathomed eaves of Ocean leave. Full many a flower is born to blush unseen and waste its fragrance on the desert air."
8) Jones, John N. S., 1 Sep 1793-17 Nov 1853. Son of Llewellyn and Mary Anderson Jones.

9) Jones, Eliza Ann Haywood, 3 Mar 1807-17 Sep 1852. Wife of J. N. S. Jones: "Born in Franklin County N.C. Died In the 46 year of her age, Blessed are the pure in heart, for they shall see God". Daughter of Judge John Haywood of N. C. and TN.

10) Jones, J. Haywood, d. 13 Aug 1866, aged 40 yrs., "Safe with Jesus."

11) Jones, Mary Louise, 8 Oct 1822-4 Jul 1823. Daughter of J. N. S. and Eliza A. Jones. Born in Davidson County Tenn. Died in Limestone County, Ala., "Farewell my poor child. Thous knowest the anguish of our hearts O God."

12) Jones, Spotswood, 23 Jun 1855-3 Oct 1869. Son of John Haywood and Sallie M. Jones.

13) Jones, Spotswood Adair, 11 Oct 1850-21 Dec 1852. Son of J. N. S. and Eliza A. Jones, "In the year of his age, Man cometh forth like a flower.....Sleep in sweet.........of...For of such is the kingdom of heaven."

14) Peck, Susie Owen Donnell, 1 Feb 1862- 9 May 1898. Wife of Benjamin C. Peck. Daughter of J. W. S. and M. L. Donnell.

Jones, John H.

John H. Jones

It appears that there were two John H. Jones in Limestone County, Alabama. The older John H. Jones was born prior to 1799 based on his listing in the 1820 Limestone County, Alabama Census.

In 1820, the older John H. Jones was living in Limestone County, Alabama. The 1820 Limestone County, Alabama Census had the following for

John H. Jones: White Males over 21: 1, White Males under 21: 2, White Females over 21: 2, White Females under 21: 0, Total Whites in Household: 5. In 1820, John owned 17 black slaves.

John Haywood Jones

On September 26, 1826, John Haywood Jones was born in Limestone County, Alabama. He was the oldest son of John Nelson Spotswood Jones and Eliza Ann Haywood Jones. He married Sarah "Sallie" Maria Collier who was born in 1830. It appears that John Haywood Jones and Sarah Collier Jones were married around 1849. They had Bouldin and Alexander who died young and William Jones who moved to Marlin, Texas, where he was an attorney.

According to the 1850 Limestone County, Alabama, United States Census, House Number 385, John Haywood Jones was a 23-year-old white male born in Alabama. Also living in his household was Sarah A. Jones, Female, 19, Alabama; Bolen C. Jones, Male, 0, Alabama, and Burkett A. Washington, Male, 12, Alabama.

In the 1850 Limestone County, Alabama, Slave Schedules, John Haywood Jones owned 53 black slaves. John Haywood Jones and his father John N. S. Jones owned a total of 168 black slaves.

According to the 1850 Limestone County, Alabama, Agricultural Census, John Haywood Jones owned 400 acres of improved land and 240 acres of unimproved land worth $45,000. He also had $900 worth of farming equipment and $3,595 worth of livestock.

According to the 1860 Limestone County, Alabama, Slave Schedules, John Haywood Jones owned 170 black slaves. He probably had the slaves of some of his sisters and brothers.

According to the 1860 Limestone County, Alabama, United States Census, Household 345, John Haywood Jones was a 33-year-old white male born in Alabama. Also in his household was Sarah M. Jones, Female, 30, Alabama; John N. S. Jones, Male, 5, Alabama; Alexander T. Jones, Male, 2, Alabama; Martha Haywood, Female, 20, Tennessee; Antonia S. Jones, Female, 15, Alabama; and

Paul L. Jones, Male, 21, Alabama. In 1850, Paul Llewellyn Jones, his brother, and Antonia Sabina Jones, his sister, were living in his household. Martha Haywood was probably the granddaughter of Judge John Haywood of Tennessee, and she was probably a cousin to John Haywood Jones.

John Haywood Jones was among the wealthiest of the cotton planters in the Limestone County area. He owned over 2,700 acres of farmland that was worked in cotton with the labor of 170 slaves. In 1860, he spared no expense in building his house with on Clinton Street. The home had 16-foot ceiling, and the rooms were twenty feet square. However, the Civil War slowed the construction of the Jones house, and it destroyed his fortune in cotton and slaves.

On August 13, 1866, John Haywood Jones died at 40 years old. He was buried in the Jones-Donnell Cemetery near Greenbrier in Limestone County, Alabama.

Jordan, Samuel - Oakland

Elizabeth "Eliza" Jane Scott was born in 1794 in Virginia; she was the wife of Samuel Jordan. In 1818, Samuel and Eliza Scott Jordan moved from Virginia to the Madison-Limestone County area of North Alabama.

Samuel Jordan and Elizabeth Scott Jordan had at least two children:
1. Palmyra Scott Jordan (1806-1864)
2. Gabriel "Gabe" Jordan

On February 3, 1818, Samuel Jordan entered 599.54 acres in Sections 28, 29, and 32 of Township 3 South and Range 2 West in Madison County, Alabama (Cowart, 1979). From February 6, 1818, through October 6, 1837, Samuel Jordan entered 1,005 acres in Sections 5, 24, 26, 27 of Townships 2, 4 South and Range 3 West in Limestone County, Alabama (Cowart, 1984).

According to the 1820, Limestone County, Alabama Census, Samuel Jordan owned 40 black slaves. His slaves farmed the cotton lands on the Oakland Plantation near Greenbrier.

In 1830 Limestone County, Alabama Census, Samuel Jordan owned 77 black slaves. Also in 1830, Elizabeth Jordan is listed with 24 slaves; together, they owned 101 slaves.

In 1840 Limestone County, Alabama Census, Samuel Jordan owned 84 black slaves. Also in 1840, Elizabeth Jordan is listed with no slaves; however, she was shown as owning 88 slaves in 1850. Samuel Jordan must have died between 1840 and 1850.

In the 1850 Limestone County, Alabama, United States Census, House Number 309, Eliza Jordan was listed as a 56-year-old white female born in Virginia. Also listed in her household was Palmyra S. Bradley, Female, 45, Virginia; Eliza Jordan Bradley, Female, 24, Alabama; Samuel Jordan (Bradley) Withers, Male, 21, Alabama; John Wright (Bradley) Withers, Male, 20 Alabama; Clement C. (Bradley) Withers, Male, 18, Alabama; Mary (Bradley) Withers, Female, 14, Mississippi; and Charles Sh, Male, 22, Alabama.

After the death of her husband Dr. John Wright Withers on March 12, 1836, Palmyra Scott Jordan Withers married a Bradley. The census taker obviously assigned the Bradley last name to all the children of Palmyra and Dr. John Withers.

According to the 1850 Limestone County, Alabama, Slave Schedules, Eliza Jordan owned 88 black slaves. Eliza was one of the largest slave holding women in Limestone County, Alabama.

According to the 1850 Limestone County, Alabama, Agricultural Census, Eliza Jordan owned 1,180 acres of improved land and 380 acres of unimproved land worth $14,000. She also had $425 worth of farming equipment and $2,924 of livestock.

Palmyra Scott Jordan Withers

On March 10, 1806, Palmyra Scott Jordan was born to Samuel Jordan and Elizabeth "Eliza" Scott Jordan. Palmyra married Dr. John Wright Withers who was born in 1796; they had the following children:

1. Dr. Samuel Jordan Withers was born on February 22, 1828, at Monroeville in Monroe County, Alabama. Samuel married Emily Goodwyn Collier (8/29/18290-7/19/1912), daughter of Charles Ephraim Collier and Elizabeth Stewart. On February 28, 1906, Dr. Samuel Jordan Withers died at Hamilton in Lonoke County, Arkansas; he was buried in the Blackwell-Collier Cemetery in Limestone County, Alabama (Find A Grave Memorial# 70532307).
2. John Wright Withers.
3. Clement C. Withers.
4. Mary Withers

On March 12, 1836, Dr. John Wright Withers died at Oakland in Limestone County, Alabama. He was buried in the Withers Cemetery near Greenbrier (Find A Grave Memorial# 143762986).

On August 16, 1864, Palmyra Scott Jordan Withers Bradley died in Limestone County, Alabama. Palmyra was buried next to her husband in the Withers Cemetery on the Oakland Plantation of her parents (Find A Grave Memorial# 23276304).

The Withers Cemetery was in Section 24 of Township 4 South and Range 3 West in Limestone County, Alabama. Samuel Jordan owned 364.24 acres in Section 24 of Township 4 South and Range 3 West in Limestone County, Alabama, where the cemetery was located.

Lane, James M.

Between 1807 and 1809, James M. Lane was born in Georgia. James was probably the son of Jonathan (John) Lane of Georgia. Jonathan Lane was married to Mary "Polly" Elizabeth Colley who was born on March 10, 1771.

In the 1830 Limestone County, Alabama Census, Mary Lane was listed as head of the household; Jonathan must have died prior to 1830. Mary Lane died prior to 1840 in Limestone County, Alabama; she was buried in the Old City Cemetery at Athens (Find A Grave Memorial# 62813284).

On November 24, 1810, John Lane entered 160 acres in Section 14 of Township 1 South and Range 2 West in Madison County of Mississippi Territory. Therefore, by 1810, the Lane family was in the area of Madison County.

Based on land and census records, John Wesley Lane, George Washington Lane, and James M. Lane were probably brothers who were born in Georgia. From 1830 through 1837, John Wesley Lane entered land in Limestone County, Alabama; in 1830 census, he is listed as owning 24 slaves. George W. Lane was listed with 44 slaves in 1840 in Limestone County. George W. Lane, who married Martha Davis, was the son of Jonathan and Mary Lane. According to the 1850 Madison County, Alabama, Slave Schedule, George W. Lane owned 66 slaves.

On March 11, 1834, James M. Lane was married to Jane J. Peete in Limestone County, Alabama. On September 8, 1834, James M. Lane entered 39.25 acres in Section 33 of Township 2 South and Range 4 West in Limestone County, Alabama (Cowart, 1984).

In 1840, James M. Lane was listed in the Limestone County, Alabama, United States Census. In 1840, James M. Lane owned 37 black slaves.

On October 24, 1848, James M. Lane married Eliza A. F. Anderson in Limestone County, Alabama. In 1838, Eliza A. F. Anderson divorced Edmund R. Anderson in Limestone County.

According to the 1850 Limestone County, Alabama, Slave Schedules, James M. Lane owned 61 black slaves. In the 1850 Limestone County, Alabama, Agricultural Census, James M. Lane owned 900 acres of improved land and 580 acres of unimproved land worth $2,000. He owned $430 worth of farming equipment and $3,020 worth of livestock.

According to the 1860 Limestone County, Alabama, United States Census, Household 533, James M. Lane was a 51-year-old white male born in Georgia. Also in his household was Eliza A. F. Lane, Female, 51, Virginia; Mary E.

Hussey, Female, 16, Alabama; Betty H. Hussey, Female, 15, Alabama; William Hayes, Male, 20, Tennessee; Benjamin Chair, Male, 43, Florida; Octavia Chair, Female, 10, Florida; and Benjamin C. Chair, Male, 12, Florida.

According to the 1860 Limestone County, Alabama, Slave Schedules, James M. Lane owned 74 black slaves. No other Lane family members are found in the 1860 census or slave schedules for Limestone County in 1860.

In 1866, James M. Lane is listed in the Limestone, Alabama State Census. Through the 1865-1867 United States Civil War Confederate Applications for Pardons, James M. Lane of Limestone County, Alabama, filed an application for amnesty as a former Confederate for a presidential pardon.

The 1870 Limestone County, Alabama, United States Census, Household 77, James M. Lane is a 63-year-old white male born in Georgia. Also in his household was Eliza Lane, Female, 64, Virginia; Hattie Tyns, Female, 27, Alabama; James S. Porter, Male, 30, Tennessee, and Rachel Lane, Female, 16, Alabama.

In 1882, Eliza A. F. Anderson Lane, wife of James M. Lane, died in Limestone County, Alabama. Eliza was buried in the Old City Cemetery at Athens.

Maclin, Captain Thomas - Slopeside

Thomas Maclin was from Brunswick County, Virginia, and he was a captain in the War of 1812. Thomas married Julia Edmunds, who died before the Maclin family moved to Limestone County, Alabama. Thomas and Julia had eight children, but only two lived beyond 1837:
1. Rebecca Edmunds Maclin was born on September 8, 1802. On June 18, 1825, Rebecca Edmunds Maclin 10/30/1888) married Ira Edward Hobbs. She was instrumental in founding the Athens Female Academy that became Athens State University. Rebecca and Ira had only one child, Thomas Hubbard Hobbs. Rebecca Edmunds Maclin

Hobbs died on October 30, 1888, and she is buried in the Maclin-Hobbs Cemetery.

2. Benjamin W. Maclin was born on November 26, 1806. In 1838, Dr. Benjamin W. Maclin married Anne Eliza Hobbs (3/22/1821-11/26/1868). Anne was the daughter of John Hobbs and Keziah Fennell and niece of Ira Edward Hobbs. Dr. Benjamin W. Maclin died on February 3, 1879, and he is buried in the Maclin-Hobbs Cemetery.

By February 1818, Thomas Maclin reportedly traveled from Brunswick County, Virginia, to Limestone County, Alabama, with his eight children and some 300 black slaves. On February 10, 1818, Thomas Maclin entered 946.98 acres in Townships 4, 5 South and Range 4 West in Limestone County, Alabama (Cowart, 1984).

From February 10, 1818, through December 8, 1845, Thomas Maclin entered a total of 1,426.73 acres. From February 7, 1833, through January 27, 1839, Benjamin Maclin entered 844.84 acres in Townships 4, 5 South and Range 4 West (Cowart, 1984). Together, Thomas and Benjamin entered 2,271.57 acres most of which was north of the Tennessee River between Limestone Creek and Swan Creek in Limestone County.

On the land entered by Thomas Maclin in Limestone County, he established a cotton farming operation known as Slopeside Plantation. The original plantation and home of Thomas Maclin was in the middle southern portion of Limestone County, Alabama. At one time, Slopeside Plantation covered some 3,000 acres of land with the plantation home located was just a few miles north of the Tennessee River on the Old Jasper Road that ran from Tuscaloosa, Alabama, to Nashville, Tennessee, via Jasper, Decatur, Athens, and Columbia.

In the 1830 Limestone County, Alabama, census records, Thomas Maclin owned 88 black slaves. In 1840, Thomas owned 76 slaves, and his son Benjamin owned 41 slaves, for a total of 117 slaves. In 1850, Benjamin W. Maclin owned 59 slaves and 77 slaves in 1860.

Between 1846 and 1847, Thomas Maclin died in Limestone County, Alabama. It is probable that he was buried in the Maclin-Hobbs Cemetery on his

Slopeside Plantation, but he was placed in an unmarked grave. Today, the Maclin-Hobbs Cemetery is located on the west side of US Highway 31 across from Calhoun Community College.

Hobbs, Thomas Hubbard

On April 19, 1826, Thomas Hubbard Hobbs was born at Athens in Limestone County, Alabama. His parents were Ira Edward Hobbs (7/8/1803-4/17/1869) and Rebecca Edmunds Maclin Hobbs; Rebecca was the daughter of Thomas Maclin and sister of Benjamin W. Maclin. Ira and Rebecca were natives of Brunswick County, Virginia; they were of Scotch-Irish ancestry. Ira E. Hobbs and at least three of his brothers, David Hobbs, John Hobbs, and Hubbard Hobbs, came to North Alabama; they were the sons of Hubbard Hobbs and Martha Meredith.

After the elder Hubbard Hobbs died, Martha and her nine children moved to Limestone and Madison Counties in North Alabama. Her son John entered land in Madison County of Mississippi Territory in 1813. According to the 1830 Madison County, Alabama Census, John Hobbs owned 53 black slaves.

On February 11, 1813, John Hobbs was the first of the brothers to enter land in Section 9 of Township 4 South and Range 1 East in Madison County of Mississippi Territory. On July 16, 1821, John entered 185.2 acres of an island in the Tennessee River in Section 32 of Township 5 South and Range 1 East. On the next day of July 17, 1821, he entered 168.4 acres of island in Section 5 of Township 6 South and Range 1 East in Madison County, Alabama (Cowart, 1979). The island was originally known as Chickasaw Island or Chickasaw Oldfields, but after John Hobbs purchased the land, the island became known as Hobbs Island. From July 28, 1821, through January 1, 1831, John Hobbs entered an additional 438.23 acres in Townships 5, 6 South and Range 1 East in Madison County, Alabama (Cowart, 1979).

From February 10, 1831, through December 4, 1837, Ira E. Hobbs, father of Thomas Hubbard Hobbs, entered 398 acres in Township 4 South and Ranges 4, 5 West in Limestone County, Alabama (Cowart, 1984). Ira entered a 79.94 tract in Section 14 of Township 4 South and Range 5 West was adjacent to a very large tract of land owned by David Hobbs. From February 11, 1818, through June 23,

1831, David Hobbs entered 1,520 acres in Township 4 South and Range 5 West in Limestone County, Alabama (Cowart, 1984).

About 1829, Ira and his brother Hubbard reportedly erected a cotton-mill near Slopeside Plantation in Limestone County, Alabama. The cotton gin operation supported the assorted members of the Hobbs-Maclin families.

On June 28, 1831, Hubbard Hobbs entered 158.59 acres in Section 8 of Township 4 South and Range 4 West in Limestone County, Alabama. In 1831, Hubbard also entered two 79.75 acre tracts with his brother Ira E. Hobbs (Cowart, 1984).

Thomas Hubbard Hobbs was named after his grandfather Thomas Maclin and his uncle Hubbard Hobbs, a United States naval lieutenant. Lieutenant Hubbard Hobbs was on the first United States vessel to circumnavigate the globe, and he spent most of his life at sea.

Thomas H. Hobbs received his academic education at LaGrange College in Franklin County, Alabama. Thomas studied law at the University of Virginia.

In 1851, Thomas Hubbard Hobbs met Indiana "Indie" Elizabeth Booth while studying law at the University of Virginia. At first, Indie was hesitant to marry Thomas because of her fear of dying during childbirth

On April 16, 1851, Thomas Hubbard Hobbs entered 80 acres in Section 5 of Township 5 South and Range 4 West in Limestone County, Alabama (Cowart, 1984). The land he entered was located on the north side of the Tennessee River west of Limestone Creek and east of Swan Creek.

On June 2 1852, Thomas Hubbard Hobbs entered 40 acres adjacent to his original entry in Section 5 of Township 5 South and Range 4 West. The land he entered was next to land of his grandfather Thomas Maclin and his uncle Benjamin W. Maclin.

On August 4, 1852, Thomas Hubbard Hobbs first married Indiana "Indie" Elizabeth Booth at Richmond, Virginia; she was born on October 2, 1828. Indie was the daughter of Benjamin Booth and Sarah Hicks Booth of Amelia County, Virginia

In October 1852, Thomas Hubbard Hobbs in partnership with George Presley Keys purchased the Athens Herald. Thomas kept a diary where he recorded about his activities.

In 1853, Thomas Hubbard Hobbs graduated from the University of Virginia as Bachelor of Arts and subsequently from the law department of the University of Pennsylvania. Thomas Hubbard Hobbs practiced law for a short time at Athens in Limestone County, Alabama. After realizing that his cotton plantation required most of his attention, Thomas quit practicing as an attorney and devoted his time as a cotton planter.

On May 17, 1854, Indiana "Indie" Elizabeth Booth Hobbs, the first wife of Thomas Hubbard Hobbs, died in childbirth in Limestone County. Indie Hobbs was buried in the Maclin-Hobbs Cemetery in Limestone County, Alabama (Find A Grave Memorial# 48358703).

On June 28, 1855, Thomas H. Hobbs entered 40 acres in Section 5 of Township 5 South and Range 4 West in Limestone County, Alabama (Cowart, 1984). This was also in the area his grandfather Thomas Maclin had land.

From 1856 to 1861, Thomas Hubbard Hobbs was elected to the Legislature, and he was one of the prime supporters of the North and South Railroad. Thomas became closely associated with Luke Pryor, and he helped promoted the establishment and completion of the rail line through Athens.

On February 17, 1858, Thomas Hubbard Hobbs married Anne Benagh at Lynchburg City, Virginia. Anne was the daughter of James Benagh and Elizabeth Richardson.

According to the 1860 Limestone County, Alabama, Slave Schedules, Thomas Hubbard Hobbs owned 83 black slaves. Thomas had inherited huge tracts of land and slaves from his family

On June 6, 1861 at the beginning of the Civil War, Captain Thomas Hubbard Hobbs left Athens with his company of Limestone Grays toward Richmond, Virginia. They entered the Confederate Army of Company F of the 9th Alabama Infantry. Captain Hobbs and his men reached the site the following day where the Battle of Manassas was being fought. He made the comment after seeing the battlefield, "I saw for the first time the awful result of war."

Captain Thomas Hubbard Hobbs and his company participated in the battles around Richmond, Virginia, in what was known as the Seven Days Fight. During these skirmishes, Captain Hobbs was shot in the knee at the Battle of Gaines Mill; the wound was the direct result of his death.

On July 22, 1862, Captain Thomas Hubbard Hobbs, Company F, 9th Alabama Infantry, died at age 36 in Virginia from complications of a severe leg wound during the Battle of Gaines Mill. He was buried in the Spring Hill Cemetery at Lynchburg, Virginia (Find A Grave Memorial# 35323092). Thomas has a memorial marker in the Athens City Cemetery at Athens in Limestone County, Alabama (Find A Grave Memorial# 35995162).

After his death, The Memphis Appeal wrote: "Among Alabama's brightest and purest sons was Major Thomas H. Hobbs, of Limestone County. He was of the cavalier stock of the Old Dominion. His education was thorough, varied and polished. He wielded a facile pen, and in writings showed his refined and tacit taste. He was gifted with a clear, cogent and convincing eloquence. Calm, dignified, self-poised, he discussed the most difficult questions with eminent ability. As a member of the Legislature, he devoted his time and talents to the development of the resources of his own State. He was foremost in all noble enterprises. In her system of popular enterprises, Alabama owed more to Thomas Hobbs than to any other one man. A politician of the old Democratic school, he was the courteous and gentlemanly opponent, never condescending to low and unmanly tricks to gain his point. Pure, and as gentle as a woman, he was the embodiment of masculine energy and heroic valor. With a courage cool, calm and daring, he was among the first to enter the army."

On August 18, 1872, Anne Benagh Hobbs died at Athens in Limestone County, Alabama. She was buried in the Athens City Cemetery at Athens in Limestone County, Alabama (Find A Grave Memorial# 35995230).

Anne Benagh Hobbs left two sons:
1. Thomas Maclin Hobbs (1858-1912) was educated at the Virginia Military Institute and Alabama State University. He married Anne Davis Richardson (1861-1928); she was the daughter of Dr. Nicholas Davis Richardson and Betty Hine. Thomas M. Hobbs lived on the Slopeside Plantation that was owned by his great grandfather, Thomas Maclin, and he was the sole successor and heir to the estates of the family. In 1921, Thomas Maclin Hobbs died and was buried in the Athens City Cemetery in Limestone County, Alabama (Find A Grave Memorial# 35995397).
2. James Benagh Hobbs (1/4/1861-2/21/1883) died from measles while a student at the University of Alabama in Tuscaloosa at the age of 21 years. He was buried in the Athens City Cemetery in Limestone County (Find A Grave Memorial# 35995613).

Malone, George - Cambridge

On October 13, 1784, George Malone was born in Sussex County, Virginia. He married Sallie Moyler in Sussex County, Virginia; she was born on July 16, 1796. They were Irish descendants and reared a family of three sons and three daughters:

1. N. C. Malone was born in Virginia on September 12, 1812 and died on September 5, 1886; he was buried in Square Rock Cemetery in Scott County, Arkansas.
2. John Nicholas Malone was born in Virginia on March 12, 1817, and died October 8, 1888.
3. Harriet J. Malone born June 15, 1819.
4. Martha E. Malone born June 11, 1821.
5. Henry Booth Malone born February 12, 1825.
6. Louisa Quarla Malone was born on October 2, 1827.
7. Sarah Benjamin Malone was born September 12, 1831.

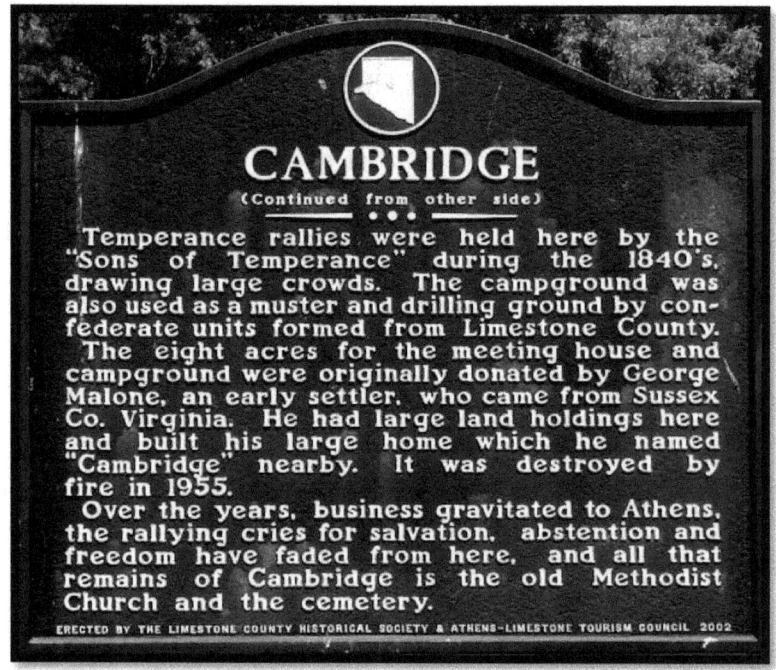

In 1818, George and Sallie Moyler Malone moved to Limestone County, Alabama. On February 5, 1818, George Malone entered 640.79 acres in Section 30 of Township 3 South and Range 3 West in Limestone County, Alabama. On February 6, 1818, Booth Malone entered 159.96 acres in Section 31 of Township 3 South and Range 3 West in Limestone County, Alabama (Cowart, 1984).

On February 9, 1818, George Malone entered 160.16 acres in Section 25 of Township 3 South and Range 4 West, and on May 26, 1831, George entered an adjacent 160.16 acres Section 25. On June 29, 1831, Booth Malone entered 160.16 acres adjacent to George in Section 25 and another 159.82 acres in Section

36 of Township 3 South and Range 4 West in Limestone County, Alabama (Cowart, 1984).

On August 20, 1847, George Malone died at the age of sixty-two years in Limestone County, Alabama. George was buried In the Cambridge Church Cemetery at Cambridge about four miles east of Athens. On September 5, 1844, Sallie Moyler Malone died in Limestone County, Alabama; she is buried in the Cambridge Church Cemetery (Find A Grave Memorial# 6149588).

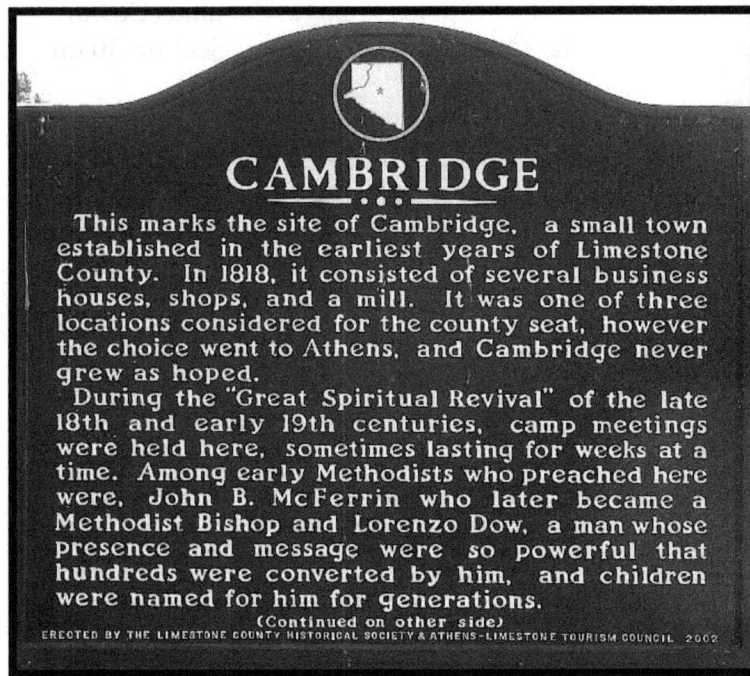

The Cambridge historic marker is in front of Cambridge Methodist Church and Cemetery. Cambridge is located about four miles east of Athens and south of United States Highway 72 on Cambridge Lane.

John Nicholas Malone

On March 12, 1817, John Nicholas Malone was born in Sussex County, Virginia. His parents were George Malone and Sallie Moyler Malone. In 1818, many members of the Malone family migrated from Virginia to Limestone County, Alabama.

In 1830, John N. Malone graduated from La Grange College, Franklin County, Alabama. He studied law with J. W. McLung at Huntsville, Alabama. In

1841, John N. Malone was admitted to the bar, and practiced law in Athens for ten years. In addition to maintaining his law office at Athens, John N. Malone devoted his time to planting.

On March 23, 1830, John N. Malone entered 160.25 acres in Section 32 of Township 3 South and Range 3 West in Limestone County, Alabama (Cowart, 1984). His father, George Malone, entered the entire acreage of Section 30 on February 5, 1818.

On May 15, 1845, John N. Malone married Mary Lucy Kernachan in Lauderdale County, Alabama. Mary was born on September 4, 1829; her parents were Abraham Kernachan and Martha Booth. Both the Kernachan and Booth families were cotton planters and slave owners.

John Nicholas Malone and Mary Lucy Kernachan Malone had the following children before she died:
1. Algernon Kernachan Malone was born in 1846 (Find A Grave Memorial# 41403797).
2. Robert Bloomfield Malone was born on March 31, 1847 and died April 1, 1933 (Find A Grave Memorial# 29733049).
3. Sarah "Sally" A. Malone was born in 1848.

On November 1, 1849, Mary Lucy Kernachan Malone died leaving one son, Robert Malone who was a planter in Limestone County. She was buried in the Cambridge Church Cemetery in Limestone County, Alabama (Find A Grave Memorial# 41403701).

In the 1850, Limestone County, Alabama, Slave Schedules, John N. Malone owned 9 black slaves. From 1851 to 1861, Judge Malone was one of the trustees of the Alabama University. In 1852, John N. Malone was a delegate to the National Convention at Baltimore, and supported Franklin Pierce and William R. King.

On October 25, 1855, John Nicholas Malone married Rebecca Ann Charlotte Jones Simmons in Lauderdale County, Alabama. Rebecca was born on March 8, 1834, and she was a cousin to the first wife of her husband, Mary Lucy Kernachan Malone. Rebecca was the former wife of John J. Simmons, and her daughter, Ann Elizabeth Ellen Simmons, married Robert Thomas Kernachan who was the brother of Mary Lucy Kernachan Malone.

John Nicholas Malone and Rebecca A. C. J. Simmons Malone had the following children:
4. Malinda "Linda" Malone Chew was born in 1856; she died in 1920 and was buried in the Athens City Cemetery (Find A Grave Memorial# 31965249).
5. George Malone was born on March 1, 1860, and died April 9, 1932 (Find A Grave Memorial# 31824077).
6. Anna T. Malone Chew was born on March 11, 1863 and died on December 27, 1924 (Find A Grave Memorial# 31942949).
7. Sarah Martha "Mattie" Malone was born on November 3, 1865 and died on March 1, 1940 (Find A Grave Memorial# 31965253).
8. Henry Booth Malone was born on September 4, 1868 and died on July 4, 1937 (Find A Grave Memorial# 25161194).

In 1860, John N. Malone took an active part in the presidential campaign of Stephen A. Douglas. John N. Malone was opposed to secession because he feared it would be followed by war. After Alabama seceded from the Union, John N. Malone was loyal to the State of Alabama and the south. He was in full sympathy with the Confederate States of America.

In the 1860, Limestone County, Alabama, Slave Schedules, John Nicholas Malone owned 45 black slaves. He probably inherited some of the slaves from relatives.

In 1874, John N. Malone was one of the trustees of the Agricultural and Mechanical School of Auburn. John had been interested in education nearly all his life. He was elected to the State Senate and stayed there for six consecutive years.

In 1881, John N. Malone was appointed probate judge to fill out an unexpired term of five years. The office had been vacated by the death of John M. Townsend.

On October 8, 1888, John Nicholas Malone died at age 71. He was buried in the Athens City Cemetery in Limestone County, Alabama (Find A Grave Memorial# 40799098). On July 28, 1893, Rebecca A. C. J. Simmons Malone died at age 59. She was buried in the Athens City Cemetery with her husband and children Find A Grave Memorial# 39554917).

Malone, Thomas

Thomas Malone

On July 14, 1777, Thomas Malone was born in Sussex County, Virginia. His parents were John Malone (1730-1794) and Mary Harper Malone (1738-1817). John Malone Jr. (1778-1860) was born a year after his brother Thomas Malone.

Thomas Malone married Rebecca Green Malone (1782-1831); they had the following children:
1. Nathaniel Burwell Malone (1800-1828) married Mary Green Jackson Wynn (1800-1898).
2. Nancy G Malone (1802-1830).
3. Sallie W Malone (1809-1827).
4. Lucy Ann Rebecca Malone (1813-1846).
5. Elizabeth Frances Malone (1821-1827).
6. Casandra Holloway Malone (1823-1827).

On October 20, 1836, Thomas Malone died in Limestone County, Alabama; the date of death was 1836 since his will was sent to probate court on November 25, 1836. Thomas was buried in the Polly Malone Cemetery (Find A Grave Memorial# 41331471).

Thomas Hill Malone

On August 8, 1794, Thomas Hill Malone was born in Virginia. He was the son of William Malone and Johanna Harper. Thomas Hill Malone married Elizabeth Tucker Malone who was his cousin. Elizabeth was born on December

21, 1798; she was the daughter of Thomas Chappell Malone (1776-1842) and Mary Chappell (1781-1848). Thomas Chappell Malone and Mary Chappell were double first cousins.

Thomas Hill Malone and Elizabeth Tucker Malone had the following children:
1. William T. Malone (1817-1836) was killed at the Alamo in Texas.
2. Joseph Smith Malone (1827-1892).
3. Martha Anderson Reese Malone Maddin (1832-1895).
4. Lucretia "Lou" Wynne Malone

On December 28, 1814, Thomas Hill Malone entered 162.35 acres in Section 13 of Township 2 South and Range 2 West in Madison County of Mississippi Territory. On September 29, 1818, Thomas Hill Malone entered 160 acres in Section 15 of Township 2 South and Range 2 West in Madison County of Mississippi Territory (Cowart, 1979). Based on the land record, it appears that Thomas Hill Malone was in Mississippi Territory by 1814.

The 1820 Limestone County, Alabama Census had the following for the household of Thomas Malone: White Males over 21: 1; White Males under 21: 4; White Females over 21: 1; White Females under 21: 2; Total Whites: 8; Free People of Color: 17; Slaves: 50; Number of Cultivated Acres 10; Number of bales of cotton 20; Average Weight per bale 350 pounds. If the free people of color were black, Thomas Malone had 67 black folks in his household in 1820.

The 1830 Limestone County, Alabama Census had the following for the household of Thomas Malone: White Males: 10-15 years: 2; 50-60 Years: 1; White Females: 5-10 Years: 1; 15-20 Years: 1; 40-50 Years: 1. In 1830, Thomas Hill Malone owned 35 black slaves.

From April 23, 1830, through December 11, 1854, Thomas Hill Malone entered 756.6 acres in Townships 3, 4 South and Range 4 West in Limestone County, Alabama (Cowart, 1984). Some of the land he entered was adjacent to his cousin Thomas Malone.

According to the 1840 Limestone County, Alabama Census, Thomas Hill Malone had 30 black slaves. In 1850, Thomas Hill Malone is not listed with any slaves in Limestone County.

In the 1850 Limestone County, Alabama, Agricultural Census, Thomas H. Malone had 180 acres of improved land and 315 acres of unimproved land worth $2,000. He also had $150 worth of farming equipment and $749 worth of livestock.

On August 11, 1857, Elizabeth Tucker Malone died in Limestone County, Alabama. She was buried in the Polly Malone Cemetery.

On August 21, 1869, Thomas Hill Malone died at age 75 in Waco, Texas. He was buried in the Oakwood Cemetery at Waco in McLennan County, Texas (Find A Grave Memorial# 29398784).

Thomas Chappell Malone

On January 9, 1776, Thomas Chappell Malone was born in Sussex County, Virginia. His parents were Daniel Malone and Amey Elizabeth Chappell, the daughter of Benjamin and Agness Binford Chappell.

Daniel Malone was born on February 13, 1750, in Surry County, Virginia, and he died on April 19, 1781, in Halifax County, Virginia (Find A Grave Memorial# 203721081). Amey Elizabeth Chappell was born on September 13, 1755, and she died in 1784 probably in Virginia.

Daniel and Amey had the following children: William Samuel Malone, Thomas Chappell Malone, Mary Malone, Thomas H. Malone, Rebecca Malone, Daniel Malone, Jacob Malone, David R. Malone, and Abraham Malone. Based on land records, the Malone family moved from Virginia to Limestone County, Alabama, with many of their relatives.

In 1797, Thomas Chappell Malone married his double first cousin Mary "Polly" Chappell who was born on January 9, 1781, in Sussex County, Virginia. Mary was the daughter of Thomas Chappell (1749-1823) and Elizabeth Tucker Malone (1755-1807).

Thomas Chappell Malone and Mary "Polly" Chappell Malone had the following children:
1. Elizabeth Tucker Malone (1798-1858) married Thomas Hill Malone, son of William Malone (1771-1850) and Johanna Harper (1772-1837).
2. Major James Chappell Malone (1800-1863) married Eliza Frances Hardiman Binford (1806-1860).
3. Martha Anderson Malone (1802-1857).
4. Mary Briggs Malone (1807-1868) married Jonathan McDonald MD (1806-1866).
5. Robert Daniel Malone (1808-1815).
6. Thomas Stith Malone MD(1812-1876) married Eliza Davis (1822-1849) in 1836. In 1851, he married Harriet Bolling Pryor (1818-1875).

In the 1830 Limestone County, Alabama Census, Thomas C. Malone owned 27 black slaves. In the 1840 Limestone County, Alabama Census, Thomas C. Malone owned 21 black slaves.

On October 29, 1842, Thomas Chappell Malone died in Limestone County, Alabama. He was buried in the Polly Malone Cemetery in Limestone County, Alabama (Find A Grave Memorial# 15359016).

On December 5, 1848, Mary Chappell Malone died at 74 years old; she was buried in the Polly Malone Cemetery in Limestone County. The inscription on her tombstone says, "Blessed are the dead that die in the Lord" (Find A Grave Memorial# 15359047).

Polly Malone Cemetery

The Polly Malone Cemetery in Limestone County, Alabama, was named after Mary "Polly" Malone 1776-1842. The following are the Malone kinfolks buried in the cemetery:
1) Malone, Thomas, July 14, 1777-October 20, 1838, born in Sussex County, Virginia was the son of John and Mary Harper Malone of Sussex County, Virginia.

2) Malone, Rebecca, April 11, 1782-May 10, 1831, wife of Thomas Malone, born in Sussex County, Virginia, daughter of James and Nancy Green also of Sussex County, Virginia.
3) Malone, Nancy Green, April 8, 1802-September 5, 1830, daughter of Thomas and Rebecca Green Malone.
4) Malone, Nathaniel Burwell, April 28, 1800-July 7, 1828, son of Thomas and Rebecca Green Malone.
5) Malone, Lucy Ann Rebecca, May 4, 1813-October 8, 1846, daughter of Thomas and Rebecca Green Malone.
6) Malone, Sallie W., April 28, 1809-August 3, 1827, daughter of Thomas and Rebecca Green Malone, died of a fever.
7) Malone, Elizabeth Frances, March 27, 1821-August 7, 1827, daughter of Thomas and Rebecca Green Malone; died of a fever.
8) Malone, Cassandra Holloway, May 22, 1823-August 11, 1827, daughter of Thomas and Rebecca Green Malone; died of a fever.
9) Malone, Elizabeth Tucker, December 21, 1798-August 11, 1857, daughter of Thomas Chappell and Mary Chappell Malone; wife of Thomas Hill Malone who died in 1869 and buried in Waco, Texas.
10) Malone, Thomas Chappell, January 9, 1776-October 29, 1842, born in Sussex County, Virginia. He married his double first cousin Mary Chappell.
11) Malone, Mary, January 9, 1781-December 5, 1848, wife of Thomas Chappell Malone, born in Sussex County, Virginia. Blessed are the dead that die in the Lord. She was the daughter of Thomas Chappell (1749-1823) and Elizabeth Tucker Malone (1755-1807); she married her double first cousin Thomas Chappell Malone.
12) Malone, Robert D., March 1, 1808-February 18, 1845, "all flesh is as grass."

Marshall, George, W.

On January 23, 1838, George W. Marshall married Ellen F. Knighten in Madison County, Alabama. According to the 1850 Limestone County, Alabama, United States Census, House Number 329, George W. Marshall was a 34-year-old white male born in Tennessee. Also living in the household was Ellen J.

Marshall, Female, 27, Alabama; Laurence W. Marshall, Male, 10, Tennessee; Elizabeth J. Marshall, Female, 8, Tennessee; Julia G. Marshall, Female, 6, Tennessee; Florence J. Marshall, Female, 5, Tennessee; Madaline Marshall, Female, 3, Alabama; William C. Marshall, Male, 2, Alabama.

In the 1850 Limestone County, Alabama, Slave Schedule, George W. Marshall owned 50 black slaves. According to the 1850 Limestone County, Alabama, Agricultural Survey, George W. Marshall owned 475 acres of improved land and 245 acres of unimproved land worth $7,680. He had $325 worth of farming equipment and livestock valued at $1,168.

In the 1860 Limestone County, Alabama, Slave Schedule, George W. Marshall not listed. Between 1850 and 1860, George and his family moved to Crawford County, Arkansas.

In the 1860 Lafayette Township, Crawford County, Arkansas, United States Census, Household 508, George W. Marshall was a 45-year-old white male born in Tennessee. Also in his household was Ellen T. Marshall, Female, 36, Georgia; Elizabeth J. Marshall, Female, 18, Tennessee; Julia G. Marshall, Female, 16, Tennessee; Florence J. Marshall, Female, 14, Tennessee; Madeline S. Marshall, Female, 12, Alabama; William Marshall, Male, 10, Alabama; Amy R. Marshall, Female, 8, Alabama; Ellen B. Marshall, Female, 6, Alabama; George A. Marshall, Male, 3, Alabama.

George W. Marshall was listed in the United States Civil War Soldiers Index as a private in the 22nd Regiment, Alabama Infantry, Company B, Confederate States of America.

Mason, Captain John Richardson

On December 23, 1803, John Richardson Mason was born in Greensville County, Virginia. He was the son of William Mason (12/24/1781-12/24/1835) and Rebecca Richardson (12/23/1781-5/5/1837).

In February 1818, John Richardson Mason came with his parents to Limestone County, Alabama, from Virginia. From February 10, 1818, through February 23, 1818, William Mason, father of John, entered 810 acres in Limestone County, Alabama. On November 29, 1829, he entered an additional 180 acres (Cowart, 1984).

In 1833, John Richardson Mason first married the daughter of Gabriel Smith in Limestone County. Gabriel Smith was a cotton planter, and in the 1830 Limestone County, Alabama Census, Gabriel owned 35 black slaves.

In 1840 Limestone County, Alabama Census, John R. Mason owned 54 black slaves. In addition to being a cotton planter, John raised livestock for resale.

In 1844, the first wife of John Richardson Mason died in Limestone County, Alabama. They had one son, William Mason, who was probably named after his grandfather. In the 1860 Limestone County census, William Mason owned 61 black slaves. By 1862, William Mason was living at Iuka, Mississippi, and he served as a Confederate soldier under General Bragg. In 1878, William Mason died in Waco Texas.

On March 28, 1845, John R. Mason was again married at Athens to Glorvinia Beaty, a daughter of Robert Beaty and Sallie Parrott. Robert Beaty was from Ireland, and he was an early settler of Limestone County. After moving to Limestone County from Virginia, Robert donated the Athens Springs and several acres for the establishment of Athens. Robert died in Missouri where he had gone on a business trip.

Glorvinia Beaty Mason inherited the Beaty home in Athens after the death of her parents, Robert and Sarah Parrott Beaty. John Richardson Mason and Glorvinia Beaty Mason had two sons:

1. Robert Beaty Mason was born on June 27, 1846. During the Civil War, Robert B. Mason was in the Confederate Army, and he served as an escort under the command of General Phillip

Dale Roddy. Robert surrendered at Pond Springs in Lawrence County, Alabama. After the war, he returned to farming and raising livestock. Robert married Mary P. Garrett (1849-1882), and they had four children: Clyde Ormond Mason, Robert Beaty Mason, John J. Greer Mason and Mary Elice Mason. Robert died on May 19, 1904, at the age of 57. He is buried in the Athens City Cemetery at Athens in Limestone County, Alabama (Find A Grave Memorial # 39554599).

2. John Ormond Mason was born on June 30, 1848, and he died at Athens on April 10, 1884, at the age of 35. He is buried in the Athens City Cemetery at Athens in Limestone County, Alabama (Find A Grave Memorial # 39554628).

At Athens, John Richardson Mason was a merchant for a few years, but he became wealthy from planting cotton and raising livestock. John was a strong supporter of the North and South Railroad, and he served as a member of its Board of Directors.

In the 1850 Limestone County, Alabama, Agricultural Survey, John Richardson Mason owned 1200 acres of improved land and 1700 acres of unimproved land worth $20,000. He owned $2,000 worth of farm equipment and $4,435 worth of livestock.

According to the 1850 Limestone County, Alabama, Slave Schedules, John R. Mason owned 106 slaves in District 4. He also owned 5 slaves in District 3 for a total of 111 slaves.

According to the 1860 Limestone County, Alabama, Slave Schedules, John R. Mason owned 134 slaves. In 1860, A. M. Weatherford was listed as the agent for John Richardson Mason.

On April 19, 1862, after the battle of Shiloh and during a visit to his son William, John Richardson Mason got very sick and died at Iuka in Tishomingo County, Mississippi. At the time of his death, Union Army forces were occupying Athens, and Federal officers were using his Robert Beaty home as their headquarters. Eventually, John was brought back home and was buried in the Athens City Cemetery (Find A Grave Memorial # 39554556).

In 1876, the Estate of John R. Mason filed a financial amount of $9,971.00 with the Southern Claims Commission. The serial number of the claim was 21,132, but the claim was disallowed.

On June 24, 1894, Glorvinia Beaty Mason died in Limestone County. Glorvinia was buried in the Athens City Cemetery at Athens, Alabama (Find A Grave Memorial# 39554519).

Matthews, Luke Sr.

Luke Matthews Sr. was born about 1767 in Brunswick County, Virginia. Luke was the son of John and Lucretia Matthews of Red Oak, and he was the grandson of Charles Matthews and great grandson of James Matthews. About 1788, Luke first married Rebecca Dameron, and she died about 1789 in Campbell County, Virginia.

About 1792, Luke Matthews married a second time to Judith Dance in Dinwiddie County, Virginia. The estate records of Luke Matthews indicate that they had a total of ten children as follows:
1. Thomas Matthews was born about 1793.
2. Elizabeth Matthews was born on November 7, 1794.
3. Luke Matthews was born September 10, 1796.
4. John Matthews was born on September 10, 1796.
5. Samuel Matthews was born December 12, 1798.
6. Edward Matthews was born about 1800.
7. Nancy Matthews was born about 1801.
8. William Washington Matthews was born about 1805, and he died about 1866.
9. Nathaniel Matthews was born about 1810.
10. Susan Ann Matthews was born about 1815.

By 1818, Thomas, Luke, John, Samuel, William W., and probably Nathaniel Matthews migrated to Limestone County, Alabama. Five of the brothers were cotton farmers, land holders, and slave owners in Limestone and Madison Counties, Alabama. Nathaniel Matthews probably followed his brother

John all the way to Texas; Nathaniel inherited the cotton plantation of his brother John in Colorado County, Texas.

In 1819, Luke Matthews Sr. died at the age of 52 in Campbell County, Virginia. His son, John Matthews, returned from Texas to Virginia where he died.

Luke Matthews Jr. - Cotton Hill

On September 10, 1796, Luke Matthews was born in Campbell County, Virginia. His parents were Luke Matthews Sr. and Judith Dance

On February 9, 1818, Luke Matthews purchased the Southeast ¼ of Section 36 in Township 3 South and Range 4 West in Limestone County, Alabama (Cowart, 1984). This parcel of land was the 1824 location of the Cotton Hill Plantation mansion. The historic marker for Cotton Hill is located about three miles southeast of Athens on the old Browns Ferry Road.

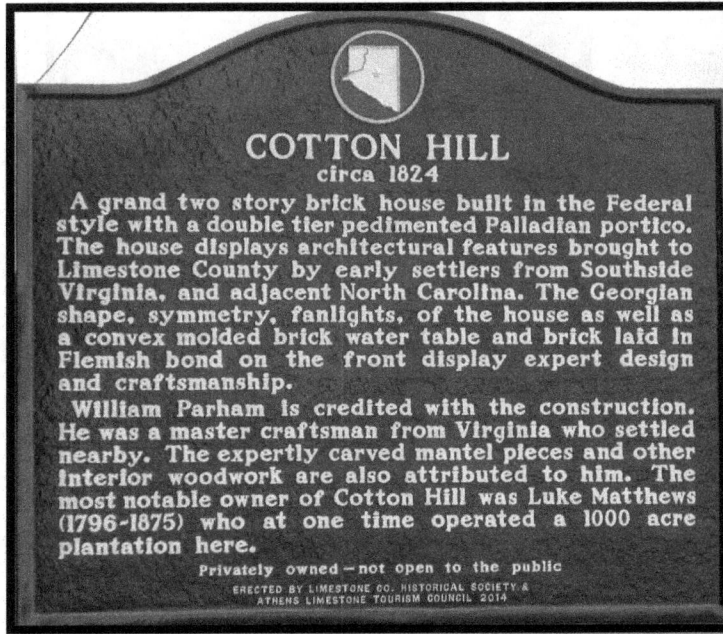

About 1824, William Parham built a large brick home on the Cotton Hill Plantation that became the residence of Luke Matthews. The home was located on a prominent hill on the north side of the Browns Ferry Road in Limestone County, Alabama, about one mile east of present-day Interstate 65.

Luke Matthews drew the plans for his plantation house and contracted his neighbor, William Parham, to build the home. Parham was an expert builder and hand made all the doors, cabinets, staircases, and fireplace mantles. The bricks for the chimneys and 18-inch-thick wall were made on the plantation by the black slaves of Luke Matthews. The house contained two large rooms downstairs and two upstairs, two hallways and a basement with three rooms.

According to Wikipedia: "Cotton Hill is a historic mansion on a former plantation in Limestone County, Alabama. The house was built in the middle of a 1,000-acre plantation by William Parham for Luke Matthews in the 1830s. It was designed in the Federal architectural style. The house was listed on the National Register of Historic Places in 2014."

Cotton Hill

Cotton Hill Plantation was located east of Tanner on the original Indian trail known as the Browns Ferry Road that ran from Big Spring (Hunt's Spring) to Gourd Settlement (Courtland). The home was in the northwest corner of the intersection of Browns Ferry Road and Cambridge Lane; it was about a mile west Peete's Corner near Piney Creek.

On March 8, 1826, Luke Matthews married Judith E. Peete in Limestone County, Alabama; she was the daughter of Benjamin and Anne Blunt Peete. Luke Matthews and Judith Peete Matthews had the following children:
1. Samuel P. Matthews.
2. Mary Jane Matthews.
3. Maria D. Matthews Erskine was born on November 29, 1835; she married Dr. Albert Russell Erskine of Huntsville. Maria died on October 1, 1920 (Find A Grave Memorial# 92826206).
4. Elizabeth Matthews.

According to the 1830 Limestone County, Alabama Census, Luke Matthews owned 41 black slaves. In the 1830 Madison County, Alabama Census, Judith Matthews owned 42 black slaves. Luke and Judith Matthews owned a total of 83 slaves in 1830.

According to the 1840 Limestone County, Alabama Census, Luke Matthews owned 112 black slaves. Luke became one of the larger southern cotton planters and slave owners of northwest Alabama. He was recognized as a kind master to his slaves.

On January 6, 1842, Judith Peete Matthews died from a fall down the stairs at the Cotton Hill Plantation Home in Limestone County, Alabama. With four small children and a large plantation on his hands, Luke lost little time in looking about for another wife.

On January 26, 1843, Luke Matthews married Lucy Anne Spotswood. Lucy was born in Virginia on February 17, 1816, to Elliott Spotswood and Sarah "Sally" Dandridge Littlepage Spotswood (1790-1854) of Madison County, Alabama. Luke and Lucy Matthews moved to a new home near Elco Switch in Limestone County.

Luke Matthews and Lucy Anne Spotswood Matthews had the following children:
5. John Nathaniel Matthews was born December 9, 1843; he married Henrietta Cecelia Tardy. John died on October 23, 1874 (Find A Grave Memorial# 10953491).

6. Elliott Robertson Matthews was born on September 4, 1845; he married Frances Weakley Scruggs. Private Elliott R. Matthews died on July 29, 1907 (Find A Grave Memorial# 10997744).
7. James Pleasant Matthews was born on March 19, 1846; he married Lucy Beirne. James died on April 16, 1909 (Find A Grave Memorial# 10965621).
8. Sallie Matthews Fletcher was born on March 5, 1847; she married James E. Fletcher. Sallie died on July 22, 1924(Find A Grave Memorial# 10945868).
9. Susan "Susie" Botts Matthews Faust was born in 1858; she married John Armstrong Faust. Susie died March 5, 1926 (Find A Grave Memorial# 160528030).
10. Lucian Turner Matthews was born on May 12, 1848; he died on September 18, 1872 (Find A Grave Memorial#10948062).
11. William Edmond Matthews was born on April 18, 1851; he married Carrie Tardy and Lina Matthews. William died on December 23, 1929 (Find A Grave Memorial# 182745191).
12. Lucy Spotswood Matthews White was born on July 29, 1854; she married David Irvine White. Lucy died on July 26, 1939(Find A Grave Memorial# 10966546).

In 1845, Luke Matthews bought from Thomas W. White some 2,138 acres of land in the area of present-day Gate 9 of the Redstone Arsenal. The property had originally belonged to James Manning who called his cotton plantation "The Grove." According to the 1830 Madison County, Alabama Census, James Manning was a cotton planter who owned 225 black slaves.

Around 1850, Luke moved his family on his newly purchased land just south of the Town of Huntsville. In the 1850 Madison County, Alabama, Agricultural Census, Luke Matthews owned 1600 acres of improved land and 800 acres of unimproved land worth $48,000. He also owned $800 worth of farming equipment and $1,200 worth of livestock.

According to the 1850 Limestone County, Alabama Census, Luke Matthews owned 57 black slaves. In the 1850 Madison County, Alabama, Slave Schedules, Luke Matthews owned 71 slaves; therefore, he owned a total of 128 slaves.

In the 1850 Limestone County, Alabama, Agricultural Census, Luke Matthews owned 600 acres of improved land and 500 acres of unimproved land worth $16,500. He also owned $630 worth of farming equipment and $1,660 worth of livestock. An additional entry for Luke Matthews in Limestone County showed that he owned 225 acres of improved land and 175 acres of unimproved land worth $6,000. Luke had $75 worth of farming equipment and $602 worth of livestock. This was probably two different farms owned by Matthews in Limestone County.

According to the 1860 Limestone County, Alabama Census, Luke Matthews owned a total 203 black slaves. In the 1860 Alabama, Slave Schedules listed as Madison City in Limestone County, Luke Matthews owned 62 slaves and under that Luke Matthews owned 98 slaves.

In the 1860 Madison County, Alabama, Agricultural Census, Luke Matthews owned 1500 acres of improved land and 1000 acres of unimproved land worth $50,000. He also owned $600 worth of farming equipment and $4,010 worth of livestock. Prior to the Civil War, Luke continued to buy land and cattle to become one of the largest landowners and wealthiest men in North Alabama.

Around 1861 during the start of the Civil War, Luke moved his family to a home on Adams Avenue in Huntsville. He probably felt that they would be more secure than living on his plantation southwest of town. Later, Luke bought a large home on McClung Street and lived there until he died.

In 1873, Luke Matthews sold the Cotton Hill Plantation to Judge John B. McClellan of Lincoln County, Tennessee. The widow of the brother-in-law of McClellan married William Parham who built the Cotton Hill home. At the time, Luke was living in Huntsville at his McClung Street home.

On November 1, 1874, Lucy Ann Spotswood Matthews died at age 58. She was buried in the Maple Hill Cemetery in Huntsville, Alabama (Find A Grave Memorial# 10948046).

On August 1, 1875, Luke Matthews died at the age of 78 in his home on McClung Street in Huntsville. Luke was buried in the Maple Hill Cemetery in Madison County, Alabama (Find A Grave Memorial# 10948025).

Samuel Matthews

On December 22, 1798, Samuel Matthews was born in Brunswick County, Virginia. Samuel was the son of Luke Matthews Sr. and Judith Dance. His siblings include the following: Martha Mathews, Thomas Matthews, Elizabeth Mathews, Luke Mathews, Simon Matthews, Edwards Mathews, Nancy Matthews, William Washington Matthews, Nathaniel Matthews, and Susan Ann Matthews.

In 1818, Samuel Matthews came to Limestone County, Alabama, with his brothers. The brothers included Luke Matthews Jr., William Washington Matthews, and Thomas Matthews; all entered land and owned slaves in Limestone County.

In the 1840 Limestone County, Alabama Census, Samuel Matthews owned 44 black slaves.

On April 25, 1844, Samuel Matthews married Sarah Elliott Spotswood. Sarah was born in March 31, 1820, and she was a sister to the wife of his brother Luke Matthews. Sarah E. Spotswood Matthews was the daughter to Elliott Spotswood and Sarah "Sally" Dandridge Littlepage Spotswood (1790-1854) of Madison County, Alabama.

According to the 1850 Limestone County, Alabama, United States Census, House Number 488, Samuel Matthews was a 51-year-old white male born in Virginia. Also in his household was Sarah C. Matthews, Female, 28, Alabama; Sarah S. Matthews, Female, 5, Alabama; and Luke Matthews, Male, 2, Alabama.

According to the 1850 Limestone County, Alabama, Slave Schedule, Samuel Matthews owned 67 black slaves.

In the 1850 Limestone County, Agricultural Census, Samuel Matthews owned 900 acres of improved land and 850 acres of unimproved land worth

$22,000. He also had $650 worth of farming equipment and livestock valued at $3,360.

In the 1860 City of Huntsville, Madison County, Alabama, United States Census, Household 387, Samuel Mathews was a 61-year-old white male born in Virginia. Also in his household was Sarah E. Matthews, Female, 38, Alabama; Sallie S. Mathews, Female, 14, Alabama; Luke Matthews, Male, 13, Alabama; and Carrie Turner, Female, 18, Alabama.

In 1866, Samuel Matthews was listed in the Limestone County, Alabama State Census. He was 67 years old.

In the 1870 Madison County, Alabama, United States Census, Household 111, Samuel Matthews was a 71-year-old white male born in Virginia. Also in the household was Edward Fletcher, Male, 30, Alabama; Sallie Fletcher, Female, 25, Alabama; and Richard Matthews, Male 5, Alabama.

On June 11, 1868, Sarah E. Spotswood Matthews died at age 48 at Huntsville in Madison County, Alabama. She was buried in the Maple Hill Cemetery (Find A Grave Memorial# 10945899). On January 5, 1883, Samuel Matthews died at age 84 at Huntsville in Madison County, Alabama. He was buried in Maple Hill Cemetery (Find A Grave Memorial# 10945908).

Thomas Matthews

In the 1820 Limestone County, Alabama Census, Thomas Matthews owned 30 black slaves. In the 1830 Limestone County, Alabama Census, Thomas Matthews owned 69 black slaves.

On March 23, 1830, Thomas Matthews entered 161 acres in Section 34 of Township 3 South and Range 3 West in Limestone County, Alabama (Cowart, 1984). On May 7, 1831, Thomas entered 78.62 acres in Section 8 of Township 4 South and Range 2 West in Madison County, Alabama (Cowart, 1979).

On May 28, 1831, Thomas Matthews entered 80 acres in Section 14 of Township 4 South and Range 7 West in Lawrence County, Alabama (Cowart,

1991). The land he entered was east of Spring Creek and about two miles south of the Tennessee River.

William Washington Matthews

On July 25, 1832, William Washington Matthews entered 80.21 acres in Section 23 of Township 4 South and Range 5 West in Limestone County, Alabama (Cowart, 1984). In the 1840 Limestone County, Alabama Census, William W. Matthews owned 22 black slaves.

In the 1840 Limestone County, Alabama Census, William W. Matthews owned 22 black slaves. In the 1850 Limestone County, Alabama Census, William W. Matthews owned 30 black slaves.

According to the 1850 Limestone County, Alabama, Agricultural Census, William Washington Matthews owned 600 acres of improved land and 360 acres of unimproved land worth $20,000. He also owned $550 worth of farming equipment and livestock valued at $2,770.

On December 18, 1854, William Washington Matthews entered 159.7 acres in Townships 5, 6 South and Range 5 West in Morgan County, Alabama (Cowart, 1981). The land was on the south side of the Tennessee River and opposite side of the river of the land he entered in Limestone County.

In the 1860 Morgan County, Alabama, Agricultural Census, William Washington Matthews was listed with $215 worth of farming equipment and $2,800 worth of livestock. His land was not mentioned in the 1860 agricultural census of Morgan County.

John Matthews - Matthews Prairie

Based on birth records, John and Luke Matthews were twin brothers. On September 10, 1796, they were both born in Campbell County, Virginia, on the same day.

In the 1830 Madison County, Alabama Census, John Matthews owned 23 black slaves. John was not shown as having slaves in Limestone County in 1830.

On June 23, 1831, John Matthews entered 181.29 acres in Section 1 of Township 5 South and Range 3 West in Limestone County, Alabama Cowart, 1984). The land was in the southeast corner of the county east of Limestone Creek and close to the Madison County line.

By 1837, John Matthews had moved to Colorado County, Texas, and lived on the east side of the Colorado River. The community of Matthews, Texas, was named in honor of John Matthews.

According to the 1840 Texas tax records, John Matthews was listed as being from Campbell County, Virginia. According to the 1840 Colorado County, Texas Census, John owned 2,222 acres and 17 black slaves.

In the 1860 Colorado County, Texas, Agricultural Census, John Matthews owned 800 acres of improved land and 140 black slaves valued at $225,000. During 1860, John and his slaves produced 589 bales of cotton and 10,000 bushels of corn.

In January 1861, John, who never married, became very sick and requested his youngest brother Nathaniel to take him back to his birthplace home in Campbell County, Virginia. Before they left Texas for Virginia, John willed his entire Texas estate to his brother Nathaniel Matthews; the children of Nathaniel inherited the plantation from their father. In 1861 after arriving in Virginia, John Matthews died and was buried in his home state of Virginia.

McDonald, Captain Jonathan R.

On November 7, 1806, Jonathan McDonald was born in Kentucky. His father was William McDonald (1766-1840) who was born in Botetourt County, Virginia. The mother of Jonathan was Ursula Hough Huff (1768-1858) who was born in Montgomery County, Virginia. William and Ursula McDonald died at Florence in Lauderdale County, Alabama.

In 1829, Jonathan McDonald married Mary Briggs Malone; she was born on April 16, 1806, in Virginia. Her parents were Thomas Chappell Malone and Mary Chappell, who were double first cousins.

Jonathan McDonald and Mary Briggs Malone had the following children born in Alabama:
1. William Augustus McDonald was born on April 28, 1830; he died on October 5, 1837(Find A Grave Memorial# 41331709).
2. Francis Lucinda McDonald was born on July 10, 1832; she died on October 5, 1837 (Find A Grave Memorial# 41331766).
3. Colonel Joseph Bibb McDonald was born on April 10, 1834; on February 10, 1858, he married Henrietta A. Bacon. Joseph died on March 11, 1883, and he was buried in the Linwood Cemetery in Muscogee County, Georgia (Find A Grave Memorial# 34103494).
4. Captain Thomas James McDonald was born on December 14, 1836; he married Margaret Simpson. Thomas died on January 6, 1903 (Find A Grave Memorial# 40372785).
5. Mary A. McDonald was born in 1839.
6. Henrietta B. McDonald was born in 1841.
7. Jonathan K. McDonald was born in 1843.
8. Sterling P. McDonald was born in 1845.
9. Stith Malone McDonald was born on December 25, 1846, and he died on November 5, 1855 (Find A Grave Memorial#41342058).
10. Eliza D. McDonald was born in 1849.

In 1836, Dr. Jonathan R. McDonald bought and lived in a beautiful southern antebellum home in Athens. The house was built about 1824 by the original owner Thomas Vining who died in 1826. After Vining died, Joseph Wood, a local cotton planter and slave owner, bought the home in 1831; he sold the house to Dr. McDonald.

In 1840, Dr. Jonathan R. McDonald was listed in the Limestone County, Alabama, United States Census. He was a cotton planter and local medical doctor serving Athens and Limestone County.

In the 1850s, Dr. Jonathan R. McDonald was a strong supporter of the development of the Tennessee and Alabama Central Railroad through Athens. He used his influence to see the rail line completed which was a big boost to the cotton industry around the Athens area.

Dr. Jonathan R. McDonald-1824

According to the 1850 Limestone County, Alabama, Agricultural Census, Jonathan McDonald owned 1,000 acres of improved land and 2,000 acres of unimproved land worth $32,000. He also had $1,440 worth of farming equipment and livestock valued at $3,490. He was one of the largest land and slave holders in Limestone County, Alabama.

In the 1850 Limestone County, Alabama, Slave Schedules, Jonathan McDonald was listed as owning 69 black slaves. By the 1860 Limestone County, Alabama, Slave Schedules, Dr. Jonathan R. McDonald owned 103 black slaves.

In 1861, Captain Jonathan R. McDonald and several members of Company F and Company H of the 9th Alabama were serving the Confederacy near Richmond, Virginia. He lived through the Civil War, but like many cotton planters suffered severe financial losses after the war.

In 1866, Jonathan McDonald was listed in the Limestone County, Alabama, State Census. Later, in the year of the state census, Jonathan McDonald died.

On July 23, 1866, Dr. Jonathan McDonald died in Limestone County, Alabama. He was buried in the in Athens City Cemetery at Athens, Alabama, (Find A Grave Memorial# 40372847)

On August 16, 1868, Mary Briggs Malone McDonald died in Limestone County, Alabama. She was buried in the Athens City Cemetery (Find A Grave Memorial# 40372839).

The Polly Malone Cemetery on the old Browns Ferry Road in Limestone County, Alabama, had the following burials for the children of Jonathan and Mary McDonald:
1. McDonald, William Augustus, April 28, 1830-October 5, 1837, was the son of Jonathan and Mary Briggs Malone McDonald; he shares box tomb top with Francis L. McDonald.
2. McDonald, Francis L. (Lucinda), July 10, 1832-October 5, 1837, was the daughter of Jonathan and Mary Briggs Malone McDonald; she shares a box tomb top with William Augustus McDonald.
3. McDonald, Stith Malone, December 25, 1846-November 5, 1855, was the son of Jonathan and Mary Briggs Malone McDonald.

Moore, John and Rebecca Fletcher

On January 1, 1757, Reverend John Moore was born in Northampton County, North Carolina. He died April 28, 1854 in Limestone County, Alabama. John, a Revolutionary War soldier, was the son of Mark Moore and Sarah Mason.

John Moore married Rebecca Fletcher, daughter of William Fletcher, a native of Virginia. Rebecca appears to come with other members of the Fletcher family that included John, Richard, and William Fletcher of Brunswick County, Virginia.

After marriage, Rebecca and John lived in Brunswick County, Virginia. Reverend John Moore and Rebecca Fletcher Leslie Moore had the following children:
1. John Fletcher Moore married Nancy Fletcher.
2. Mary Moore married Thomas Kent Harris.
3. Dr. David Moore was born 1787 in Brunswick County, Virginia, and died in 1845 in Huntsville, Alabama.
4. Richard Moore married Eliza Turner. On February 5, 1818, Richard entered 397.61 acres in Sections 2, 11, 14 of Township 3 south and Range 3 West in Limestone County, Alabama (Cowart, 1984). He entered 158.94 acres with his brother David Moore.
5. Dr. Alfred Moore (1790-1856) of Huntsville, surgeon in the War of 1812, married Elizabeth Jones, parents of Colonel Sydenham Moore of Eutaw.
6. Judge John Edmund Moore of Florence.

In 1807, the Moore family moved from Brunswick County, Virginia to Davidson County, Tennessee. By 1808, the family of Rebecca Fletcher moved to Madison County in Mississippi Territory, and by 1818, they were in Limestone County, Alabama.

Dr. Alfred Moore

On September 11, 1791, Dr. Alfred Moore was born in Brunswick County, Virginia. In 1814, Alfred married and Eliza Jones (2/2/1796-6/19/18??); his second marriage was to Mary Jane Watson (1816-4/1/1892) of Richmond, Virginia. Dr. Alfred Moore fathered the following children:
1. Ella Moore Donegan (unknown-1887) (Find A Grave Memorial# 95670696).
2. Colonel John Edmund Moore (1815-1865) (Find A Grave Memorial# 83330955).
3. Sydenham Moore (1817-1862) (Find A Grave Memorial# 7120940).
4. Olivia Moore O'Neal (1819-1909) (Find A Grave Memorial# 38526610).

5. Dr. George H. Moore (1821-1860). (Find A Grave Memorial# 134134377)
6. Elizabeth Jones Moore Phelan (1828-1860) (Find A Grave Memorial# 18561323).

On February 6, 1818, Alfred Moore entered 320 acres in Section 2 of Township 4 South and Range 3 West in Limestone County. On July 25, 1831, Alfred entered 80 acres in Section 2 of Township 4 South and Range 3 West in Limestone County, Alabama (Cowart, 1984).

In the 1830 Madison County, Alabama Census, Alfred Moore owned 32 black slaves. In the 1850 Limestone County, Alabama, Slave Schedules, Alfred Moore owned 61 black slaves.

On January 7, 1856, Dr. Alfred Moore died at Huntsville. He was buried in Maple Hill Cemetery in Madison County, Alabama (Find A Grave Memorial# 10968605).

Dr. David Moore

On August 25, 1787, Dr. David Moore, the son of John and Rebecca Fletcher Moore, was born in Brunswick County, Virginia. He received his early education in Virginia, and he graduated in medicine from the University of Pennsylvania. After becoming a doctor, Moore moved to Nashville, Tennessee, where he began practicing as a local doctor in the area. He became a friend and the family physician of General Andrew Jackson.

In 1808, Dr. Moore moved from Davidson County, Tennessee, south along the Great South Trail or Old Huntsville Road from Nashville to Madison County in Mississippi Territory. As other soldiers who served under General Andrew Jackson, David was able to enter vast tracts of property in North Alabama and become a wealthy land speculator and cotton planter.

In 1809 within present-day downtown Huntsville, Dr. David Moore was deeded 30 acres by LeRoy Pope. David served as a trustee for the new Town of Huntsville of Mississippi Territory in 1809.

On August 26, 1809, David Moore first entered about 320 acres in Section 1 of Township 4 South and Range 1 West in Madison County of Mississippi Territory. On August 28, 1809, David entered another 320 acres in Section 12 of Township 4 South and Range 1 West (Cowart, 1979).

From 1813 until March 1814, Dr. David Moore and his brother Dr. Alfred Moore served as the army surgeons for General Andrew Jackson during the Creek Indian War. After the Battle of Horseshoe Bend, David and Alfred returned home to Madison County.

After Alabama became a state, Dr. David Moore was elected 13 times to the House of Representatives. From 1822 through 1825, David was elected to the Alabama Senate, but he preferred the role as representative.

From August 26, 1809, through August 25, 1846, Dr. David Moore entered a total of 4,155 acres of land in Madison County of Mississippi Territory (Cowart, 1979). In 1817, Madison County would become part of Alabama Territory, and in 1819, it would be a county in the State of Alabama.

On February 5, 1818, Dr. David Moore entered 398 acres in Sections 2, 11 of Township 3 South and Range 3 West. On February 6, 1818, he entered 160 acres in Section 20 of Township 4 South and Range 3 West. On June 22, 1825, David entered 80 acres in Section 2 of Township 3 South and Range 3 West. From July 29, 1830, through May 30, 1831, he entered an additional 240 acres in Section 2 of Township 5 South and Range 3 West in Limestone County, Alabama (Cowart, 1984). Therefore, Dr. David Moore entered a total of 878 acres in Limestone County.

On March 11, 1818, David Moore entered 240 acres in Sections 4, 22 in Township 3 South and Range 12 West in Lauderdale County. On July 28, 1831, he entered an additional 80 acres in Section 7 of Township 3 South and Range 10 West in Lauderdale County, Alabama, for a total of 320 acres (Cowart, 1996).

In September 1818, David Moore entered 1,925 acres in Lawrence County, Alabama. On October 6, 1818, he entered an additional 160 acres of land, and on March 9, 1830, he entered an additional 160 acres. Dr. David Moore entered a total of 2,245 acres in Lawrence County, Alabama, with most of the property being along the south bank of the Tennessee River (Cowart, 1991).

From September 16, 1818, through November 12, 1818, David Moore entered about 1,205 acres in present-day Colbert County which was originally Lawrence and Franklin Counties. Colbert County was established after the Civil War in 1867. On November 6, 1818, David entered an additional 1,027 acres in Franklin County, Alabama. Part of the land he entered in Franklin County was with the Russellville Land Company which included the following trustees: David Moore, Anthony Winston, Brice M. Garner, G. W. Martin, and Richard Ellis.

In the 1830 Madison County, Alabama Census, David Moore owned 100 black slaves. His slaves included 56 males and 44 females.

Dr. David Moore was first married to Harriet Haywood, daughter of Judge John Haywood of Tennessee. In 1834 after the death of Harriet, he married Martha Leslie Harrison Moore Patton (11/5/1811-11/6/1881), daughter of Benjamin Harrison of Brunswick County, Virginia. David was the father of three sons and three daughters with only two sons and two daughters reaching adulthood. The known children of Dr. David Moore are as follows:
1. David Leslie Moore (CSA) 6/12/1837-6/21/1887.
2. Samuel B. Moore (26th Alabama Infantry Regiment, CSA) owned 112 slaves in 1860.
3. Harriet Moore Rhett (1836-1902)

In the counties of Franklin, Lawrence, Limestone, and Madison Counties of northwest Alabama, Dr. David Moore entered a total of 9,830 acres of land. He also owned land and a plantation in Noxubee County, Mississippi. Supposedly, he owned and managed nine cotton plantations and produced 1,000 bales of cotton annually some of which he shipped to Liverpool, England.

On September 23, 1845, Dr. David Moore died as a wealthy landowner and cotton planter. He was buried in the Maple Hill Cemetery at Huntsville in Madison County, Alabama (Find A Grave Memorial# 8758742).

In the 1850 Madison County, Alabama, Agricultural Census, Thomas J. Bibb was listed as the agent for David Moore. According to the census, David Moore estate had 700 acres of improved land and 1,000 acres of unimproved land worth $20,000. There was $500 worth of farming equipment and $1,900 worth of livestock.

In the 1850 Madison County, Alabama, Slave Schedules, Dr. David Moore's Estate owned 231 black slaves. These slaves were in five different locations in Madison County with three different agents. The agents included Thomas Bibb, William C. Bibb, and James F. Pittcock.

Peebles/Peoples, Sterling

Sterling Peebles (1760-1811) and Martha Wilkins Peebles were the parents of four sons who made their way from North Carolina to Mississippi Territory in what is now North Alabama. The Peebles brothers were seeking better cotton grounds along the Tennessee River Valley. There were also other cousins who made the perilous journey from Northampton County, North Carolina.

In 1815, several male cousins and/or brothers of the Peebles family came to the Madison County area of Mississippi Territory with their families and black slaves. Eventually, most all the Peebles owned land and slaves in Limestone County, Alabama. They were basically cotton farmers trying to get wealthy with the labor of their black slaves.

The four sons of Sterling and Martha Peebles that migrated southwest from North Carolina were Dudley Robinson Peebles, Joseph Douglas Peebles, Edmund Peebles, and Henry Wyche Peebles. Their father Sterling had died in North Carolina before the brothers made their way to the Tennessee Valley.

The other cousins, who were thought to be nephews of Sterling, were Howell Peebles, son of Ephraim and Hannah Peebles, and Henry Peeples Jr., son of Henry Peebles Sr. and Ann Taylor. Howell Peebles was not a prominent figure in Limestone County; in 1857, Howell Peebles died in Limestone County, Alabama.

Peebles, Dudley Robinson

On September 10, 1818, Dudley and Henry Peebles entered 800 acres in Township 4 South and Range 7 West in Lawrence County, Alabama. The land they entered was at the headwaters of Spring Creek just east of Courtland, Alabama.

On March 16, 1819, Lawrence County Commissioner Court appointed Dudley Peoples and several other men to work on a Courtland road project. On June 22, 1819, Dudley Peoples is mentioned in the document concerning building of road from Courtland toward Big Spring in Franklin County.

According to the 1820 Lawrence County, Alabama Census, the Dudley H. Peoples household had three white males over 21. Those three white males over 21 were probably Dudley Robinson Peebles, Edmund Peebles, and Henry Wyche Peebles, since their other brother Joseph D. Peebles was listed in Limestone County in 1820. In the 1820 Lawrence County, Alabama Census, Dudley R. Peebles owned 64 black slaves.

Before October 1828, Dudley Robinson Peoples died, and his brother Henry Wyche Peebles was appointed as administrator of the Dudley Peebles Estate. In 1834, the estate of Dudley Peebles was in the Orphans Court in Lawrence County, Alabama.

Peebles, Joseph Douglas

On November 28, 1815, Joseph D. Peebles entered 160 in Madison County of Mississippi Territory that was assigned to George Lowe (Cowart, 1979). On February 5, 1818, Joseph Douglas Peebles entered over 370.49 acres of land in Limestone County, Alabama (Cowart, 1984).

The 1820 Limestone County, Alabama Census had the following for Joseph D. Peebles: White Males over 21: 2; White Males under 21: 2; White Females over 21: 1; Total Whites: 5; Slaves: 32; Acres Cultivated: 200; Number of Hands: 11; Number of Bales: 45; Average Weight per bale: 280 pounds; Gins: 1; Saws: 52; Mills: 0. According to the 1820, Limestone County, Alabama Census, Joseph D. Peebles owned 32 black slaves.

On January 21, 1830, Joseph D. Peebles entered three tracts of land containing some 370 acres of land in Township 3 South and Range 3 West in Limestone County, Alabama (Cowart, 1984). In the 1830 Limestone County, Alabama census, Joseph Douglas Peebles owned 67 black slaves.

The 1830 Limestone County, Alabama Census had the following for Joseph D. Peebles: White Males: 10-15: 1; 15-20: 1; 40-50: 1; White Females: 5-10: 1; 30-40: 1; Slaves: 67.

Peebles, Henry Wyche

In the 1830 Lawrence County, Alabama census, Henry W. Peebles owned 59 black slaves. Since Henry W. Peebles was not shown with any slaves in 1820, he must have inherited his slaves from his brother Dudley who died in 1828.

In the 1830 Lawrence County, Alabama Census, Henry W. Peebles was between 30-40 years old. Henry W. Peebles was a brother of Dudley Peebles, and the only Peebles in the 1830 Lawrence County census.

Peebles, Henry Jr.

About 1784, Henry Peeples Jr. was born in Virginia. His father was Henry Peebles Sr., and his mother was Ann Taylor. Henry was married three times; he married Mary Barclay about 1807, at Jackson in Northampton, North Carolina.

About 1814, Henry Jr. and his wife Mary Barclay Peebles came to Mississippi Territory from Northampton County, North Carolina. Henry Jr. and Mary Peebles brought their young sons: Washington Peebles, Robert Barclay Peebles, and John T. Peebles. It is believed that shortly after Henry Jr. arrived, his wife Mary Barclay Peebles died.

On February 15, 1815, he married Writher Waters in Madison County of Mississippi Territory. For some reason, the marriage lasted about one- and one-half years before Henry Peebles Jr. married for the third time.

On May 8, 1815, Andrew Metcalf was assigned the property that was originally entered by Henry Peeples Jr. for 159.84 acres of land in Section 31 of Township 1 South and Range 1 East in Madison County in Mississippi Territory (Cowart, 1979). The land he entered was about six miles south of the Tennessee State Line and about three miles north of Meridianville close to the prime meridian.

On August 3, 1816, Henry Peeples Jr. married Rebecca Vinson of Madison, Alabama. Rebecca was the third wife of Henry Peeples Jr.

On February 6, 1818, Henry Peebles entered 182.41 acres in Section 12 of Township 4 South and Range 3 West in Limestone County. On February 7, 1818, he entered 160.25 acres in Section 9 of Township 5 South and Range 3 West in Limestone County, Alabama, near Mooresville (Cowart, 1984).

The 1820 Limestone County, Alabama census for Henry Peoples had the following: 1 Male over 21; 6 males under 21; 1 female over 21; 6 people of color; 30 slaves; 3 acres cultivated; 5 bales at 350 pounds/bale of cotton.

In the 1820 in Limestone County, Alabama Census, Henry Peoples owned 30 black slaves and had six free people of color. If the free persons of color were black, there were 36 black folks living in the household of Henry Peebles in 1820.

The 1830 Limestone County, Alabama Census had the following for Henry Peebles: White Males: 10-15: 2; 15-20:2; 20-30: 2; 40-50: 1; White Females: Under 5: 1; 30-40:1; Slaves: 21. In the1830 Limestone County, Alabama census, Henry Peebles owned 21 black slaves.

The 1840 Limestone County, Alabama Census had the following for Henry Peebles: White Males: 5-10: 1; 20-30: 2; 50-60: 1; White Females: 10-15: 1; 40-50: 1; Free Persons of Color: 6; Total Slaves: 32; Total Working in

Agriculture: 15. In 1840 in Limestone County, Henry Peebles had 38 black folks living in his household.

Around 1846-1847, Henry Peeples Jr. died in Limestone County, Alabama. His burial site is not known.

Robert Barclay Peebles

On July 4, 1808, Robert Barclay Peebles was born in Northampton County, North Carolina. He was the son of Henry Peebles and Mary Barclay Peebles. Robert moved to Limestone County, Alabama, with other family members.

Robert B. Peebles was a merchant at Mooresville in Limestone County. His brother John T. Peebles also helped him in the retail business.

In 1839, Robert B. Peebles married Sophia Sheldon Cooley. Sophia was born on September 22, 1806.

According to the 1850 Limestone County, Alabama, Agricultural Census, Robert B. Peebles owned 400 acres of improved land and 420 acres of unimproved land worth $14,000. He also had $325 worth of farming equipment and livestock worth $1,324.

In the 1860 Limestone County, Alabama, Slave Schedules, Robert B. Peebles owned 80 black slaves. After the Civil War, Robert lost much of his fortune, but still owned many acres of land. In 1860, Washington Peebles, who was supposedly the brother of Robert, owned 37 slaves.

On October 30, 1873, Robert Barclay Peebles died in Limestone County, Alabama. Robert was buried in the Peebles Cemetery at Mooresville in Limestone County, Alabama (Find A Grave Memorial# 72930665).

On February 25, 1882, Sophia Sheldon Cooley Peebles died in Limestone County. She was buried in the Peebles Cemetery (Find A Grave Memorial# 72930680).

John Turner Peebles

On May 10, 1812, John Turner Peebles was born in Northampton County, North Carolina. In 1815, the Henry Peebles family moved from North Carolina to Mississippi Territory when John was just three years old.

On December 2, 1842, John T. Peebles married Martha Tisdale; she was the daughter of Shirley and Anne Blick Tisdale, natives of Virginia. In 1839, the Tisdales had moved from Virginia to Limestone County.

John and Martha T. Peebles had the following children:
1. Sergeant Thomas Washington Peebles (1844-1864) died from a wound he received at the Battle of Franklin.
2. Henderson Tisdale Peebles (1845-1898).
3. Mary Elizabeth Peebles (1849-1855).
4. Mary Ann Peebles was born on July 20, 1860; she married Benjamin Farley Harn. On September 26, 1913, Mary died in Ashville, North Carolina, and she was buried in the Peebles Cemetery at Mooresville in Limestone County, Alabama (Find A Grave Memorial# 188606237).
5. John Henry Peebles (1851-1931) married Elizabeth Withers; she was the daughter of Dr. S. and Emily Stewart Withers. John became a merchant in Mooresville.
6. Ann Sophia Peebles (1853-1855).
7. Robert Kellog Peebles (1856-1887).
8. Charles Edward Peebles (1858-1892).

In 1850 Limestone County, Alabama, Slave Schedules, John T. Peebles owned 9 black slaves. In addition to farming, John helped his brother Robert operate the merchandize store business at Mooresville.

On September 29, 1874, about 11 months after the death of his brother Robert, John T. Peeples died in Limestone County, Alabama. He was buried in the Peebles Cemetery at Mooresville in Limestone County, Alabama (Find A Grave Memorial# 18860651).

Pickett, Sarah Orrick - Myrtle Grove

On June 22, 1790, Colonel Steptoe Pickett Sr. was born in Virginia. He was the son of Colonel Martin Pickett (12/251736-4/25/1804) and Ann Blackwell of Paradise Plantation in Fauquier County, Virginia. Ann Blackwell Pickett was the daughter of Joseph Blackwell (1715-1787), who was a lieutenant in the Revolutionary War, and Lucy Steptoe, daughter of Captain John Steptoe. Martin Pickett served in both the French and Indian War and the American Revolutionary War.

Steptoe Pickett Sr. was a cousin to Harry "Light Horse" Lee who was the ninth Governor of Virginia and father of Robert E. Lee. Steptoe Pickett Sr. was a school classmate of President James Buchanan, Chief Justice John Marshall, and General George E. Pickett of "Pickett's Charge" at Gettysburg.

On October 2, 1793, Sarah Orrick Chilton Pickett was born on Currioman Plantation in Westmoreland County, Virginia. Her parents were Orrick Chilton and Felitia Corbin Chilton.

On January 10, 1811, Sarah and Steptoe Pickett Sr. were married at the Currioman Plantation in Westmoreland County, Virginia. Steptoe Pickett Sr. and Sarah Orrick Chilton Pickett had the following children:
1. Martin Pickett was born on October 23, 1811, in Fauquier County, Virginia; on April 14, 1840, he married Louisa Randolph. Martin died in June 1899, at Mobile in Mobile County, Alabama.
2. Joanna Tucker Pickett was born and died in 1812.
3. Richard Orrick Pickett was born in Fauquier County, Virginia, on August 22, 1814; he married Fannie Louisa Boggs (1817-1907). On November 23, 1898, Richard died in Leighton, Alabama; he was buried in Florence Cemetery in Lauderdale County, Alabama (Find A Grave Memorial# 36476083).
4. Steptoe Pickett Jr. was born in Fauquier County, Virginia, on November 17, 1816; he died on August 29, 1882. He was buried in the Madison Cemetery in Madison County, Alabama (Find A Grave Memorial #10167485).

5. Alexander Corbin Pickett was born on April 11, 1821, in Limestone County, Alabama; he died January 17, 1883. He was buried in the Augusta Memorial Park in Woodruff County, Arkansas (Find A Grave Memorial# 189853844).
6. Felicia Ann Chilton Pickett was born in 1822; she married Governor Reuben Chapman in 1838 when she was 16, becoming the youngest First Lady of Alabama. At the time of their marriage, Governor Reuben Chapman was 39 years old. In 1874, she died in Huntsville in Madison County, Alabama.
7. Dr. John Scott Pickett was born in 1823; he married Martha Blackwell, daughter of William Henry Blackwell and Eliza Collier. John died in 1887.
8. Charles William Pickett was born on March 25, 1825; he died September 22, 1826.
9. Dr. William Henry Pickett was born on December 22, 1826; in 1850, he married Amy Raines Collier (1836-1885), daughter of Edward Collier. On February 8, 1890, William died at age 63; he was buried in Oaklawn Cemetery in Independence County, Arkansas (Find A Grave Memorial# 119758855).
10. Elizabeth Jane Pickett was born on June 26, 1829; she died on April 30, 1833.
11. Sarah Virginia Pickett was born on November 23, 1831; she married Samuel Blackwell, a son of William Henry Blackwell and Eliza Collier.
12. Annastasia "Anna" R. Corbin Pickett was born October 1, 1836; she married Thomas Bibb who died in 1861. She then married Julian Temple Edwards of Riverview Plantation. On February 4, 1913, Anna died at age 76; she was buried in the Lanesville Cemetery in King William County, Virginia (Find A Grave Memorial# 87288110).

In 1821, Steptoe Sr. and his family moved from Fauquier County, Virginia, to the southeastern portion of Limestone County, Alabama. Steptoe and Sarah O. Pickett lived near their Collier and Blackwell relatives at their Myrtle Grove Plantation between Triana and Mooresville.

From March 10, 1830, through April 20, 1830, Steptoe Pickett entered 550.42 acres in Sections 20 and 28 of Township 5 South and Range 3 West in

Limestone County, Alabama (Cowart, 1984). Some of his land was near William H. Blackwell who was a trustee of Sarah Orrick Pickett on June 6, 1842.

According to the 1830 Limestone County, Alabama Census, Steptoe Pickett Sr. owned 30 black slaves. In the 1840 Limestone County census, he owned 46 slaves.

On December 12, 1843, Colonel Steptoe Pickett Sr. died in Morgan County, Alabama. Some say he died in Limestone County, but the place of his burial is not known.

In the 1850 Limestone County, Alabama, United States Census, House Number 333, Sarah O. Pickett was a 58-year-old white female born in Virginia. Also living in her household was Virginia Pickett, Female, 18, Alabama; Annastasia R. Pickett, Female, 14, Alabama; Stephen Pickett, Male, 33, Virginia; Frances W. Pickett, Male, 0, Alabama; William H. Pickett, Male, 23, Alabama; and Amy R. Pickett, Female, 20, Alabama.

According to the 1850 Limestone County, Alabama, Slave Schedule, Sarah O. Pickett owned 61 black slaves. Sarah was another female slave holder in Limestone County who inherited the slaves of her deceased husband. Her son Steptoe Jr. owned 57 slaves; therefore, together they owned 118 slaves.

In the 1850 Limestone County, Alabama, Agricultural Census, Sarah O. Pickett owned 500 acres of improved land and 220 acres of unimproved land worth $8,640. She had $590 worth of farming equipment and $2,092 worth of livestock.

In the 1860 Limestone, County, Alabama, United States Census, Household 353, Sarah O. Pickett was a 69-year-old white female born in Virginia. Also living in her household was Steptoe Pickett, Male, 41, Virginia; Eugenie S. Pickett, Female, 25, Alabama; Fanny Pickett, Female, 1, Alabama; and illegible Pickett Female, 26, Alabama.

In the 1860 Limestone County Largest Slave Owners: Sarah O. Pickett owned 69 slaves. Her son Steptoe had only 16 slaves in 1860 Limestone County census.

On February 19, 1865, Sarah Orrick Chilton Pickett died at age 71 in Limestone County, Alabama. She was buried in the old part of the Madison Cemetery in Madison County, Alabama (Find A Grave Memorial# 10167495).

Major Steptoe Pickett Jr. - Madison Station

On November 17, 1816, Captain Steptoe Pickett Jr. was born in Fauquier County, Virginia. In 1821, he moved as a young boy to Limestone County with his parents Steptoe Pickett Sr. and Sarah Orrick Chilton Pickett.

On January 16, 1849, Steptoe Pickett Jr. married Mary Frances Ward. She was the daughter of Francis Everett Ward and sister of John J. Ward.

In the 1850, Limestone County, Alabama, Slave Schedules, Steptoe Pickett Jr. owned 57 black slaves. He probably inherited the slaves from his father who died in 1843.

On March 17, 1850, Mary Frances Ward Pickett died at 21 years of age in Limestone County, Alabama. She was buried in the old Triana City Cemetery in Madison County. Alabama.

On September 25, 1851, the Memphis Eagle reported the death of the son of Steptoe Pickett Jr. as follows: "Frank Ward Pickett, only child of the late Mrs. Mary Frances Pickett, wife of Steptoe Pickett" died at the age of 18 months and 8 days. He is commemorated on his mother's tombstone in the Triana City Cemetery. His age at death reveals that his mother died in childbirth."

In September 1855, Steptoe Pickett Jr. married Eugenia Sale (1834-1907). Eugenia Sale was a granddaughter of Dudley Sale, born 1782 in Virginia. In the 1830 Madison County, Alabama Census, Dudley Sale owned 26 black slaves.

In the 1860, Limestone County, Alabama, Slave Schedules, Steptoe Pickett Jr. owned only 16 black slaves. He probably had slaves at another location but only 16 in Limestone County.

From 1861 through 1865, Major Steptoe Pickett Jr. was a Civil War Confederate Staff Officer in the Army of Northern Virginia. He served in the 9th Alabama Infantry as Assistant Quartermaster to General Cadmus Wilcox.

On August 27, 1873, Steptoe Pickett lost his twelve-year-old daughter Felicia to a freak accident. Her death was reported in the Huntsville Advocate which stated, "Died on Wednesday August 27, Felicia Pickett, daughter of Major Steptoe Pickett at home at Madison Station from inadvertently swallowing a glass bead. She was about 12 years of age and a bright and interesting child."

On August 31, 1882, The Huntsville Weekly Independence reported the death of Major Steptoe Pickett as printed: "Died, Mr. Steptoe Pickett, one of our best-known citizens at Madison, Tuesday, August 29th in his 66th year. For many years, he has been a respectable citizen of this county."

On January 27, 1892, the Mercury Advocate reported the death of the son of Steptoe Pickett Jr. as stated: "Died Sunday last at the residence of his uncle, Mr. John S. Nance, Adams Avenue, Henry S. Pickett, aged about 23, second son of Mr. Steptoe Pickett, a resident of Madison till his death. He was a loving son, a source of comfort and joy to his widowed mother."

On December 9, 1868, as reported in The Daily Memphis Avalanche, Steptoe Pickett Jr. had 1,200 pounds of his cotton burned in Limestone County by a bunch of horsemen in disguise as Ku Klux Klan. The cotton was destroyed by 12 men on horseback some seven miles from Madison Station. Earlier, the men had been to the plantation of Samuel H. Moore, but the damage there was not reported. Based on the report, cotton was still a major product of the former plantation slave owners who were turning to sharecroppers to farm their lands.

On August 29, 1882, Captain Steptoe Pickett Jr. died at Madison in Madison County, Alabama. Steptoe was buried in the old part of the Madison Cemetery (Find A Grave Memorial# 10167485).

Pryor, Luke Sr. - Sugar Creek

On April 3, 1770, Luke Pryor Sr. was born in Hanover County, Virginia; his parents were Senator John Luke Pryor and Ann Poythress. He was first marriage was to Martha Scott, a sister of General Winfield Scott. Luke and Martha Scott Pryor had the following children:
1. George Pryor was born on October 19, 1802; he died on October 24, 1803.
2. Elizabeth Pryor Douglas was born in 1802 in Hanover County, Virginia; she married Fleming Douglas.

The second marriage of Luke Pryor Sr. was to Ann "Nancy" Batte Lane in Virginia. Ann was born on June 21, 1790, in Virginia. They had the following children:
3. Ann Batte Pryor Shelton was born in 1812 in Westmoreland County, Virginia; she married Fredrick R. Shelton. On October 27, 1856, she died at Mooresville in Limestone County, Alabama.
4. John Benjamin Pryor was born in 1812 in Virginia; he married Frances Ann Bingaman. John Benjamin Pryor of Natchez, Mississippi, would become a noted racehorse trainer. On December 26, 1890, John died and was buried in the Athens City Cemetery (Find A Grave Memorial# 194676148).
5. Mary Dennis Pryor was born on November 22, 1816; she married H. W. Kimbell (Campbell) who owned 38 slaves in 1860. On March 11, 1896, Mary died and was buried in the Athens City Cemetery (Find A Grave Memorial# 3954927).
6. Martha Pryor Allison was born in 1818 in Honover County, Virginia; she married William Davis Allison.
7. Harriett Bolling Pryor was born on July 30, 1818; she married Dr. Thomas Stith Malone. On April 20, 1875, Harriett died and was buried in the Athens City Cemetery (Find A Grave Memorial# 40785359).
8. Virginia Pryor was born in 1819; she died in 1828.
9. Luke Pryor Jr. was born on July 5, 1820, in Huntsville, Alabama; he married Isabella Virginia Harris. On August 5, 1900, Luke died and

was buried in the Athens City Cemetery (Find A Grave Memorial# 6421229).
10. Richard Pryor was born in 1822.
11. Emily Pryor McWilliams was born on September 15, 1826, in Limestone County, Alabama; she married Andrew Jackson McWilliams. On March 8, 1884, Emily died at Tupelo in Lee County, Mississippi.
12. Eliza James Pryor Davis was born in 1822 in Jefferson County, Kentucky; on November 3, 1849, Eliza died in Limestone County, Alabama.

In 1820, Luke and Ann Pryor move from Brunswick County, Virginia, to Madison County, Alabama. The Pryors were natives of the State of Virginia, and descendants of English ancestry.

Around 1822, Luke and Ann Pryor moved to Limestone County, Alabama, and settled on their Sugar Creek Plantation. By occupation Luke Pryor Sr. was a cotton planter and slave owner. He was considered a good citizen and a quiet, unassuming gentleman.

In the 1840 Census, Luke Pryor was recorded as having six free blacks under the age of 10 as well as one male slave child under 10 and an older female over 55 years old. By 1850, Luke Pryor was recorded with 39 slaves from four months to 70 years old.

In the 1850 Limestone County, Agricultural Census, Luke Pryor owned 520 acres of improved land and 360 acres of unimproved land worth $12,000. He also owned $760 worth of farming equipment and $1,302 worth of livestock.

On June 12, 1851, Luke Pryor Sr. died at the age of 81. He was buried in the Athens City Cemetery in Limestone County, Alabama (Find A Grave Memorial# 39560046). Luke Pryor Sr. was mourned by all who knew him.

On March 2, 1864, Ann "Nancy" Batte Lane Pryor, widow of Luke Sr., died at age 73. She was buried in the Athens City Cemetery in Limestone County, Alabama (Find A Grave Memorial# 39560075).

Luke Pryor Jr. - Sugar Creek

On July 5, 1820, Luke Pryor Jr. was born at the Green Bottom Inn of Huntsville in Madison County, Alabama. He was the son of Luke Pryor Sr. and Ann Batte Lane Pryor.

In 1824, the Pryor family moved near Athens, and Luke Jr. attended school at Mooresville in Limestone County, Alabama. Later, Luke Pryor Jr. attended Washington College in Natchez, Mississippi, where he studied law.

In 1841 after studying law under Judge Daniel Coleman at Athens, Luke Pryor Jr. passed the bar and was an attorney for some 40 years. Initially, he became a partner in the law firm of Robert C. Brickell, a distinguished attorney in Huntsville. Later, he worked with Egbert J. Jones, General Leroy Pope Walker, and George Smith Houston.

On August 18, 1845, Luke Pryor Jr. married Isabella Virginia Harris in Limestone County. Isabella was born on January 7, 1826; she was a daughter of John Henry Harris (1778-1843) and Frances Rowzee (1781-1842), natives of Virginia. The siblings of Isabella were Sarah Ann Harris Roberts (1806-1871); John R. Harris (1810-1863); Elizabeth Tate Harris Washington (1818-1893); Benjamin M. Harris (1820-1837); and Schuyler Harris (1823-1880).

Luke Pryor Jr. and Isabella Virginia Harris Pryor had the following children all born in Limestone County, Alabama.
1. Aurora Pryor was born on May 28, 1846; she married Robert Anderson McClellan (1842-1898). On January 15, 1926, Aurora died and was buried in the Athens City Cemetery (Find A Grave Memorial# 31965732).
2. William Richard Pryor was born on August 6, 1848; he married Ida Harris (1849-1915). On February 5, 1908, William died and was buried in the Athens City Cemetery (Find A Grave Memorial# 41147486).
3. Memory Pryor was born on September 27, 1850; she married William S. Peebles. On January 21, 1929, Memory died and was buried in the Athens City Cemetery (Find A Grave Memorial# 39560984).

4. Ann B. Pryor was born on May 10, 1853; she married Maclin Sloss. On May 2, 1902, Ann died and was buried in the Athens City Cemetery (Find A Grave Memorial# 39581455).
5. Fannie Snow Pryor was born on January 21, 1856; on April 19, 1935, Fannie died and was buried in the Athens City Cemetery (Find A Grave Memorial# 39560209).
6. Mary Pryor was born on May 13, 1859; she married Thomas Bass Leslie (1858-1917). On March 10, 1917, Mary died and was buried in the Greenwood Cemetery in Clay County, Mississippi (Find A Grave Memorial# 121379469).
7. Francis Pryor was the son of Luke and Isabella, but his date of birth and death are unknown.
8. Hattie Pryor was born on September 13, 1866; she married Robert Joseph Lowe (1861-1910). On March 25, 1901, Hattie died and was buried in the Athens City Cemetery (Find A Grave Memorial# 29085631).

According to the 1850 United States Census, Luke Pryor Jr. recorded his occupation as a lawyer. Luke Pryor Jr. lived at the Sugar Creek Plantation near Athens, Alabama, for some 40 years before moving to Flower Hill Plantation south of Tanner.

In 1854, Luke and Isabella Pryor lived in the Pryor House with their family at Athens in Limestone County, Alabama. The photograph of the Pryor House was taken on March 23, 1934, by W. N. Manning for the Library of Congress Historic American Buildings Survey.

About 1854, Luke Pryor Jr. became an advocate of the railroad system for Limestone County. In 1855, Luke Pryor Jr., a member of to the Democratic Party, was elected to the state legislature. He supported the railroad through Athens and Limestone County that would improve the economy by providing access to markets and increase the price of farm products. Luke and Major

Pryor House-1826

Thomas H. Hobbs passed a bill supporting the railroad that ran from Nashville to Montgomery by way of Athens.

In the 1860 Slave Schedules for Limestone County, Alabama, Luke Pryor Jr. was listed as owning 76 black slaves. In addition to his law practice, Pryor was a wealthy cotton planter and landowner. During the 1860s, Luke Pryor Jr. and his family moved to the Flower Hill Plantation south of Tanner in Limestone County.

On April 12, 1861, the Civil War started and by 1865 slavery was completely abolished. The planters who did not lose everything after the war turned to sharecroppers to continue their cotton farming operations.

Luke Pryor Jr.

From January 7, 1880, through November 23, 1880, Luke Pryor Jr. served as United States Senator from Limestone County, Alabama. Governor Rufus W. Cobb appointed Pryor to fill the senate seat opened by the death of Senator George Smith Houston, but Pryor did not run for re-election after his term was completed and was succeeded by James L. Pugh.

In 1883, Luke Pryor Jr. was elected to a two-year term in the United States House of Representatives. From March 4, 1883, through March 3, 1885, Luke Pryor Jr. served 8th congressional district of Alabama. He was preceded by General Joseph Wheeler of Lawrence County, and he succeeded by Joseph Wheeler.

On June 16, 1889, Isabella Virginia Harris Pryor died at age 63. She was buried in the Athens City Cemetery in Limestone County, Alabama (Find A Grave Memorial# 39560184).

On August 5, 1900, Luke Pryor Jr. died at the age of 80. He had lived at the Flower Hill Plantation south of Tanner in Limestone County until his death. Luke Pryor Jr. was buried in Athens City Cemetery (Find A Grave Memorial# 6421229).

Ragland, Samuel Major - Triana

In 1773, Samuel Ragland was born in Louisa County, Virginia. He was the son of John Ragland Jr. (1721-1784) and Anne Beverly Dudley. John and Anne B. Dudley Ragland had the following children that were born in Louisa County, Virginia:

1. Nathaniel Ragland was born in 1764; he died in 1833 at Huntsville in Madison County, Alabama.
2. John Dudley Ragland was born on April 4, 1763; he married Margaret Swift Thompson. John died June 17, 1832, in Goochland, Virginia.
3. Sallie Dudley Ragland was born on April 4, 1763; she was a twin to John Dudley Ragland. Sallie married James Davis; she died about 1851 in Virginia.
4. Beverly Ragland was born about 1767; he married Frances Rowe. Beverly died in 1803 in Louisa County, Virginia.
5. Susanna "Suky" Ragland Davis was born about 1770; she married Charles Davis. Suky died about 1847 in Virginia.
6. Edward Mercer Ragland was born about 1771; he married Urusa Dudley Brown. Edward died in 1813 in Smith County, Tennessee.
7. Samuel Ragland (1773-1852).
8. James Ragland was born in 1775; he died in 1817 in Smith County, Tennessee.

By 1813, it appears that Nathaniel, Edward, Samuel, and James Ragland moved from Virginia to Smith County, Tennessee. From there Samuel and his brother Nathaniel moved to Madison County, Alabama.

By 1818, Samuel and Nathaniel Ragland were in Madison County, Alabama. Nathaniel and Samuel were cotton planters and slave owners. On February 4, 1818, Nathaniel entered 620.82 acres in Sections 20 and 21 of Township 5 South and Range 2 West in Madison County, Alabama (Cowart, 1979).

In the 1830 Madison County, Alabama Census, Nathaniel Ragland owned 92 black slaves. He had 57 black males and 35 female slaves.

On March 4, 1833, the two brothers entered land in the same area Samuel Ragland entered 320 acres in Section 22 and Nathaniel Ragland entered 301.82 adjacent acres in Section 23 of Township 5 South and Range 2 West in Madison County, Alabama (Cowart, 1979).

On November 20, 1834, Nathaniel Ragland entered 160.81 acres in Section 23 of Township 5 South and Range 5 West in Morgan County, Alabama

(Cowart, 1981). It is believed that Nathaniel died in 1834 or 1835; his land was probably inherited by his brother Samuel. The Ragland property in Madison and Limestone Counties was near Thomas Bibb, Charles Collier and James Collier.

In 1835, Major Samuel Ragland of Madison County, Alabama, advertised his horse Polly Balloo had a foal. The mare was bred by Dancy's Old Timoleon owned by Colonel David Dancy.

On June 12, 1837, Samuel Ragland entered 240.55 acres in Section 22 of Township 4 South and Range 3 West in Limestone County, Alabama (Cowart, 1984). His land was adjacent to Benjamin Dickson.

On December 23, 1837, Samuel Ragland advertised in the Huntsville Advocate, and on February 21, 1838, he advertised in a Nashville newspaper offering a reward for a runaway slave as follows: "$250 Reward for the apprehension and confinement in jail for my negro man Isham, so that I get him again, if taken out of the state, I will give $100. He left my Plantation near Triana, Madison County, Alabama, early in September last; he is of dark complexion, about 35 years old, five feet five or six inches high, has a scar on the breast, a slight scar on the under lip, occasioned by a bite; he is a blacksmith by trade, has full prominent eyes, short thick fingers, and rather hoarse voice. He runaway two years since, and was committed to jail in Columbia, Tennessee. It is probable he will try to pass through that State again. I will give the above reward for his delivery to me at my residence, near Triana, or agreeable to the terms above."

The advertisement was also noted in 1974 by Dr. Kenneth Johnson in his paper Some Aspects of Slavery in the Muscle Shoals Area as follows: "When dogs were used to hunt slaves, they were usually kept on a leash. On other occasions, they were turned loose to run the slave the same way they would run a deer or fox. In such cases, the slave could be severely injured or killed by the dogs unless he could find safety in a tree. Samuel Ragland of Madison County advertised that his runaway slave, Isham, could be identified by scar on the breast and the under lip which resulted from the bite of a dog. The use of slave catchers with dogs was unpleasant but apparently a common aspect of the slave system."

According to the 1850 Madison County, Alabama, United States Census, House Number 276, Samuel Ragland was a 66-year-old white male born in Virginia. Also living in the household of Samuel Ragland was Robert Morlamore a 27-year-old male born in New York.

According to the 1850 Madison County, Alabama, Agricultural Census, Samuel Ragland owned 495 acres of improved land and 200 acres of unimproved land worth $5,000. He also had $125 worth of farming equipment and $4,370 worth of livestock.

In the 1850 Limestone County, Alabama, Slave Schedule, Samuel Ragland owned 54 black slaves. In 1850, Samuel Ragland of Madison County had 108 slaves in two different locations. In Limestone and Madison Counties, Samuel Ragland had a total of 162 slaves. Another Samuel J. Ragland of Franklin County, Alabama, had 53 slaves.

Until his death in 1852, Samuel Ragland lived on his Triana Plantation in Madison County, Alabama. His plantation was in the southwest corner of Madison County and the southeast corner of Limestone County not far from the north bank of the Tennessee River. In 1852, Samuel Riley died in Madison County, Alabama.

Rowe, William

On September 1, 1792, William Rowe was born in Louisa County, Virginia; he was the son of John Rowe and Sarah Anderson. William served in the War of 1812.

In 1819, William and his family came from Virginia to Madison County, Alabama. The Rowe children went to school at Triana in Madison County and Pettusville in Limestone County, Alabama.

In the 1830 Limestone County, Alabama Census, William Rowe owned 24 black slaves. He was a Virginian seeking prime cotton land in the Tennessee Valley of northwest Alabama.

In 1834, William Rowe married Nancy Gooch (1806-1875) in Limestone County, Alabama. The father of Nancy was Roland Gooch who was born on April 22, 1778, in Albemarle County, Virginia. On April 14, 1801, Roland married Elizabeth "Betsy" McGehee in Louisa County, Virginia; she was the mother of Nancy Gooch Rowe. Betsy Gooch died on February 25, 1858. Roland Gooch died in Madison County, Alabama, on August 29, 1850, and was buried in Gooch Cemetery.

In the 1840 Limestone County, Alabama Census, William Rowe owned 44 black slaves. He was farming cotton in Limestone and Madison Counties of North Alabama.

On May 1, 1847, William and Nancy Gooch Rowe had Nathan Matson Rowe who was born in Limestone County, Alabama. On October 26, 1875, Nathan married Alice Cornelia Toney near Triana.

In the 1850 Madison County, Alabama, Agricultural Census, William Rowe owned 165 acres of improved land and 120 acres of unimproved land worth $3,000. He owned $800 worth of farming equipment and $1,500 worth of livestock.

According to the 1860 Madison County, Alabama, Agricultural Census, William Rowe owned 180 acres of improved land and 120 acres of unimproved land worth $5,000. He owned $350 worth of farming equipment and $1,125 worth of livestock.

Tate, Waddy

In 1786, Waddy Tate was born at Lynchburg in Campbell County, Virginia. He was the son of Jesse Tate and Margaret Miller of Virginia. The children of Jesse Tate and Margaret Miller Tate are as follows:
1. Sally A. Tate was born about 1772; she married Armstead Ellis Stokes who died 1823. On August 11, 1792, Sally married Micajah Anthony (1759-1793).

2. Elizabeth P. Tate was born about 1774.
3. Henry Tate (1776-1835) married Martha C. Yancey (1790-1839) on November 4, 1817, in Campbell County, Virginia.
4. John Tate was born about 1778 in Bedford County, Virginia; on February 19, 1802, he married Sophia Harris (1781-1822). On December 16, 1822, Sophia died in Limestone County, Alabama. On October 19, 1823, John married Mary Logwood in Limestone County, Alabama; Mary died on September 30, 1824, in Limestone County, Alabama. On January 27, 1825, John married Ann Jones in Limestone County, Alabama.
5. Euphan Tate was born about 1780; on February 22, 1807, she married Edmund Logwood in Bedford County, Virginia.
6. Mary Tate was born about 1782; on December 7, 1805, she married Gross Scruggs. On September 19, 1832, Mary died in Bedford County, Virginia. In 1856, Gross Scruggs died in Madison County, Alabama.
7. Caleb Tate was born on August 27, 1783, in Lynchburg, Virginia. On December 25, 1806, he married Mary Middleton in Elbert County, Georgia; on January 12, 1838, Mary died in Dallas County, Alabama. On June 15, 1840, Caleb married Martha Ann Taylor in Coosa County, Alabama. On September 15, 1841, Caleb died in Dallas County, Alabama.
8. Waddy Tate (1786-1864).

On January 14, 1808, Dr. Waddy Tate married Eliza E. Thompson in Elbert County, Georgia. Eliza was born about 1790; she and Waddy Tate had three children.

By 1811, Dr. Waddy Tate and his older brother John Tate were in Madison County of Mississippi Territory. On April 5, 1811, Waddy Tate entered 159.9 acres in Section 1 of Township 2 South and Range 1 West in Madison County (Cowart, 1979).

In 1811, Dr. Waddy Tate fought a duel at Huntsville in Mississippi Territory with Clement Comer Clay, who had entered 159.25 acres in Madison County on March 30, 1810. The duel evolved from a dispute between Dr. Waddy Tate who was 25 and Clement Comer Clay who was 22. Waddy Tate would become the Alabama State Representative of Limestone County, and Clement Comer Clay would become the Alabama Governor and State Supreme Court Justice from Madison County. If either man was wounded, it was obviously not enough to stop their careers, but the duel probably solved their disagreement because they worked together in future endeavors.

On December 21, 1811, John Tate, older brother of Waddy Tate, entered 166.14 acres in Section 22 of Township 1 South and Range 1 East in Madison County of Mississippi Territory. On June 29, 1815, John Tate entered 166.14 acres in Section 22 of Township 1 South and Range 1 East in Madison County (Cowart, 1979).

In 1816, Waddy Tate Jr. was born to Waddy Tate and Eliza E. Thompson Tate. Waddy Tate Jr. died in 1865, and he was buried in the Maple Hill Cemetery at Hustsville, Alabama.

In 1817, Eliza E. Thompson Tate, wife of Waddy Tate, died in Madison County of Mississippi Territory. The location of her grave is not known.

On February 2 and 4, 1818, Waddy Tate entered 345.5 acres in Township 2 South and Range 1 West in Madison County. On February 4, 1818, Dr. Waddy Tate along with other trustees Henry Chambers, William J. Adair, John Lindsay, and Thomas Bibb of the Town of Triana entered 276.94 acres in Section 22 of Township 5 South and Range 2 West in Madison County, Alabama (Cowart, 1979). The Town of Triana was located at the junction of Indian Creek with the Tennessee River. In 1819, the Alabama state legislature approved the incorporation Triana, and it became the second incorporated town in Madison County.

From February 6, 1818, through January 25, 1833, Waddy Tate entered approximately 1,036 acres in Townships 3, 4 South and Range 3 West in Limestone County, Alabama (Cowart, 1984). Waddy Tate was shown on slave records as living in Limestone County, Alabama.

On March 9 and 11, 1818, Waddy Tate entered about 968 acres in Township 3 South and Ranges 11, 12 West in Lauderdale County, Alabama

(Cowart, 1996). Waddy Tate was a land speculator in addition to being a cotton planter and slave owner.

On June 18, 1818, Dr. Waddy Tate married Julia Matilda Coleman at Nashville in Davidson County, Tennessee. On April 21, 1820, Julia died in Limestone County, Alabama. Waddy Tate and Julia Matilda Coleman Tate did not have any children.

On September 14 and 16, 1818, Waddy Tate entered some 638 acres in Sections 7 and 12 of Township 4 South and Ranges 8, 9 West in Lawrence County, Alabama (Cowart, 1991).

In the 1820 Limestone County, Alabama Census, Waddy Tate owned 100 black slaves. In 1820, John Tate owned 16 black slaves in Limestone County.

On May 2, 1823, Dr. Waddy Tate married Mary Scruggs in Madison County, Alabama; Mary was born on September 30, 1803. She died on February 26, 1836, at Florence in Lauderdale County, Alabama. She was a daughter of Gross Scruggs and Nancy Logwood. Waddy Tate and Mary Scruggs Tate had four children.

In 1830, Colonel Benjamin Sherrod sold the island that became known as Patton Island at Florence to Waddy Tate. The island contained nearly 600 acres and was in Sections 12, 13, and 14 of Township 3 South and Range 11 West in Lauderdale County, Alabama. The island extends from near Wilson Dam to O'Neal Bridge at Florence.

In the 1830 Limestone County, Alabama Census, Waddy Tate owned 80 black slaves. John Tate was not listed in the 1830 Limestone County, Alabama Census; he may have migrated to Texas. Waddy Tate was the executor of his estate in Fayette County, Texas; Waddy was sued by members of the family over the handling of the estate of his brother, John Tate.

In 1839, Waddy Tate was involved in a number of ventures in Florence, but he was reportedly wiped out by a severe economic depression. Waddy sold his interest in the island in the Tennessee River at Florence labeled as Tinnin's Island on an 1844 map. The daughter of Dr. Waddy Tate, Margaret Tate Tinnin

(1811-1833), was to married Robert Tinnin, who at one time was the principal of Athens Male Academy. The Tinnin family is where the island got its 1844 name.

Waddy Tate sold the island to Governor Robert Miller Patton of the Sweetwater Plantation in Florence, Alabama. After Robert Miller Patton purchased the island from Waddy Tate, it became known as Patton Island. Today, the Singing River Bridge on Highway 133 crosses Patton Island in the Tennessee River downstream of Wilson Dam.

According to the 1840 Limestone County, Alabama Census, Waddy Tate was a 50-60-year-old white male. In 1840, there were six males and one female in the Waddy Tate household. In the 1840 Limestone County, Alabama Census, Waddy Tate owned 83 black slaves.

According to the 1843, Deed Book G, page 14 of Tishmingo County, Mississippi: "Benjamin Reynolds and his wife Catherine Reynolds of Franklin County, Alabama, for the sum of $400.00, deeds to Waddy Tate Sr. of Limestone County, Alabama, 160 acres more of less of land in the county of Tishomingo County, Mississippi, the NE¼ of Section 5 in Township 3 South and Range 6 East."

On October 11, 1848, Frederick Tate, son of Waddy Tate and Mary Scruggs Tate, married Mary Branch Fletcher in Limestone County, Alabama. Mary Branch Fletcher (1831-1853) was the daughter of James Nicholas Fletcher and Matilda G. Golden Cheatham Fletcher of Limestone County.

In the 1850 Limestone County, Alabama, Slave Schedules, Waddy Tate owned 38 black slaves and William R. Tate owned 30 slaves. In 1850, Waddy was living with the family of his son Fred and Mary B. Tate.

According to the 1850 Huntsville, Madison County, Alabama, United States Census, House Number 519, Waddy Tate was a 64-year-old white male born in Virginia living in his household of his son Frederick Tate. Fred Tate was a 25-year-old white male born in Alabama. Also living in the household of Fred Tate was Mary B. Tate, Female, 20, Virginia; Irwin Tate, Male, 1, Alabama; and William Tate, Male, 19, Alabama.

On October 30, 1851, Frederick "Fred" Tate moved his family to LaGrange, Texas; Waddy Tate moved with the family. Fred run a large cotton plantation on the Colorado River in Fayette County, Texas; he also practiced law in LaGrange and for the surrounding citizens.

On May 16, 1853, Mary Branch Tate died in Fayette County, Texas. The location of her grave is not known. On January 19, 1855, Fred Tate married Lucy Croom in Greene County, Alabama. Fred and Lucy Croom Tate had three children.

In 1860 Fayette County, Texas, Slave Schedules, Frederick Tate was listed as owning 31 black slaves. He had moved to Texas to find more and better cotton land for his plantation.

On September 5, 1861, in LaGrange, Texas, Waddy Tate was one of the signers who organized the Volunteer Aid Society for the citizens of Fayette County, Texas. They were to meet on September 7, 1861, at the courthouse in LaGrange to support the families of the volunteers of war.

By November 1861, Major Fred Tate was mustered into service during the Civil War. Fred was an officer with the 9th Texas Infantry of the Confederate States Army.

On April 24, 1864, Waddy Tate died at LaGrange in Fayette County, Texas. The location of his grave is not known.

By the time of the 1870 Fayette County, Texas, United States Census, Lucy Tate was listed as a widow of Fred Tate. Fred died sometime during the 1860s.

Trice, William

The 1820 Limestone County, Alabama Census had the following for William Trice: White Males over 21: 1; White Males under 21: 5; White Females over 21: 2; White Females under 21: 3; Total Whites: 11; Free Persons of Color:

4; Slaves: 35; Acres Cultivated: 5; Bales 11; Approximate Weight per Bale 400 pounds. If the free persons of color were black, William Trice had 39 black folks living in his household in 1820.

On February 1, 1830, William Trice entered land in the southeast ¼ of Section 13 of Township 5 South and Range 3 West in Limestone County, Alabama. His property was adjacent to William H. Blackwell and Bouldin Collier.

Vest, Samuel M.

About 1775, Samuel Vest Sr. was born in Virginia; he was one of the first of the Vest family to come to North Alabama. Around 1815, Samuel and his family moved from Virginia to Madison County in Mississippi Territory. By 1818, Samuel was living in Madison County, Alabama.

Samuel Vest was married to Elizabeth W. Betsey; she was born about 1785. Samuel Vest Sr. and Elizabeth W. Betsey Vest had the following children:
1. Elizabeth Vest was living in Green County, Alabama, by 1843.
2. Susan H. Vest died in Madison County, Alabama, after 1834. On March 8, 1821, Susan married Archibald T. Maddera in Madison County, Alabama.
3. Samuel M. Vest Jr. was born in 1821. He was living in Green County, Alabama, in 1845. Samuel Jr. was married three times:
    I. On January 24, 1844, Samuel M. Vest Jr. married Sarah Ann Adams Darwin in Madison County, Alabama. Sarah Ann Adams Darwin was born in 1826; on April 5, 1847, she died in Madison County, Alabama, with burial in Humphey-True Cemetery or Liberty Hill Cemetery in Madison. Samuel M. Vest and Sarah Ann Adams Darwin had Sidney A. Vest who married to Mary A. Power on December 29, 1866, in Madison County, Alabama.
    II. On July 5, 1851, Samuel M. Vest Jr. married Margaret T. Springer in Madison. On April 1, 1853, Margaret died at 20 years 8 months 22 days; she is buried in Triana Cemetery in Madison County, Alabama. Samuel Jr. and Margaret had A. Charles Vest in 1853 in

Madison County, Alabama. In 1880, Charles was living in Madison County, Alabama, where he died on January 17, 1881. Charles had a daughter Matilda E. Vest.

III. On August 13, 1855, Samuel M. Vest Jr. married to Sarah "Sallie" Amy Watkins (7/27/1831-9/30/1910) in Madison County, Alabama. On January 6, 1860, they had James Waddie Vest in Madison County, Alabama. James married Martha E. Sandlin, daughter of William Gordon Sandlin and Nancy Ann Watkins. On May 20, 1915, James Waddie Vest died in Morgan County, Alabama.

On April 3, 1823, the following notice was printed in the newspaper as follows: "NOTICE, On Saturday, the 18th day of April, there will be an Election held at Samuel Vest's, for the purpose of electing THREE AGENTS, for the 16th Section in Township Three, Range One, West of Basis Meridian in Madison County. DAVID MAXWELL, LEWIS FINLAY, J. S. CALVERT, Agents."

On November 16, 1830, Samuel Vest Sr. died in Madison County, Alabama. On November 30, 1843, Elizabeth W. Betsey Vest died in Madison County, Alabama.

In the 1850 Limestone County, Alabama, United States Census, House Number 326, Samuel M. Vest Jr. was a 29-year-old white male born in Alabama. He was the son of Samuel M. Vest Sr.

According to the 1850 Limestone County, Alabama, Slave Schedule, Samuel M. Vest Jr. owned 52 black slaves. In the 1850 Limestone County, Alabama, Agricultural Census, Samuel M. Vest Jr. owned 800 acres of improved land and 160 acres of unimproved land valued at $12,000. He also owned $500 worth of farming equipment and livestock valued at $1,835.

In the 1860 South Western Division, Madison County, Alabama, United States Census, Household 102, Samuel M. Vest Jr. was a 39-year-old white male born in Alabama. Also living in the household of Samuel M. Vest was Sallie A. Vest, Female, 27, Alabama; Sidna A. Vest, Female, 14, Alabama; Charles S. Vest, Male, 9, Alabama; and James W. Vest, Male, 0, Alabama.

Ward, William

On October 5, 1831, William Ward married Elizabeth Bransford in Madison County, Alabama. William and Elizabeth lived in Limestone County, Alabama, before moving to Arkansas.

According to the 1850 Limestone County, Alabama, United States Census, House Number 395, William Ward was a 43-year-old white male born in South Carolina. Also living in the household of William Ward was William H. Ward, Male, 14, Alabama; James Ward, Male, 12, Alabama; Benjamin N. F. Ward, Male, 9, Alabama; and Thomas M. Ward, Male, 6, Alabama.

In the 1850 Limestone County, Alabama, Slave Schedule, William Ward owned 68 black slaves. He was listed twice with one indicating 58 slaves and the other 10 slaves.

In the 1850 Limestone County, Alabama, Agricultural Census, William Ward owned 190 acres of improved land and 50 acres of unimproved land valued at $2,400. He also owned $100 worth of farming equipment and livestock valued at $780.

In the 1860 Crockett Township, Arkansas, United States Census, Household 344, William Ward was a 53-year-old white male born in South Carolina. Also living in the household of William Ward was James Ward, Male, 21, Alabama; Benjamin Ward, Male, 19, Alabama; and Thomas M. Ward, Male, 16, Alabama.

Washington, Starke

The 1820 Limestone County, Alabama Census listed Starke Washington with the following: White Males over 21: 2; White Males under 21: 3; White Females over 21: 1; White Females under 21: 2; Total Whites: 8; Free Persons of Color: 12; Slaves: 22; Number of Acres Cultivated: 4; bales: 11; Average Weight per Bale: 350 pounds. If the free persons of color were black, there were 34 black folks living in the household of Starke Washington in 1820.

The 1830 Limestone County, Alabama Census had the following for the household of Starke Washington: White Males: Under 5 years: 1; 30-40 Years: 1; White Females: Under 5 years: 1; 5-10 years: 1; 30-40 Years: 1; Slaves: 14.

White, Samuel D.

Samuel Dedman White was born in Virginia about 1799; he married Susan Blackburn. Susan was born on March 30, 1808, in Lunenburg County, Virginia

In the 1830 Limestone County, Alabama Census, Samuel D. White owned 22 black slaves. Samuel brought his slaves from Virginia to Limestone County, Alabama.

According to the 1840 Limestone County, Alabama Census, Samuel D. White owned 61 black slaves. Samuel was engaged in farming cotton and raising livestock with the help of his slaves.

In the 1850 Limestone County, Alabama United States Census, House Number 413, Samuel D. White was a 51-year-old white male born in Virginia. Also living in the household of Samuel D. White was Susan White, Female, 38, Virginia; Jane Ward White, Female, 27, Alabama; William L. White, Male, 24, Alabama; Marion E. White, Female, 18, Alabama; James S. White, Male, 16, Alabama; Thomas White, Male, 14, Alabama; Robert H. White, Male, 12, Alabama; Virginia White, Female, 8, Alabama; and Edward White, Male, 3, Alabama.

According to the 1850 Limestone County, Alabama, Slave Schedules, Samuel D. White owned 118 black slaves. In the 1850 Limestone County, Alabama, Agricultural Census, Samuel D. White owned 800 acres of improved land and 1,140 acres of unimproved land valued at $40,000. He also owned $950 worth of farming equipment and livestock valued at $4,269.

On May 17, 1856, Susan Blackburn White died in Giles County, Tennessee. Susan was buried in the White-Lewis-Hilliard Cemetery at Jeff in Madison County, Alabama. The tombstone inscription reads, "Erected as a token of her many virtues by her children" (Find A Grave Memorial# 68249280).

On December 25, 1856, Samuel Dedman White died in Giles County, Tennessee; he was the husband of Susan Blackburn White (1808-1856). Samuel was buried in the White-Lewis-Hilliard Cemetery at Jeff in Madison County, Alabama (Find A Grave Memorial# 68503873).

References

1820 Limestone County, Alabama, United States Census

1830 Limestone County, Alabama, United States Census

1840 Limestone County, Alabama, United States Census

1850 Limestone County, Alabama, Agricultural Census

1850 Limestone County, Alabama, United States Census

1860 Limestone County, Alabama, United States Census

1860 Limestone County, Alabama, Slave Schedule

1870 Limestone County, Alabama, United States Census

1880 Limestone County, Alabama, United States Census

Carter, Clarence Edwin, Editor, "Territorial Papers of the United States," United States Government Publishing Company, Washington, DC, 1934.

Cowart, Margaret Matthews, "Old Land Records of Colbert County, Alabama," 7801 Tea Garden Road Southeast, Huntsville, Alabama, 1985.

Cowart, Margaret Matthews, "Old Land Records of Franklin County, Alabama," 7801 Tea Garden Road Southeast, Huntsville, Alabama, 1986.

Cowart, Margaret Matthews, "Old Land Records of Lauderdale County, Alabama," 7801 Tea Garden Road Southeast, Huntsville, Alabama, 1996.

Cowart, Margaret Matthews, "Old Land Records of Lawrence County, Alabama," 7801 Tea Garden Road Southeast, Huntsville, Alabama, 1991.

Cowart, Margaret Matthews, Old Land Records of Limestone County, Alabama," 7801 Tea Garden Road Southeast, Huntsville, Alabama, 1984.

Cowart, Margaret Matthews, "Old Land Records of Madison County, Alabama, 7801 Tea Garden Road Southeast, Huntsville, Alabama, 1979.

Cowart, Margaret Matthews, "Old Land Records of Morgan County, Alabama," 7801 Tea Garden Road Southeast, Huntsville, Alabama, 1981.

Crockett, David, "A Narrative of the Life of David Crockett of the State of Tennessee," Introduction by Paul Andrew Hutton, University of Nebraska Press, Lincoln, Nebraska, Reprinted 1834 edition, 1987.

Dunnavant, Robert Jr., "Historic Limestone County," Volume I, Pea Ridge Press, Athens, Alabama, 1993.

Find a Grave, www.findagrave.com

Gentry, Dorthy, "Life and Legends of Lawrence County, Alabama, Nottingham-SWS, Inc., Tuscaloosa, Alabama, 1962.

Hatley, Tom, "The Dividing Paths, Cherokees and South Carolinians Through the Era of Revolution," Oxford University Press, New York, 1995.

Hyatt, Ratford, "Old Lawrence Reminscences," Lawrence County Historical Commission, Moulton, Alabama (date unknown)

James, Marquis, "Andrew Jackson, Portrait of a President," The Bobbs-Merill Company, New York, 1937.

Leftwich, Nina, "Two Hundred Years at the Shoals," The American Southern Publishing Company, Northport, Alabama, 1935.

M.A.H., "Historical Traditions of Tennessee, The Captivity of Jane Brown and Her Family," The American Whig Review, Volume 15, Issue 87, Cornersville, Tennessee, December 25, 1851, Nassau Street, New York, 1852.

Powell, John Wesley, Matthew Williams Stirling, Jesse Walter Fewkes, Frederick Webb Hodge, William Henry Holmes, "Annual Report," Volume 5, Parts 1883-1884, Library of American Civilization PCMI Collection, Smithsonian Institution, Bureau of American Ethnology, Government Printing Office, Pennsylvania State University, page 272, 1887.

Royall, Anne Newport, "Letters from Alabama 1817-1822," University of Alabama Press, Tuscaloosa, Alabama, 1969.

Saunders, James Edmund, "Early Settlers of Alabama," Southern Historical Press, 1977, Reprint edition of 1899.

Swanton, John R., "The Indians of the Southeastern United States," Smithsonia Institution Press, Washington, D.C., 1987.

Watts, C. Wilder, "Indians at the Muscle Shoals," The Journal of Muscle Shoals History, Volume 1, 1973.

Index

Alba Wood, 125, 128, 129, 130
Anderson, Charles Dandridge, 91, 92
Anderson, Eliza A. F., 228, 229
Athens, 55, 56, 65, 66, 67, 68, 70, 93, 94, 95, 118, 142, 143, 144, 145, 151, 153, 154, 162, 166, 167, 168, 169, 171, 176, 192, 193, 194, 195, 199, 200, 202, 203, 204, 205, 206, 209, 210, 211, 212, 214, 228, 229, 230, 231, 233, 234, 235, 237, 238, 239, 240, 246, 247, 248, 249, 258, 259, 260, 276, 277, 278, 279, 281, 289
Beaty, Glorvinia, 67, 93, 246, 248
Beaty, Robert W., 66, 210
Bedingfield, Charles, 46
Bedingfield, Meredith, 46
Bell Tavern, 126
Belle Mina, 96, 98, 99, 100, 101, 102, 103, 104, 185, 189, 190, 193, 194, 195
Bibb, David Porter, 97, 101, 103, 104, 105, 194
Bibb, Henry C., 103, 111
Bibb, Robert Thompson, 97, 106
Bibb, Thomas, 64, 67, 96, 97, 98, 99, 100, 101, 102, 103, 104, 106, 126, 167, 265, 272, 283, 287
Bibb, William Wyatt, 63, 67, 96, 98
Big Spring, 66, 126, 250, 266
Black Warriors' Path, 13, 54
Blackbourn, Clement, 131, 133, 134
Blackbourn, Sarah, 130, 131, 132, 133
Blackburn, Susan, 294, 295
Blackwell, Eliza W., 108

Blackwell, William H., 107, 108, 109, 273, 291
Blackwell, William Henry, 106, 107, 108, 109, 147, 272
Bluewater Creek, 20, 51
Bond, John, 112, 113
Bond, Nicholas Pirtle, 109, 110, 111, 112
Bond, Samuel, 110, 111, 112
Booth, Elizabeth, 137, 140, 232, 233
Boxwood Plantation, 60
Bradley, Angeline Permelia, 114, 116
Bradley, James, 97, 101
Bradley, Joseph H., 113, 114
Bridgewater, 49, 54
Brown, John, 52, 53
Brown, Joseph, 47, 48
Brown, William L., 116, 117
Browns Ferry, 20, 39, 48, 51, 52, 53, 57, 65, 92, 249, 250, 260
Browns Ferry Road, 20, 51, 52, 92, 249, 250, 260
Burleson, James, 33, 57, 58, 59
Burleson, Joseph, 33, 57, 58, 59, 60, 61
Burleson's Trace, 57, 60, 61
Cain, Allison Chappell, 118, 119, 120
Cambridge, 235, 237, 238, 250
Carroll, Grief, 121, 122, 123
Carroll, John D., 66, 94
Cheatham, Christopher, 126, 127, 128, 129, 130
Chickamauga Confederacy, 15, 21, 22
Chickamauga War, 20, 21, 22, 25, 47

Chickasaw, 15, 19, 20, 21, 22, 24, 25, 27, 29, 30, 36, 37, 38, 54, 57, 63, 96, 231
Chickasaw Island, 15, 24, 25, 26
Chickasaw Old Fields, 15, 27
Chickasaw Oldfields, 231
Chilton, Sarah Orrick, 107, 271, 274
Clark, William Robert, 130, 131, 133
Coe, Jesse, 135, 136, 137, 138, 139, 140, 141, 142
Colbert, George, 25, 29, 128
Colbert's Ferry, 20, 25
Coldwater, 20
Coleman, Daniel, 142, 143, 144, 145, 278
Coleman, Ruffin, 76, 144, 186, 187, 189, 190
Collier, Henry Watkins, 145, 147, 148
Collier, James, 106, 145, 146, 149, 283
Collier, Thomas Bouldin, 148, 150
Collier, Wyatt, 106, 107, 108, 109, 146, 147, 148
Cotton Gin Treaty, 23, 24, 26, 27, 28, 62, 63
Cotton Hill, 249, 250, 251, 253
Cow Ford Landing, 20, 57, 60
Cox, Joshua, 53
Creek Indians, 16, 57
Critz, George F., 150, 151
Crockett, David, 48, 49, 54
Crockett, Robert, 49
Cumberland River, 15, 20, 136, 165
Cuttyatoy, 47, 48, 53
Davis, Nicholas, 136, 143, 151, 153, 154, 155, 156, 157, 159, 167, 235
Dillard, Huldah Jones, 163, 164, 185
Donnell, James Webb Smith, 166, 167, 169, 170, 171, 220

Donnell, Robert, 112, 164, 165, 166, 167, 168, 169, 170, 172
Doublehead, 14, 15, 16, 17, 19, 20, 21, 22, 23, 24, 26, 27, 28, 29, 32, 36, 37, 38, 39, 47, 51, 52, 55, 62, 63, 65, 126, 165
Druid's Grove, 91, 218, 220
Duncan, James M., 164, 188
Duncan, James Madison, 188
Eggleston, William F., 104
Elk County, 63, 64
Elk River Mills, 66
Elk River Shoals, 11
English Spring, 197
English, James, 197
Fisher, Jacob, 171, 173, 174
Fletcher, Edward A., 177, 178, 179, 182, 183, 184
Fletcher, James Nicholas, 177, 178, 179, 180, 182, 289
Fletcher, John Jacob, 175, 176, 177, 181
Fletcher, John James, 177, 178, 179, 180, 181, 182
Fletcher, Rebecca, 175, 177, 184, 260, 261, 262
Fletcher, Richard, 176, 177
Fletcher, William, 176, 177, 184, 260, 261
Flint River, 24, 55, 62
Flower Hill, 196, 197, 198, 199, 200, 202, 279, 280, 281
Fort Hampton, 14, 29, 37, 38, 40, 45, 47, 48, 49, 52, 53, 54, 55, 63, 66
Fox's Creek, 20, 57, 58, 59, 60, 61
Gaines Trace, 51, 54
Gamble, James Hurt, 163, 185, 186, 187
Garner, Brice M., 53, 264
Garrett, Edmond, 191, 192, 193, 194

Garrett, Edmond Peter, 95
Garrett, Jesse, 191
Garrett, Peter Francisco, 192, 193, 194, 195
Gilchrist, Malcolm, 45, 64, 65
Gooch, Nancy, 285
Gourd's Settlement, 20, 51, 52
Halbert, Henry Sale, 14, 15
Hampton, Wade, 52
Harris Cemetery, 197, 198, 199, 200, 201, 202
Harris, John Henry, 196, 197, 198, 199, 200, 278
Harris, John R., 196, 198, 199, 278
Harris, Schuyler, 196, 199, 200, 202, 278
Harrison, Mary Anne, 91, 92
Harrison, Temperance, 202, 204
Haywood, Eliza Ann, 219, 221, 223, 224
Hine, James, 204
Hine, Silas, 138, 202, 203, 204, 206
Hine, William A., 204, 205
Hine-Malone Cemetery, 206
Hobbs, Hubbard, 231, 232
Hobbs, Ira Edward, 229, 230, 231
Hobbs, John, 230, 231
Hobbs, Thomas Hubbard, 170, 229, 231, 232, 233, 234
Hopewell Treaty, 24, 25, 26, 37
Horton, James E., 66, 207, 208, 209
Horton, James Edwin, 208, 209
Horton, Rodah, 207, 208
Houston, George Smith, 67, 93, 153, 210, 211, 212, 213, 214, 278, 281
Hunt's Spring, 51, 52, 250

Jackson, Andrew, 46, 47, 49, 110, 136, 172, 185, 208, 209, 262, 263, 277, 297
Jackson, James, 214, 215, 216, 217, 218
Jackson, Rufus, 216, 217, 218
Jones, John H., 223, 224
Jones, John N. S., 219, 220, 221, 222, 224
Jones, Llewellyn, 91, 198, 218, 219, 220, 225
Jordan, Eliza, 226
Jordan, Palmyra Scott, 225, 226, 227
Jordan, Samuel, 225, 226, 227
Katagiskee, 16
Kernachan, Mary Lucy, 238, 239
Lane, James M., 227, 228, 229
Lucy's Branch, 45, 46, 47, 163
Maclin, Benjamin W., 230, 231, 232
Maclin, Thomas, 229, 230, 231, 232, 233, 235
Madison County, 24, 26, 37, 55, 58, 62, 63, 64, 66, 91, 93, 96, 100, 101, 102, 103, 107, 110, 113, 116, 121, 122, 131, 132, 133, 143, 146, 147, 148, 149, 150, 152, 153, 154, 156, 159, 163, 166, 171, 175, 176, 177, 178, 180, 181, 184, 191, 199, 207, 208, 214, 219, 225, 228, 231, 241, 244, 251, 252, 253, 254, 255, 256, 257, 261, 262, 263, 264, 265, 266, 268, 271, 272, 274, 275, 277, 278, 282, 283, 284, 285, 286, 287, 288, 289, 291, 292, 293, 295
Madison, James, 30, 36, 63, 113, 185, 188, 189
Malone, George, 118, 119, 235, 236, 237, 238, 239

Malone, John Nicholas, 236, 237, 238, 239, 240
Malone, Mary, 118, 242
Malone, Mary Briggs, 243, 258, 260
Malone, Mary H., 204
Malone, Thomas, 240, 241, 244
Malone, Thomas Chappell, 118, 119, 241, 242, 243, 244, 258
Malone, Thomas Hill, 119, 240, 241, 242, 243, 244
Marshall, George W., 244, 245
Mason, John Richardson, 67, 93, 245, 246, 247
Mason, William, 245, 246
Matthews, John, 248, 249, 256, 257
Matthews, Luke, 166, 248, 249, 250, 251, 252, 253, 254, 255, 256
Matthews, Samuel, 248, 254, 255
Matthews, Thomas, 248, 254, 255
Matthews, William Washington, 248, 254, 256
McDonald, John, 19
McDonald, Jonathan, 243, 257, 258, 259, 260
McDonald, William, 257
Meigs, Return J., 40, 62
Melton, John, 23, 26, 38, 39, 40, 45, 46, 47, 126
Melton's Bluff, 20, 23, 27, 39, 40, 48, 49, 50, 51, 52, 54, 65
Mississippi Territory, 30, 37, 57, 58, 63, 64, 93, 96, 102, 103, 110, 113, 116, 121, 126, 148, 166, 175, 176, 177, 178, 184, 191, 214, 219, 228, 231, 241, 261, 262, 263, 265, 266, 267, 268, 270, 286, 287, 291
Mitchell Trace, 14, 54
Moore, Alfred, 261, 262, 263
Moore, David, 261, 262, 263, 264, 265
Moore, John, 260, 261
Mouse Town, 20, 57, 58, 59, 60
Myrtle Grove, 145, 149, 150, 271, 272
North River Road, 37, 38, 55, 56
Nubbin Ridge, 178, 180
Oak Mount, 163, 164, 185, 187, 189, 190
Oakland, 107, 225, 227
Ocuma, 38, 39, 40, 45
Old Jasper Road, 51, 56, 230
Over Elk, 26, 65
Parrott, Sarah, 93, 95, 246
Patrick Stagecoach Line, 56
Patton Island, 288, 289
Peck's Landing, 60, 61
Peebles, Dudley, 266, 267
Peebles, Henry W., 267
Peebles, John Turner, 270
Peebles, Joseph D., 266, 267
Peebles, Joseph Douglas, 265, 266, 267
Peebles, Robert Barclay, 267, 269
Peebles, Sterling, 265
Peeples, Henry, 265, 267, 268, 269
Peete, Mary Goodson, 193, 194, 195
Peete's Corner, 194, 250
Perkins, Benjamin, 198
Pickett, Sarah O., 272, 273
Pickett, Steptoe, 271, 272, 273, 274, 275
Pleasant Hill, 164, 167, 168, 170
Polly Malone Cemetery, 240, 242, 243, 260
Pryor, Luke, 200, 214, 233, 276, 277, 278, 279, 280, 281
Ragland, Nathaniel, 158, 282
Ragland, Samuel, 281, 282, 283, 284
Rhodes Ferry, 56
Robertson, James, 20, 29

Rowe, William, 284, 285
Rowell, Neal, 129, 130
Royall, Anne Newport, 40, 50, 55
Seclusion, 91, 169, 170, 220
Shawnee, 15, 19, 21, 22
Sims Settlements, 24, 29
Sims, James, 28, 35
Slopeside, 229, 230, 231, 232, 235
Sloss, Leticia C., 203, 204, 205
Smith, Gabriel, 138, 246
Spotswood, Lucy Ann, 253
Spotswood, Sarah E., 254, 255
Standing Turkey, 19, 39
Stuart, John, 19
Sugar Creek, 23, 27, 276, 277, 278, 279
Tanner, Samuel, 67
Tate, Frederick, 289, 290
Tate, John, 286, 287, 288
Tate, Waddy, 285, 286, 287, 288, 289, 290

The Cedars, 193, 195
Thompson, Parmelia, 96, 106
Tisdale, Martha, 270
Trice, William, 290, 291
Tucker, Elizabeth, 240, 241, 242, 243, 244
Turkey Town Treaty, 23, 25, 26, 28, 38, 51, 53, 55, 64, 192
Vaughn, James, 66
Vest, Samuel, 291, 292
Walker, William H., 117, 118
Walnut Grove Plantation, 61, 155, 157
Ward, William, 293
Washington, Starke, 293, 294
White, Samuel D., 134, 135, 294
Winston, Louis, 58, 59
Withers, John Wright, 226, 227
Woodside, 103, 104, 105, 194
Yuchi, 13, 14, 15

I am extremely honored and humbled by the many people who read my books. I greatly appreciate the readers that enjoy truthful historical stories of the Warrior Mountains and the great Tennessee River Valley. I send all the followers of my books a heartfelt thank you; without people who love local history, about the North Alabama, all my research and work would be in vain.

I graciously request that each of you who acquire one of my books from Amazon, please post an honest review. A short two-to-three-line evaluation of my books would be greatly appreciated. Again, thank you to all who take the time to educate yourself on local history.

www.ingramcontent.com/pod-product-compliance
Lightning Source LLC
Chambersburg PA
CBHW081846170426
43199CB00018B/2830